INTERSTELLAR FLIGHT MAGAZINE

BEST OF YEAR THREE

PRAISE FOR INTERSTELLAR FLIGHT MAGAZINE

“Interstellar Flight Magazine does have a lighter side full of fun discussions about the writing process, as well as dozens of recommendations readers from space operas to horror novels that readers will not want to miss. Picking up this one-of-a-kind collection will be sure to lead you to your next favorite indie Science Fiction and Fantasy book." —Reedsy

"Unsure what’s going on in contemporary speculative fiction? Learn about modern voices in genre, both through their own words and criticism." —Warp Speed Odyssey

EDITED BY

Holly Lyn Walrath
Sydney Richardson

CONTRIBUTORS

Leslie Archibald
Erin Becker
Andrea Blythe
Alexandra Casale
Laura Díaz de Arce
Bri Downing
Michael Glazner
J.D. Harlock
Henry L. Herz
Jeana Jorgensen
Annika Barranti Klein
Len Lawson
Hesper Leveret
vanessa maki
Archita Mittra
Anushmita Mohanty
J.T. Morse
Julie Reeser
Elyse Ribbons 柳素英
Christina Sng
Presley Thomas
A.A. Voigt
T.D. Walker
J.Z. Weston
Corey J. White

INTERSTELLAR FLIGHT PRESS BEST OF YEAR THREE

Cover Illustration by Chaz Kemp.

Edited by Holly Lyn Walrath and Sydney Richardson.

Published by Interstellar Flight Press, Houston, Texas.

www.interstellarflightpress.com

ISBN (eBook): 978-1-953736-15-4

ISBN (paperback): 978-1-953736-14-7

First Edition: September 2022

INTERSTELLAR FLIGHT MAGAZINE

BEST OF YEAR THREE

CONTENTS

INTERVIEWS

EDITOR'S NOTE

BY HOLLY LYN WALRATH

We made it another year. Running a small press during the pandemic has been eye-opening. Interstellar Flight Magazine has been a point of light for me. I'm constantly amazed by the wonderful work we are able to highlight in these pages. Both in terms of supporting marginalized voices, but also we are one of the few nonfiction SFF outlets out there.

This year's anthology highlights indie authors and creators who are working outside the lines of traditional publishing venues. I was lucky enough to attend Fantastic Fest in Austin to bring several reviews of new, unpublished-as-of-yet films. Several articles this year highlight what it's like to be a creator in a pandemic.

In terms of the press, we've got interviews with all the authors who wrote our new releases for 2021. We just wrapped up our short story collection call, so I'm excited for what is coming our way in terms of new books.

I want to say thank you as always to our contributors, volunteers, authors who we've interviewed, and everyone who puts in their own little effort to keep this spaceship afloat. I truly could not do this without y'all.

Holly Lyn Walrath

Managing Editor

Interstellar Flight Press

ORIGINAL ARTICLES

SCI-FI, AI AND THE FUTURE OF NEW CHINA: HOW CHINA USES SCIENCE FICTION TO DEFINE ITS FUTURE

BY ALEXANDRA CASALE

> "This powerful medium of the sci-fi genre works as both inspiration and introduction to the possibilities of the potential. Moreover, its ability to inspire and educate the masses is not lost on those who wish to guide the future."

In 2061, the sun is dying, and the people of earth must band together to save the planet . . . or at the very least, save the human race. This is the plot of the popular Chinese Sci-fi book and its 2019 movie adaptation entitled *The Wandering Earth* by Liu Cixin (currently streaming on Netflix). A pivotal scene in the movie depicts a battle of wits between the advanced AI computer called MOSS and our rebel human hero, astronaut Liu Peiqiang.

The scene reveals a clash between the logical, utilitarian-based MOSS and our hero's illogical, almost selfish goal—which is to save his children on earth. In a nutshell, MOSS runs the numbers and concludes that for humanity to survive, the earth and its current inhabitants cannot be saved. On the contrary, our human protagonist Liu sees something quite different . . . he sees a small chance to save the earth, its inhabitants, and the future of humanity—he sees hope.

As the scene progresses, each entity attempts to stifle the other, until Peiqiang prevails. Ultimately, he does what heroes do—he makes the right decision, sacrifices himself, and saves the world.

The Wandering Earth not only depicts a Chinese hero but also a new China with superior science and technology. This blockbuster presentation played to Chinese audiences who were ready to enjoy the entertainment factor and were also excited to envision the potential for China's superior technological future.

The powerful medium of the sci-fi genre works as both inspiration and introduction to the possibilities of the potential. Moreover, its ability to inspire and educate the masses is not lost on those who wish to guide the future.

For instance, American tech companies such as Microsoft, Google, and Apple often commission sci-fi writers to do something called: "design fiction." Here, science fiction think-tanks run through futuristic narratives with the goal of leading to marketable products and services. For example, the head of the National Aeronautics and Space Administration (NASA) recently confirmed that they are working with actor Tom Cruise to create a science fiction film in space. While not design fiction, NASA hopes this film will inspire a new generation of engineers and scientists throughout the US.

Ironically, we also see similar methodology playing out in today's Covid-19 scenario. The screenwriter of the then-futuristic 2011 pandemic movie *Contagion,* Scott Z. Burns, has been asked by policymakers what can we expect with this novel virus. In fact, the stars of the film were brought together to make Public Service Announcements warning of coronavirus and how to stay safe.

America isn't the only country utilizing the power and influence of sci-fi, the world's second-largest economy has also taken notice. For example, the CEO of Xiaomi, one of China's largest smartphone companies, has made Liu Cixin's *Three Body* Trilogy, a sci-fi trilogy about humanity's first contact with an alien civilization, required reading for employees. This may be because Liu's work focuses on innovative concepts of science and technology.

Further, in 2015—a few days after Liu received the Hugo Award—the Vice President of the People's Republic of China, Li Yuanchao, met with Liu and a delegation of science fiction writers. During this visit, Vice President Li called on Chinese science fiction writers to "fuel the faith of the youth in realizing the fulfillment of the Chinese Dream." The Chinese Dream can mean different things to different people, but Li is aptly referencing President Xi's version, a version that includes China becoming the global leader in emerging technology—artificial intelligence (AI) being the pinnacle of this emerging technology.

This idea likely gained strength in 2017, when an AI gaming system called AlphaGo defeated the world champion, Chinese Go player Ke Jie. Here, a machine recently invented by a California company conquered a game invented over 2,500 years ago in Asia. The country and the Chinese government took notice. Later that year, China unveiled its "Next Generation Artificial Intelligence Development Plan" (China Embassy), a document laying out the country's strategy to become the AI global leader by 2030. This plan gave Chinese citizens a new vision of the future and made it clear that the future was coming fast.

Kai-fu Lee, author and former head of Google China, declared: "AI is going to change everything. To not understand the coming AI revolution is to risk getting left behind." President Xi agrees and is betting that AI will indeed be a geopolitical game-changer. Hence, one could say that China's "Artificial Intelligence Development Plan" merged with the Chinese Dream to create Xi's AI dominance Dream.

Markedly, the sci-fi genre, with its unique ability to inspire innovation and futuristic thought, is being tapped to help China achieve this dream. As noted, this is something we see in both China and the West; however, China faces a distinct problem compared to its western counterpart. The issue for China is, the country has struggled in modern times to successfully toggle between historical governmental controls and releasing the reins of artistic freedom—something vital for innovation. While the genre has been steadily thriving for a couple of decades, it is still subject to that approval and censorship, especially as Xi Jinping's government seeks to establish increasingly rigid cultural control.

For example, to get a movie or book released in the states, government approval is not needed; in China, however, these creative works are subject to approval, censorship, and in some cases must undergo complete revisions. A problem for the Chinese government is that the most popular sci-fi writers are often the ones that push the limits of imagination as well as push the limits against authority. Chinese sci-fi writers have to toggle between exploring their full artistic expression while not pushing so far that their work never gets released to audiences, and clever sci-fi writers must toe the line between conveying their art properly without being labeled a dissident. Working to maintain this delicate balance may hinder their artistic expression, and ultimately this would be counterproductive for both the artist and Xi's mission. For example, Liu Cixin's publisher worried that the opening scene of his book *The Three Body Problem* was too politically charged and would never make it past government censors. Reluctantly, Liu revised his book to appease the government. While this move allowed his book to be published, Liu felt the change diminished his story.

Ken Liu, a translator of Chinese science fiction (and of *The Three Body Problem*), has become adept in navigating such political obstacles. He finds creative ways to transmit the writer's political or social critiques without being too inflammatory. Liu argues that in the effort to maintain this delicate balance, many sci-fi writers have skillfully learned to convey their art in an ambiguous manner, creating multiple possibilities of interpretation. Such ambiguity works as loopholes for authors to publish daring material without explicitly challenging the government—while readers are left to read between the lines.

It should be noted that in recent times, there is good news for these writers, as China is experiencing a science fiction renaissance of sorts, perhaps because President Xi's AI dominance message and mission need sci-fi's help. Today, the genre is receiving its longest run of quasi-government support. For example, after the success of *The Wandering Earth*, a headline in *People's Daily*—the Chinese Communist Party newspaper—proudly proclaimed: "Only the Chinese Can Save the Planet!" Authors such as Liu Cixin believe this trend may signal a deeper shift within the government and societal mindset, one where rapid technological change has fostered a new excitement about sci-fi's depiction of China's future possibilities.

Ultimately, it's an interesting dilemma that the Chinese government faces. President Xi wishes to utilize the popularity and inspirational vision of Sci-fi to foster innovation and lead China into the technological future. However, Xi's expanding governmental cultural controls actually work to stifle this very mission. While the country's sci-fi artists are not only creative in their storytelling but also creative in their rebellion, as they strive for artistic expression without being shut down. Just as with Liu Cixin's *The Wandering Earth*, we see our rebel hero fight against the machine's authority—where man prevails against the powers that be. Furthermore, the rebel saves humanity with something very human—hope.

THE LEGACY OF UNUS ANNUS: EPHEMERAL ART IN A CYBERPUNK WORLD

BY ANDREA BLYTHE

> *"For its part, Unus Annus is situated within this crossroads of art and technology, embodying fine art traditions through a digital medium well suited to the cyberpunk world in which we live."*

What would you do if you knew you only had a year to live? This philosophical question lies at the heart of *Unus Annus* (latin for "one year"), a creative experiment developed by gamers Mark Fischbach (Markiplier) and Ethan Nestor (Crankgameplays). The YouTube channel served as their own answer to the question. Embracing the idea of making every second count, the pair set themselves the challenge of creating and posting one new video every day for a year.

Featuring a variety of stunts and absurdist humor, *Unus Annus* garnered immediate popularity, reaching over one million subscribers within a week of being launched and accumulating 4.44 million by the year's end. One of the compelling aspects of the channel was not only its daily upload of videos, but its promise to self-destruct at the end of the appointed year.

What's more, is that Fischbach and Nestor followed through with that promise. At the stroke of midnight on Friday, November 13, 2020, the *Unus Annus* channel and all of its content was deleted.

Though confounding to some, the decision positions *Unus Annus* as a landmark in our current cultural landscape. The channel is simultaneously connected to our increasingly digital and technology-infused world and bound to artistic traditions (such as absurdism and ephemeral art), marking it as a creative project that should be remembered long after its passing.

LIVING IN A CYBERPUNK WORLD

Cyberpunk as a science fiction genre began in the 1980s through the works of authors such as Neal Stephenson, William Gibson, and Bruce Sterling. Rather than presenting the hopeful technological ideals of earlier science fiction, these authors envisioned dystopian futures in which advanced technologies, such as artificial intelligence, virtual reality, and cybernetics, are juxtaposed against bleak societies with mega-corporation overlords and high levels of poverty and crime. The highly influential genre has had a significant impact on science fiction and media as a whole, spawning numerous dark, neon-infused landscapes across novels, comics, movies, and video games.

A recent iteration of the genre was the highly anticipated video game, *Cyberpunk 2077* (*CD Projekt Red*), which launched just this year to mixed reviews. Many critics have noted that while the game echoes the gritty neon-infused aesthetics of cyberpunk, it seems to lack the revolutionary heart. This disconnect between the visual cyberpunk style and any deep social commentary against capitalism typical of the genre has led some critics to question whether cyberpunk as a genre is still relevant in today's world.

Part of the reasoning is that many of the futuristic technologies envisioned in Gibson and Sterling's early novels have now come to pass. Technology floods our everyday lives—and concepts like surveillance capitalism, genetic engineering, artificial intelligence, virtual and augmented realities, and drone technologies (for delivery and weaponization) have become the norm.

In other words, we're already living in a cyberpunk world.

The pandemic has further cemented us within this cyberpunk landscape. As we have withdrawn from public activities during quarantine isolation, we have become even more dependent on the digital realm to maintain social interactions and business relationships. A number of corporations are experiencing immense growth in these challenging times, while smaller businesses and individual workers are struggling.

Living in a cyberpunk reality means that technology, particularly computers and robotics, has become integrated into nearly every aspect of our lives. This includes how we create and interact with the arts—an area traditionally known for its connection to physical spaces.

When discussing "art", the concept tends to dredge up images of sculptors chiseling away at marble or painters in color-splattered studios attacking a canvas with paint and brush. For the more theatrically inclined, the word may provide visions of Shakespearian stage productions. In each of these cases, the audience's interaction with the work also requires traveling to a physical space in the forms of art museums, galleries, or theaters.

With the advent of digital technology and social media, the creation of and interaction with the arts is shifting a few degrees—an adaptation that has been further exaggerated by the pandemic. While a great amount of film and television have been available streaming services for years now, a number of theatrical productions have also begun producing live streams and recordings to provide audiences access. Likewise, art and history museums have curated virtual exhibits, allowing visitors to explore the exhibits from their couch in true cyberpunk fashion.

The creation of art has also been fully infused with the digital. Almost as soon as the first computers were invented, people began attempting to make art using the new technologies available. Some of the first original pieces of art appeared in the 50s and 60s, and artists have continued to use computers to make art ever since, ranging from digital paintings to experimental works incorporating light and sound. In particular, digital painting has become a common medium, with artists across the web creating and sharing digital works on par with creators using traditional tools.

The realm of digital art creation has even progressed beyond the human. Programmed to use machine learning to gather immense amounts of data about a particular art form, artificial intelligence then creates new works extrapolated from this learning. The results have proven to be at turns interesting, humorous, and eerie.

As with any newer artistic medium, a debate has been raised about the value of digital art compared to traditional methods. One of the advantages of physical painting and sculptures is that they represent a unique physical product that can thus be deemed the "original" that represents a special cultural value that can grow over time. In the cases of fine art, pieces can eventually become valued at hundreds of thousands (if not millions) of dollars due their rarity.

Digital art has faced a challenge in this regard, as the format can be easily duplicated with the copy being identical to the original. But never fear, a cyberpunk-worthy solution to this challenge has been developed through the development of cryptoart. Through blockchain technology, "a digital work can be imbued with programmatic scarcity by its creator, a first step to indicating authenticity."

These intersections between the creation and consumption of art and the digital are continually evolving, with some artists pulling away from computer technology to rely on more physical mediums, while others lean into it. For its part, *Unus Annus* is situated within this crossroads of art and technology, embodying fine art traditions through a digital medium well suited to the cyberpunk world in which we live.

THE ART OF SHITPOSTING

When Fischbach and Nestor set themselves the challenge of producing one video a day for a year, they provided few parameters as to what those videos might actually be. The resulting content, with its wild variety of subject matters and filming styles, made the channel difficult to pin down.

Lauren Milici of *Fanbyte* described the channel as an "existential *Jackass* for a new generation," comparing the antics of Fishbach and Nestor to the dangerous and disgusting stunts that the *Jackass* comedians performed in the 90s. It's an apt comparison, encompassing a multitude of the pair's adventures, including creating their own bungee jump, sitting inside pee saunas, and (under the guidance of professionals) attempting fire breathing, learning aerial hoop acrobatics, and getting hit with pepper spray. A series of stunts carried darkly comedic undertones, parodying horror themes through attempts at ghost hunting, calling forth spirits, staged kidnappings, and exploring escape rooms.

And yet, a vast number of videos fall outside of the confines of stunts—particularly when the pandemic struck. When the lockdowns in March and April 2020 hit, Fischbach and Nestor went into lockdown, which forced them to adapt to the use of video conferencing along with much of the world. Their videos during this time shifted to more conversation-based content, many focused on memes and other oddities of the internet.

Few videos bothered to hold any kind of narrative thread. However, one of particular note was "Hunting HeeHoo" (the 290th episode), which represented one of the most sophisticated videos on the channel in terms of its storytelling and cinematography. The video was essentially a mockumentary short film in the cinematic style of paranormal documentaries, such as *Finding Bigfoot* (*Animal Planet,* 2011). As the story goes, Markiplier (Fischbach) devolves into the terrifying creature known as HeeHoo, leaving Nestor to pick up the pieces and track down and save his friend. Narration by Dave Pettitt brought a gravity to the project and cemented the dry humor and documentary-style tone.

When you take in the whole of the *Unus Annus* content—ranging from brick soccer to video hypnotism, to seeing how many slaps it would take to cook a raw chicken—perhaps the best way to sum up the channel is through the concept of **shitposting**.

As its most basic, shitposting is an expression of absurdity or randomness, which can be intentionally meaningless or satirical in nature. Although often associated with internet memes, shitposting hails from art history.

A notable example is the Dada movement, which started in the 1910s. Following WWI and facing economic and political frustrations, the artists of the movement pushed back against the status quo by presenting art situated in absurdity. A well-known piece of the movement is Marcel Duchamp's "Fountain", which was a "readymade" art piece composed of a porcelain urinal signed "R. Mutt".

According to Sam Greszes at *Polygon* ("Shitposting Is An Art, If History Is Any Indication," December 17, 2018), the Dada movement was drawn from disgust at the world. "A society that victimizes its own most vulnerable elements doesn't deserve context, humor, or decadence, the artists insisted," he explains. "That society instead deserves nonsense."

Such absurdist humor can also be found littered throughout the classical music world, as well. As Matt Brazel explains ("Historical Shitposting and the Importance of Absurdist Humour in Music," Happy Mag, July 15, 2020), composers such as Mozart and Igor Stravinsky were known to have infused their work with musical jokes that poked fun at conventions of the time (which later became legitimate tools of the craft). One could also look at the work of experimental composer John Cage created *4'33"*, which "instructs its performers to not play their instruments—at all."

As an art form, shitposting thrives in our modern cyberpunk world, since the digital medium makes it infinitely easier to create and spread. The constant onslaught of anxieties and absurdities throughout 2020, in particular, have provided fodder for shitposting and memes to be fed and nurtured. Faced with a constant barrage of strange, unsettling news over the past few years, it's only natural to turn to works that offer amusement and humor through demonstration of nonsense.

As such, the launch of *Unus Annus* was perfectly timed to suit the zeitgeist of this moment, while continuing the traditions of artists who came before. Displaying a urinal in an art museum alongside more traditional works resonates the same energy as Fishbach and Nestor delightedly making breakfast using sex toys as utensils. Neither work in and of itself is trying to make sense. The absurdity is the point.

And yet, *Unus Annus* also contained an element that went beyond mere shitposting and wild stunts, namely the existentialism of which Milici makes note. The channel was based on the premise of its own eventual destruction, with each video counting down to its inevitable end. No matter the absurdity or nonsense that may unveil itself in various individual videos, the constant ticking of the clock was an ever-present reminder of the impermanence of life.

WHEN DIGITAL MEETS THE EPHEMERAL

Ephemeral art—or art that is intended to only exist once or for a short period of time—has been around for almost as long as the concept of art itself. A common form of ephemerality is represented by musical concerts, stage plays, or performance art (such as "The Artist is Present" by Artist Marina Abramovic). Though they can be recorded, the performance in the moment is unique and can only be truly experienced once.

Ephemeral art can take on physical manifestations as well, as in the case of street art that can be painted over at any moment, exterior sculptural works intended to fade from or change along with the environment, henna tattoos that fade over time, elaborate icing decorations on cookies or cakes designed to be eaten, or various other temporal mediums.

A number of living artists have become known for their ephemeral works, such as land artist Andy Goldsworthy who tunes into his surroundings to create site-specific art out of the materials around him—leaves, sticks, snow, bark, rocks, etc.—providing an intense shock of beauty in relation to the natural world.

As another example, Néle Azevedo, a Brazilian artist, created an installation in which she shaped 1,000 figures out of ice on the steps of a concert hall in Berlin, Germany in 2009. Designed to send a message about global warming, the figures quickly melted into puddles in the sun. The figures have since been recreated at other monuments around the world.

Ephemeral art is often used to signify the transitory nature of life, the reality that everything changes and fades. As the artist Dina Goebel at the Creative Feeling writes ("Ephemeral Art: What a Beautiful Thing"), "It allows the artist to make a link between the relationships of existence, decay, and loss. It is this transition between life and death where many religious cultures, myths and rituals exist. Where the purpose of the art is to celebrate or acknowledge a transition period, not necessarily between life and death but also for example, from child to adult."

Unus Annus played directly into this concept, through the creator's plan to delete the channel after a year of work. Not only was this ephemerality planned, but it was intertwined with a clear message. "Memento Mori," stated the creators, intoning the channel's motto. The Latin phrase translated to "remember death," acting more as an affirmation of the value of life rather than nihilism.

"On a video to video basis, it wasn't [that] deep," said Nestor in the final video of the project, "But the overarching theme of the channel was make the most out of your life, because it's going to end and you have to do everything you can with the time that you have."

From a thematic standpoint, *Unus Annus'* connection to ephemeral art is obvious. However, its implementation of YouTube videos as its medium brings into question whether or not digital art can actually be ephemeral.

Documentation and preservation have long been topics of discussion when it comes to ephemeral art. A general understanding is that the level and form of documentation of the original work should be determined by the artist—which has been complicated by the technologies available. Smartphones are prevalent, providing both a high-quality digital camera and the capability of instantly sharing photos across social media.

Many street and land artists actively photograph and share their own work, as building a social media presence has become a vital aspect of building their reputation and careers. Some street artists and muralists even print their social media handles and hashtags onto their work, so that photographs can be easily found when shared.

It's also important to note that this kind of documentation permitted by the author is typically transformative. In other words, a photograph of street or land art is not an exact replica of the work itself. Therefore, the original work is able to remain ephemeral, fading or being erased as intended.

Working within a digital medium makes the issue of documentation even more complex. Digital paintings, photographs, videos, and even complete websites can be instantaneously preserved through caching, screenshots, and downloads—copies that are indistinguishable from the original, bringing ownership of the work into question. Furthermore, nothing shared online ever really dies. Digital works thought to be lost can often resurface weeks, months, or even years later.

Unus Annus is situated at the heart of this issue. From the start, the project was designed to be ephemeral, and Fischbach and Nestor have been clear about their intentions to that end, periodically reminding viewers that the videos once gone were meant to stay gone. Although the pair has stated that transformative works (such as fan art and some compilation videos) would be permitted, they requested that any downloads of their videos be deleted along with the channel. For those cases when cases in which their wishes are violated (as in the reupload of complete *Unus Annus* videos), Fischbach and Nestor have promised to pursue their removal, even through litigation, if necessary.

Ensuring the deletion of *Unus Annus* will likely provide to be an ongoing and lengthy battle. Even as I write this, copycat channels have already sprung up and vanished, like digital doppelgangers. Almost as soon as one seems to be removed, another takes its place. Or seems to take its place, as it's sometimes difficult to tell the difference between each copy—ghosts of ghosts of ghosts.

Much of the control is outside of the creator's hands. Ensuring that a digital ephemeral work remains ephemeral therefore becomes a communal act. The audience actively participates in the ephemerality of a work by choosing to *not* engage in the consumption of that work. Just as Fishbach and Nestor held true to their promise to delete the channel, fans of *Unus Annus* seem likewise committed to honoring the intent of the project. Any copycats will thus have little impact on the overall effect of the project. Those who were present during the journey—whether they discovered it at the beginning of the end—shared in the experience of loving something and then letting it go.

MEMENTO MORI

The last year has felt like we've been trapped in a cyberpunk dystopian nightmare. Locked inside our homes by the pandemic, we have had to rely on Zoom calls and social media for our human interactions, each of which presents its own benefits and frustrations. All the while, news about the world has seemed to get worse and worse—with things only tentatively starting to improve in the new year.

In the midst of this anxiety-inducing chaos, *Unus Annus* provided consistency through a daily dose of absurd humor, while also reminding viewers to take advantage of what life we are given. It's hard to let something like that go.

The final hours of *Unus Annus* provided a memorial for what the channel achieved. Fischbach and Nestor hosted a twelve-hour Livestream, during which they reflected on their efforts over the past year, shared fanart and memes, and thanked crew, guests, and viewers for being a part of the journey.

All the while, the seconds ticked down on the clock behind them.

Over 1.5 million people were present to witness these final moments, a gathering of the community that loved these videos. While Fischbach and Nestor spoke on the Livestream, the viewers took to social media, sharing their favorite moments of the channel and expressing thoughts about what it meant to them personally and how it helped them through a tumultuous year.

Then as the seconds ticked down to zero, Fischbach and Nestor hit delete—and *Unus Annus* vanished. "It was a year's worth of work to build up to one moment, that one second before we hit the delete button. That last second; that was everything," said Fischbach in his post mortem video. He explained that the point was to elicit heavy emotions of grieving, to deal with and accept loss. "I wanted to make something that was so important that people would hate to let it go—and that's what we did."

Watching the screen go black, it was hard not to feel that I had witnessed the conclusion to something important. The full significance of *Unus Annus* and its impact on the creation of digital ephemeral art still remains to be seen. Other digital and artistic experiments will come, and the ways in which art interacts with technology will continue to evolve. Regardless of what's to come, *Unus Annus*—with its particular blend of absurdity, existentialism, and experimentation in digital ephemeral art—stood as a marker along the path.

A NEW HALLOWEEN: HOW COVID-19 CHANGED THE WAY WE CELEBRATE HALLOWEEN

BY CHRISTINA SNG

The COVID-19 pandemic has greatly affected the way we live and socialize over the past 2 years. One of the most beloved celebrations affected is Halloween, especially for the horror community.

I asked some members of the Horror Writers Association how the pandemic has changed how they celebrate Halloween. Their answers were both delightful and inspiring! Read on.

John C. Mannone: I was staying at my daughter's for a couple of weeks while my house was being sold (finally did in April) when Halloween "arrived". She and others decorated the house, especially externally to keep the spirit alive.

Steve Stred: Usually each Halloween we'd meet up with my sister and her family to trick or treat as Halloween is also my nephew's birthday. For last year, we rented an AirBnB in the mountains and did a trick or treat scavenger hunt for them throughout the two levels so that they could still find stuff but not worry about the uncertainty of knocking on strangers doors!

Lisa Morton: We stage a small yard haunt each year. Last year we redesigned it so that it was completely viewable from the street, rather than including a walk up to the door, and on Halloween night we livestreamed it via Facebook Live for half-an-hour. I think we ended up with more people visiting virtually than we've ever had in person (we're hidden in a cul-de-sac), so we plan on continuing to livestream each year.

Jacqueline West: My six-year-old has respiratory issues, so we didn't trick-or-treat last year (except to a couple of relatives' houses)—but because we live in a neighborhood with lots of kids who we know, we did reverse trick-or-treating instead.

We made little paper bags full of treats, and my son helped decorate and label them, and we dropped them off of the porches or doorsteps of his friends early on Halloween afternoon.

We still got to walk the neighborhood and see all the decorations, while avoiding any crowds/close contact, and he loved leaving the special surprises for everyone.

Rami Ungar: Since I celebrate Halloween year-round as well, I try to find something fun to do each year. Last year, I saw a couple of movies and wished I was having a more exciting Halloween.

This year, however, I plan to be in Vegas for Halloween come heck or high water. I plan to start on the 30th ghost hunting at Zak Bagan's museum and end the day at the Adventure Dome's Fright Night festivities.

Cecile Grimm-Cabeen: We LOVE throwing a big Halloween Bash at our house each year. But because of COVID, our last "Bash" was 2019. Not sure when we can resume our big bashes.

In 2020 on Halloween, our daughter decided to have a formal, sit-down Halloween dinner party just for our family "pod".

She even staged a scavenger hunt throughout the house for us to find our Halloween bags of customized treats. It was just the 6 of us. We played a Werewolf game of puzzles too. It was fun.

Ken Vaughan: We normally get between 2 and 500 kids. Last year we just didn't have the spoons and kept closed for the night. There was virtually no traffic in any case. Will probably do something this year.

Lou Rera: It didn't. I set up a Halloween-themed installation in the graveyard behind my house, replete with a ghoul to scare the hell out of my granddaughters.

H.R. Boldwood: I made up personalized treat bags and set them on a table on the driveway and waved from the front door, chatting with them.

Lorna Dickson-Keach: My husband ran a Ravenloft DnD game for me and my son, and we both dressed up as skeletons.

The story included an investigation where our characters had to interview the residents of a spooky village to solve the puzzle and with every house we "found" candy treasure, which he doled out and we munched on while playing.

It was awesome.

Larry Hinkle: We drew pictures on little treat bags and set them out at the end of the driveway.

Colleen Anderson: Well, not much for me but some of the houses around where I lived have porches and stairs. They rigged up a slide for passing the goodies down the rail to the waiting kiddies. Safe and fun!

And a special feature from Lee Murray on Halloween in New Zealand:

In the past, Halloween wasn't widely celebrated in New Zealand—was even strongly objected to by some groups as being overly commercial and promoting satanic practices among children!—but a general interest in global traditions and a plethora of fun Halloween merchandise has resulted in a surge in participation in recent years. After all, who doesn't like free candy/lollies. Plastic spiders. Orange balloons. Dressing up? And downunder in New Zealand, October is springtime, so you don't have to wear a coat over your carefully crafted costume.

In 2020, when Halloween came around, we'd not long come out of lock-down and since we had no vaccine yet, people here were naturally cautious. Sending your children out to knock on strangers' doors seemed a particularly bad thing to do in a pandemic. And New Zealand has adopted a total elimination policy, which means we act to isolate any COVID in the community.

But the government also recognized that people were looking for ways to celebrate and connect, so they introduced a household contact tracing system. All it required was that I go to the national health website, put in my address and the site spat out an individual QR scan code for my household.

Hello! Horror writer. I *love* Halloween. I laminated the posters, taped one to my front door and another where it could be seen at the far end of the house, and those posters have been there ever since. Now anyone who comes to my house can hold up their phone and scan their details and the information is recorded.

I need to be clear here: I have no record of those people's names and addresses, but, *if* there were an outbreak associated with my household or anyone who visited my home, I could give permission for the government health trackers to access contact information for the period of interest.

Those details, stored in the cloud, cannot be used for any other purpose than contact tracing and they are deleted three weeks after the contact date. Having those contact tracing posters gave me confidence that if we were unlucky enough to have COVID-19 circulating in the community, any spread might be readily contained.

So armed with that tracking app (highlighted with a balloon on Halloween), a fun mask, and a huge bowl of wrapped candy, we celebrated Halloween as usual—*almost.* Each time the doorbell rang, I opened the door, shooed the kids back a bit (kids will do almost anything when bribed with candy), put the candy bowl out on a stool, and the kids helped themselves to large handfuls.

Prompted by their parents (typically standing back on the driveway), the kids said thank you, and then off they went to the next house. When I'd waved the little demons goodbye, I brought the candy in, so it didn't melt (NZ springtime, remember). Repeat.

There were fewer visitors than usual, but I can say without a doubt, those little ghouls and witches were super excited—even those whose smiles I couldn't see behind their masks. And the mums and dads scanning their details seemed happy, too. It worked so well, I'm planning to do the same this year.

FUTURISM IN THE LAND OF THE FUTURE: FINDING SOLACE IN CHINESE SCIENCE FICTION

BY ELYSE RIBBONS 柳素英

I have recently relocated from sunny Chapel Hill, North Carolina to the other side of the world, Chengdu, China. Something of note about the Sichuan provincial capital, home to more than sixteen million people and several thousand pandas, is that it is also the base of the Chinese Sci-fi World Publishing group. While you might not be familiar with the magazine Kehuan Shijie 科幻世界, you are likely familiar with the worldwide hit they published, *Three Body Problem* (2008) by Liu Cixin.

Since I have recently moved, I am still suffering through the many weeks of quarantine. Between desperate acts of creativity to engage my toddler in anything other than screen time, I have found much solace in reading the wonderful short stories in Kehuan Shijie. Chinese sci-fi is a joy for many reasons, but a large part is that it feels a little less like fiction and more like near-future realities.

A short story published by Kehuan Shijie in 2019 has recently been making waves as it was the most highly fought over for film rights at the Shanghai Film Fest this year. But this science fiction story, "**Tuse Shijie**" 涂色世界 (or "Coloring the World") is very different from the typical stories vied for in the Chinese film market.

Written by Mu Ming, a woman who has extensive experience in computer science and has worked at Google, "Tuse Shijie" is a story of a near-future world grappling with the benefits of technology at the cost of human individuality. The main key to the story is a retinal implant that provides tetrachromacy as well as other visual enhancements. A mother with Ludditeleanings has to deal with the desires of her color-blind daughter to be like the rest of her classmates. As a winner of the 31st Annual Chinese Literature Awards, this story clearly hit a note with readers, many of whom are parents grappling with their own expectations and technological philosophies for their children. This is in noted correlation with the recent revamping of educational regulations and the banning of tutoring companies.

Another great example of social issues at the heart of Chinese Sci-fi is the 2016 Hugo award-winning short story, "Folding Beijing," also written by a women, Hao Jingfang. She writes of a world where space is folded to create three separate geographical realities that inhabit the same space when opened up. The first tier is for the moneyed classes, and it represents a world of clean air, green parks, refinement, and they get most of the time in the space. The second tier is for the middle classes and is more densely populated and a little bit less nice, they also get less time in the space. And finally, the third tier is for the laboring masses, who live in towers of tiny apartments and subsist off of meager meals and have never seen an open sky or green trees. They also get the least amount of time, with only eight hours of access to the space in every 48-hour cycle.

This stratification of the three classes is not too far from the current reality of modern Chinese cities. I write this as I look out my own window in the university district of Chengdu, and instead of lovely green parks, I see a massive ocean of giant buildings. Thousands and thousands of people live in the apartments within my view. It's a little bit like sitting on the beach and staring out at the sea, one feels very small and insignificant in the face of it.

And yet that story reflects the fraught relationship for physical space and class, and recent rent controls and landlord rules being placed in Beijing is a reaction to this friction. To me, this is yet another example of the prescience of futurism in science fiction. And one of the many reasons why living in China, in certain aspects, is a little bit like taking a look at life in the future.

Recently, Kai-Fu Lee, the computer scientist who previously ran Google's operations in China, wrote the book *A.I. 2041: Ten Visions for Our Future* (*Currency*, 2021) which lays out his vision of our A.I.-enabled future. While this book is non-fiction, he collaborated with a previous employee and award-winning science fiction writer Chen Qiufan. What makes this book so truly unique is that it pairs ten essays penned by Lee with ten short works of speculative fiction by Chen. As one journalist wrote, "The effect is a little bit like reading an issue of McKinsey Quarterly and then watching an episode of the dark sci-fi TV series Black Mirror" ("What Will A.I. Make Possible by 2041? Technologist Kai-Fu Lee Has Some Ideas," in Fortune, September 14, 2021).

Being based in metropolis China makes thinking of futurism in present-day terms a surprisingly easy thing to do. I currently live in a very average University-housing complex and the gate at my compound has a facial recognition system to open all the gates and entrances. It will alert authorities if I break my quarantine. I was impressed that it recognized my face, even with my mask, when I came back from my most recent COVID test.

It is a world where one has to carry their phone with them at all times not because they're addicted to their screens, but because it contains an interactive QR health code. This code is scanned at access points to almost all buildings and public transport. If someone has been in contact with anyone who later tests positive for COVID-19, this health code will then turn red. Only when it's green are you able to walk around freely and use public transportation.

I am looking forward to the end of quarantine, and proudly being able to show my green QR code to other parents, after I've checked theirs so that I know that our children can play together safely. This is something that I could not do in America outside of our pod, as it was impossible to know exactly who people had shared air with. I am also looking forward to going out and attending nerdy futurist talks and other events that I'd be more wary of in the U.S. And so I wait, with bated breath, for the end of my quarantining. Biding my time between Teletubbies with the toddler and Kehuan Shijie when she naps.

TRUE CRIME IS A FEMINIST HOBBY: STUDYING THE HISTORY OF CRIME HELPS US UNDERSTAND VIOLENCE AGAINST WOMEN

BY HOLLY LYN WALRATH

If you're a true crime fan, you're probably a feminist. Searches for "true crime" and "women" on Google come up with a slew of articles discussing how a huge portion of true crime fans are women, particularly young women. These articles are often written by women who love the genre, and the majority of them begin with some story of their own trauma related to crime or else the reality of being a woman in today's world:

> "I was walking down the street wearing big headphones. I wear them everywhere, like many women, trans, and queer people I know, to avoid hearing men's street harassment. And in my headphones I was listening to a Dateline NBC podcast episode about a woman being murdered. It struck me as kind of sick—listening to stories of women's suffering for my enjoyment in order to avoid a milder form of suffering in the real world. But that's the appeal of the true crime genre: We like it because it confirms that the world is dangerous and bad. But unlike the real world, in which men harass and assault and murder women, true crime can always be switched off." — P.E. Moskowitz, "True Crime is Cathartic for Women. It's Also Cop Propaganda," in Mother Jones, May/June 2020 Issue

Rape. Murder. Mutilation. Kidnapping. Torture. These are some of the topics often covered in true crime, a genre that is perhaps more horrific because of its basis in reality. When we see the words "based on a true story," we're immediately hooked. The way we hurt each other as humans is terrifyingly fascinating and intrinsically skewed against women.

When you start to explore true crime stories, several patterns stand out. Victims of violent crimes are primarily women. According to the National Organization for Women, an average of three women a day are killed in the US, and one-third of women are killed by an intimate partner. According to the National Center for Injury Prevention and Control, about 4.8 million intimate partner-related physical assaults and rapes occur yearly. The National Crime Victimization Survey showed that in 2006, 600 women were raped each day in the US. The primary targets of crimes are young women, low-income women, black women, queer women, and women with disabilities. ("Violence Against Women in the United States: Statistics," National Organization for Women)

True crime forces us to acknowledge that crime often targets the most vulnerable of our society and that women who are in "double jeopardy" by nature of being a woman and black (or triple, or quadruple in the case of women by nature of their race, gender, sexuality, class, dis/ability, ethnicity, and economic status) are very often the most targeted of victims.

Violence against women needs to be stopped, clearly, but it can't change without society's viewpoint completely shifting. How do you get people to not just recognize the statistics, but to change? How do you stop the mindset that puts men in power and then doesn't hold them accountable?

One answer might lie in true crime.

THE PSYCHOLOGY OF FEAR

Something happens to our minds when we hear a story. We immediately insert ourselves into the narrative, into the shoes of the main character. Our brains churn the scenario, wondering, "What would I do in this situation?"

Uri Hasson, a researcher from Princeton, studied what happens to the human brain when it hears a story. He had one person watch an episode of *Sherlock*. Then, he had another person listen to a retelling of the episode. It turns out both people shared similar brain wave patterns, despite hearing different versions of the same story. Thus, story activates the brain and gets a listener to apply that story to their own experience, working the same way in different people. ("Clicking: How Our Brains Are in Sync," by Katherine Hobson in Princeton Alumni Weekly, April 11, 2018).

Story is a shared, cultural understanding. Stories are often passed down from generation to generation. So it makes sense that women are among the biggest fans of true crime. After all, what story have our mothers taught us better than to fear men?

The last few years have seen a massive outpouring of true crime-related media, and in particular, true crime media by women. From podcasts to books, women creators are able to synthesize crime in ways that make their work wildly popular to readers and viewers.

When I started getting into true crime, I realized that the majority of people who had interviewed serial killers were women. Books like Katharine Ramsland's *Confession of a Serial Killer: The Untold Story of Dennis Rader, the BTK Killer* (*ForeEdge*, 2017), written during a long correspondence Ramsland had with Rader while he was in jail.

> "Danger is strangely attractive. It's arousing, and makes us feel alive. When we read true crime accounts, we can experience this shivering dread within a protective frame. The stories fascinate us, but we also know we can put the book down and walk away. We can feel the energy without being overwhelmed by anxiety. We get close to the bodies without having to do the autopsy, or see through a killer's eyes without concern over being arrested. We're voyeurs. We step through a massacre to satisfy our morbid curiosity, but also to raise our sense of anger: we want good to prevail, limping along though it may be, and the perp to go down. The investigation that probes closer and closer provides tension and relief, and the court case with a final just verdict is cathartic. If the story is well told, we feel for the victims, the investigators, and the families who must suffer through it. With the exception of crimes not solved or bodies never found, these stories feel right. They restore our sense of safety and hope" (Ramsland in an interview, "Neither Fear Nor Symmetry in the World of Katherine Ramsland," by Mark Danowsky in Schuylkill Valley Journal Online).

I was fascinated by the grit it took to start corresponding with a known killer. And I also knew, it was the kind of thing society didn't expect a woman to do. But women LOVE true crime. They consume it at such a rate that true crime podcasts increased 16% among women in 2019 compared to 2018 ("Social Psychologist Amanda Vicary and Spotify Reveal Why Women Are so Obsessed with True Crime—and Share 4 New Podcasts Coming in 2020," in For the Record, Spotify, January 29, 2020), according to researcher and psychologist Amanda Vicary. Her study showed that women not only prefer true crime books over books about say, gang violence, but they also prefer true crime stories with female protagonists ("Women, More than Men, Choose True Crime Over Other Violent Nonfiction," by Diana Yates, Illinois News, February 15, 2010).

Vicary surmises that women love true crime because of the brain's story mechanism. True crime stories allow women to insert themselves into the narrative and figure out how they would react in a situation. Some of the most popular true crime stories are survivor tales, like that of Ted Bundy's only living victim, Kathy Kleiner.

> "It could be the fact that we're just in tune and interested in these things that are dangerous to us because understanding and knowing about them can increase our chances that it's not going to happen to us." Vicary explains in an article in The Atlantic ("How a True Crime Podcast Became a Mental-Health Support Group," by Andrea Marks, February 21, 2017).

True crime geared toward women has become so common that it has spawned an entire world of consumerism, with shirts that read "dogs, wine, and true crime" or "murder shows and comfy clothes." Like most feminist movements, true crime has quickly been co-opted for profit.

The women taking over the genre are extremely talented. There are hundreds upon hundreds of true crime podcasts, and a very many of them are hosted by women, including my favorite, *Morbid* (2018-present), hosted by Alaina & Ash. Alaina is an autopsy technician who often lends her expertise to the show's most gory details. They come up with quippy sayings "fresh air is for dead people" and "better a rude bitch than a dead bitch" that encourage women (and men) to be alert to patterns in crime, like the fact that serial killers often target houses with open doors and windows (see Richard Chase), or that nice women who help men often end up dead (see Ted Bundy).

The genre has made way for women to become pivotal in industries that are now a major part of our society. Sarah Koenig's work on *Serial* (*This American Life*, 2014-2022) was a major part of the revivification of the podcast industry, for example. Season One was the most popular, and it followed the case of Hae Min Lee, who was murdered in 1999. Koenig dived into the trial of the accused Adnan Masud Syed and her investigative journalism was in part responsible for the appeal of Syed's case in 2014, which was eventually denied by the Supreme Court. Listeners remain convinced of Syed's innocence based on Koenig's work on the podcast.

Phoebe Judge and Lauren Spohrer were on the forefront of the genre with the podcast *Criminal* (*Vox Media Podcast Network*, 2014-Present) started in January of 2014. In the early world of podcasting, the stage was dominated by men. *Criminal* is hosted and produced by women who own the company that runs it, but it wasn't always that way. "We've performed at podcast festivals where we could count the number of women on one hand" ("Interview: Criminal and This is Love Co-Founders 'Proud to Be a Woman-Run Shop'," by Charline Jao in The Mary Sue, May 9th, 2018). What I like best about *Criminal* is how it doesn't apply any kind of judgment to the crime. It simply tells the story. But even then, you can tell the producers are aware of the placement of a story in context. For example, when they told the story of the early lottery, "the numbers," they made a point to include the game's history and its landmark status of having been started by black women.

SURVIVAL OR MERELY REPRESENTATION?

While it's tempting to peg the interest women have in true crime on our desire to find ways to survive men, and that's likely a part of it, I think the answer is more feminist. We're finally seeing women talking about crime in an authentic and inclusive way. Women are leading podcasts, tv shows, and writing about true crime in a way that a patriarchal society never intended. The women who have made true crime their lives and careers are a form of representation that allows women to feel comfortable in the true crime world.

If you consume enough true crime content, you start to recognize patterns. And those patterns point to a society which has allowed men to kill women for years on end. It's not just about this one fact—that men kill more than women. It's also about the larger system. Over and over again, you will hear how police ignore women's testimony, how they disregard crimes because the victim is a sex worker, how they listen to men more than women, and that leads to more deaths, how they often disbelieve women who have been raped, how having a woman cop on the scene of a sex crime can make a major difference, how male police officers use their status to commit sex crimes.

Studying true crime can open your eyes to the facts you may have missed before. These are statistics we should know already—that we shouldn't be surprised by. But something about the compelling format of say, a podcast telling the story of a murder in detail, gives them authenticity. These are statistics we gloss over when we hear them, such as this excerpt from a report on the efficacy of prevention of violence against women and girls:

> "WHO estimates that more than 30% of women worldwide have experienced either physical or sexual partner violence. 7% of women worldwide have experienced non-partner sexual assault. About 100–140 million girls and women worldwide have undergone female genital mutilation (FGM) and more than 3 million girls are at risk for FGM every year in Africa alone. Nearly 70 million girls worldwide have been married before the age of 18 years, many of them against their will. The effect of violence against women and girls on their health and welfare, their families, and communities is substantial. The costs of violence against women and girls, both direct and indirect, are a staggering burden for households and economies." — Ellsberg et al, *The Lancet* (March 2018)

The city of Juarez, Mexico has the highest rate of femicide (murder of women) in the world. As one researcher explains, "Ciudad Juarez was built around capitalist factories; low wages and poor working conditions combined with Ciudad Juarez's border location gave rise to poverty, drug use and criminal gangs. Women, particularly those who were employed, became a target for murder and sexual violence" ("Gender and Violence: Feminist Theories, Deadly Economies, and Damaging Discourse," by Janine Shaw in E-International Relations, November 3, 2017).

Shaw goes on to explain why femicide is by nature, a problem that must be explored intersectionally: "The theory of femicide also places victims within patriarchal power structures of economics and politics, allowing for a deeper insight into how violence is connected to patriarchy and masculinity. Femicide thus highlights the complex relationship between violence, economics, politics and gender ideology."

Studying true crime is intersectional. For example, look at the theory of canon. If we consider women writers in the canon of books that are published, for example, it's clear that more women are published today than they used to be. This is because of the shift of power that feminism created—allowing more women to be literate, to seek out and demand books by women and for women, and for more publishers to publish women writers successfully.

The same can be said of the "true crime canon" or list of popular crimes that are regularly covered in true crime shows. Sure, you're bound to cover Ted Bundy and the white, middle-class, attractive women he targeted. But true crime fans want more than just the well-known, well-trodden canon. And the introduction of a feminist lens allows the canon to be looked at in a different frame of reference. What crimes were investigated by the police and what crimes were reported? How much did the media cover a crime and why? (Studies show that the media often overreports violent crime, overrepresents black men as perpetrators of crime, and overreports missing white women in what is called "the missing white girl syndrome"). These factors ultimately determine what crimes are part of the true crime canon.

Examining crime means we are forced to consider things like race, gender, sexuality, class, dis/ability, ethnicity, and economic status because they often end up being relevant to the crime. Was it a hate crime? A sex crime? A crime motivated by money? All the angles have to be examined or something might be missed.

The more we can understand why crimes against women occur, the more we'll be able to prevent them in the future. That's the hope anyway. And you can't separate preventing violence against women from feminism. The issue here is not that women haven't been taught how to survive, because they have.

And they are going to keep on surviving, and thriving, until the system changes.

HOW DUNGEONS & DRAGONS SAVED LIFE IN LOCKDOWN: D&D AND THE FREEDOM OF IMAGINATION

BY HESPER LEVERETT

> *"We got to kick butt and fight dragons too and feel like we were doing things that were cool and important and made a difference—and that we had a choice in doing them."*

As the pandemic grinds on and on, many of the things which once sustained us feel like they're fizzling out. It's hard to maintain a virtual social life when nobody ever has anything new to talk about, and even as things open up again it can be difficult to remember how to behave like a human around other humans. The exception to this awkwardness—for me, at any rate—has been my Dungeons & Dragons game, which was a lifesaver in lockdown. Never has the promise of a second life, filled with adventure, cool loot, and—perhaps most crucially—a clear sense of progression—seemed sweeter. And never has an escape from the limitations of a singular body seemed more important.

The fantasy role-playing game (RPG) *Dungeons & Dragons* has been around since the 1970s, with a period of 'Satanic Panic' notoriety in the 1980s when RPGs, along with heavy metal music, were unjustly accused by Christian campaigners of luring young people into Satanism and suicide. After that came a slow slide into relative obscurity. When I was growing up in the 1990s, it wasn't something that touched my life at all—I knew about it, vaguely, but assumed it was something of no possible interest to me. And I say that as someone who loved fantasy fiction and video RPGs. In more recent years, *D&D* has undergone a renaissance, with endless pop-culture references, celebrity endorsements, real-play podcasts, and more. I'd seen and enjoyed the memes about alignment charts and rolling natural 20s, but I never played before the pandemic.

Then came a conversation over Zoom with some friends on the topic of terrible ex-boyfriends who are sticklers for the rules when playing games and suck all the fun out of everything, and who had ruined my friends' previous attempts to play *Dungeons & Dragons*. And I came up with a crazy idea—perhaps we didn't need the boyfriends, WE could play *D&D* together! One appeal via my creative writing group for someone who could Dungeon Master a clueless group of newbies through their first campaign later, and we were setting off on our adventures. In the starter-level campaign "Dragon of Icespire Peak," we visited the town of Phandalin, and worked our way through the quests on the board—visiting monster-infested mines, ruins, and a gnome warren—before facing down the eponymous dragon.

We had no idea what we were doing, and it was glorious. We bumbled our way through dungeons, fired eldritch blasts at a lightning pig, got caught taking a bath at an inopportune moment, talked our way out of a confrontation with a manticore, and generally made it up as we went along. Without preconceptions about how *D&D* was supposed to work, we were free to invent our own ways of doing things, and our Dungeon Master let us do it. And this, I realize, *is* in fact how *D&D* is supposed to work—you're supposed to have fun role-playing a character of your own invention, and the DM is there to facilitate your fun, not to control what you do.

In a world which felt drab, dreary, and (literally) locked down, we were free to play around with whatever we felt like. We could experiment with gender roles (incidentally, for all I might have previously thought of *D&D* as predominantly a hobby for cis men, our gaming group currently consists of one (1) cis man, three cis women, one trans demigirl, and one non-binary person), with mental states, imaginary religions, with bodies and ways of being very different from our own.

Oh, and we got to kick butt and fight dragons too and feel like we were doing things that were cool and important and made a difference—and that we had a choice in doing them. What *Dungeons & Dragons* gives you,

I think, more than anything else, is a feeling of freedom. You're free to choose who you want to be and what you want to do. Sure, you still need to roll the dice, but that uncertainty just adds to the fun—when every day feels exactly the same, you find yourself longing for a bit of unpredictability.

THE BLOOD LIBEL IS BACK, BABY: ANTISEMITIC TROPES IN FOLKLORE, CULTURE, AND SFF

BY JEANA JORGENSEN

> *"What are Tolkien's dwarves if not diminutive, bearded hoarders who are made to suffer for their greed? What are Rowlings's goblins if not an updated, bank-controlling rendition of the same, or the Ferengi in Star Trek, for that matter? Are Jewish people doomed to be forever the Other in folklore and fantasy?"*

Fans of the Mel Brooks 1981 film *History of the World Part I* may recall the spoof trailer at the end for the sequel film featuring "Jews in Space." *Spaceballs*, released in 1987 by Mel Brooks, also features Jews in space, though mostly via allusion to Jewish humor and stereotypes juxtaposed with *Star Wars* parody. Recently, conspiracy theories have gone in the same direction, positing not just Jews in space but quite specifically Jewish lasers in space.

For instance, Republican Representative Marjorie Greene Taylor alleged that the 2018 California wildfires were caused by Jewish space lasers, though she later walked back this theory as fake news. Outlandish as this may seem, it represents the resurgence of one of the oldest antisemitic tropes in folklore and culture: the blood libel. In both modern conspiracy theories ranging from Jewish space lasers to omnipotent lizard people and in medieval legends about Jews kidnapping Christian babies, the common theme is one of canny Jewish people stealing the futures of ordinary Christian folk. This story, unlike its alleged victims, just won't die.

The blood libel legend is at least one thousand years old. As folklorist Alan

Dundes documents, court records dating from 1144 onward show that European Jews were tried and executed for the crime of kidnapping and murdering Christian children in order to obtain their blood for ritual purposes (1). This motif shows up in ballads, such as "Sir Hugh, or, The Jew's Daughter" as well as in Chaucer's Prioress's Tale in *The Canterbury Tales*. Places where such murders allegedly took place were commemorated with altars and became pilgrimage sites in Austria, with child and adult visitors streaming in through the 1950s (1).

Classical Western fairy tales, the wonder tales that would in many ways fuel the development of the genres of fantasy, science fiction, and horror, also depict these same antisemitic tropes. In the Grimms' nineteenth-century collection of fairy tales, stories like "The Jew in the Thornbush" and "The Good Bargain" feature antagonistic Jews who are punished and tortured and killed. Even more subtly, "Rumplestiltskin" makes no mention of Jewish people but features an antagonist with access to endless gold, who wishes to obtain a baby, and whose name is unpronounceable, if not unknowable. In many picture-book depictions, Rumplestiltskin wears an odd hat and has a long beard, adding to the iconographic clues that perhaps this traditional fairy-tale figure is a parody of a Jewish money-lender (2).

Indeed, antisemitic stereotypes abound in classic fantasy literature. What are

Tolkien's dwarves if not diminutive, bearded hoarders who are made to suffer for their greed? What are Rowlings's goblins if not an updated, bank-controlling rendition of the same, or the Ferengi in *Star Trek*, for that matter? Are Jewish people doomed to be forever the Other in folklore and fantasy? Fortunately, there are other voices to be counted: Jane Yolen's intertwining of "Sleeping Beauty" with a Holocaust family story in her novel *Briar Rose*; Naomi Novik's response to "Rumplestiltskin" in her novel *Spinning Silver*; and Veronica Schanoes's novella "Among the Thorns," which presents a revenge-driven sequel to "The Jew in the Thornbush." Schanoes does us the favor of compiling even more resources in this recommendation ("Stories Based on Jewish Folklore and Magic," by Veronica Schanoes, in Electric Literature, April 27, 2021) of books on Jewish magic, mysticism, and more.

As a folklorist, I can attest to the longevity of tradition, for good or for ill; the blood libel has persisted for a millennium, and as long as there is some cultural resonance to it, some function that it fulfills, it will continue to adapt. Unfortunately, I see echoes in the blood libel in not just the Jewish space laser conspiracy theory and the belief that Jews were responsible for COVID-19, but also in other conspiracy theories positing harm to children, everything from the Satanic Panic of the 1980s and 1990s to the Pizzagate conspiracy theory about child pornography rings.

Flip over an urban legend or conspiracy theory, and disgust often lines its

underbelly. Urban legends from the 1990s and 2000s mingle disgust and threat with a conservative-leaning examination of modern city life: you're only in danger of consuming a Kentucky Fried Rat or McPus Sandwich or Taco Bell Roach Burrito if you don't have a woman at home to cook every meal for you, naturally. Tales of immigrants and refugees and welfare recipients lining their refrigerators and their pockets at the expense of the honest taxpayer elicit disgusted rage.

But who is the proper recipient of the disgust? I find Dundes's admittedly psychoanalytic approach to the blood libel compelling: he reads it as revealing the Christian need for a Jewish scapegoat, a form of projective inversion whereby (medieval and beyond) Christians justify their hatred for Jews by pushing a narrative wherein the Jews hated them first, hated them enough to steal and murder their children (1).

Here, too, I see a similarity with the modern versions of the blood libel that do not explicitly name Jews when outlining a threat to children (Pizzagate) or the environment (space lasers). Using the theory of projective inversion might lead us to ask why scapegoats are needed in this instance; could it be that the QAnon conservative-leaning conspiracy theory believers need to believe that someone other than their chosen allies is assaulting children (*cough* Matt Gaetz) or destroying the environment (*cough* the GOP party)? Far easier to tune in to rumors about killer clowns and poisoned Halloween candy and kidnappers in white vans than to accept the fact that child abuse is far more common in the home and in the church than from instances of stranger danger, after all.

The identity of the scapegoat may shift, but popular narrative can perform a powerful "look-away" spell on almost any atrocious act.

Wandering briefly through urban legend and fairy tale, fantasy and science fiction, it is evident that antisemitic tropes have deep roots and a tendency to shape-shift to remain relevant. Whether stealing babies to murder them or molest them, or whether collecting debts with interest to impoverish hard-working Christians, the Jews of lore and legend are thieves of the future (and as a Jewish person myself, I feel tired just reading this sentence because first I'm already quite sick of antisemitism, and second, I must really be working overtime to accomplish all these dastardly deeds!).

When studying up on the blood libel or its echoes in speculative fiction, we should always be asking who is telling these stories . . . and why.

Stories do far more than simply entertain.

REFERENCES:

(1) Dundes, Alan. "The Ritual Murder of Blood Libel Legend: A Study of Anti-Semitic Victimization through Projective Inversion." In *The Meaning of Folklore: The Analytical Essays of Alan Dundes*, ed Simon Bronner. Utah State University Press, 2007. 386–409.

(2) Schanoes, Veronica. "Thorns into Gold: Contemporary Jewish American Responses to Antisemitism in Traditional Fairy Tales." *Journal of American Folklore* 132.525 (2019): 291–309.

SEEING BEYOND SIGHT: MY JOURNEY TO AFROFUTURISM

BY LEN LAWSON

"Afrofuturism, at its core, is invading spaces with blackness that said black is inferior. At its nucleus, the black imagination has always been Afrofuturistic because it yearns for its roots in Africa, the place that birthed it, where communion with the supernatural originated in tribal culture."

In the 80s, black was weak. Our orphaned boys were rescued by millionaires on TV. Fresh off being pimps, hustlers, and gangsters in movies in the 70s, we were running scared on screen while being comic relief, tokenized, and looking for white folks to save us on stage.

That was unless we had a ball or a microphone in our hands, or unless we got the crazy idea that we could be President of the United States, and even in that, we were still just running. *Run, Jesse, run!*

If you were born black in the 80s, then you didn't want to be black in the 80s. After the Civil Rights and Black Arts Movements of the 60s and 70s, the 80s taught us that it wasn't enough to be black. We set our sights on everything that whiteness told us we couldn't have, so black, for the most part, was not the thing to be in the 80s until we made it the thing to be by turning those balls and microphones into profit, escape, and flight. This is where affirmative action, gangsta rap, Eddie Murphy, and Denzel Washington come in. In the late 80s and 90s, we figured it out. This blackness was a commodity just like it was during slavery, except we had buying power now.

But allow me to return to those early 80s when I grew up in single- and double-wide trailers, reading any book I could find with a cassette tape attached and catching the school bus at my neighbor's house where we watched early morning cartoons. Enter *Go-Bots*. Enter *Transformers*.

Enter *Thundercats* and *Superfriends*. And then on Saturday mornings, I stared for hours at our floor model, living room television on my belly with elbows on the carpet and hands holding up my face to the screen to see *He-Man*, *Spider-Man*, and *Dungeons and Dragons*, hardly one damn black face in the whole lot. At least none that mattered.

Yes, there was the occasional appearance of Black Lightning, and the one black girl on *D & D*. I didn't accept this until I became an adult, but clearly, Panthro on *Thundercats* was black (another essay). None of these shows, however, taught me (not that they had to) that being black was something to be proud of or even accept as intentional in this world. So why would I even want to be? White heroes, both men and women, dominated the screen, so in order to be something of value to this world, I had to become, as depicted in my opening, something better than black, as my black boy thought process went.

This was coupled with being one of few black boys in my classes up through high school. It amazes me to this day how I made my best grades in high-level classes while classmates that did not look like me coasted, making poor grades without the threat of being removed from those same classes. Therefore, I made the connection that my brains weren't enough to be considered their equal. They got more opportunities and did less, while I got no opportunities and did more.

I was completely baffled when I was passed over for Palmetto Boys State, a highly coveted mentoring program for boys in South Carolina, some that didn't even read their textbooks and didn't desire to be called on in class like me. I knew it was because I was black, but I didn't know why blackness was the reason. That was the only thing that separated me from them. Since I wasn't much of an athlete (of course, I could run) and had no claims to popularity, I dived headfirst into our blue carpet on Saturday mornings to absorb life from our floor model TV screen. With the advent of Nintendo, aside from *Mike Tyson's Punch-Out* and Bo Jackson and Christian Okoye on *Tecmo Bowl*, there were no strong black leads to live vicariously through in video games either. But in front of the TV, I was super through Superman. I was a genius through Batman. I was different yet special through X-Men, and for those few minutes in that living room from the 80s, until I graduated high school, I definitely wasn't and didn't want to be black.

I rejected *black* movies even though all my friends loved them. I watched and knew the words to *Beverly Hills Cop, The Color Purple*, *Boyz N the Hood*, and of course, *Friday*. But I knew they weren't *real cinema*. They didn't win Oscars, so in my head, they were just movies for black people to make money. To this day, my top five movies do not have a strong black lead. At this moment, I confess that I didn't know what an HBCU (historically black college/university) was until I taught at one beginning in 2010, and I lived within fifteen miles of two HBCU's separated within feet of each other in the same small, adjacent town in South Carolina. I chose a PWI (Predominantly White Institution) to attend college in my home state because I knew I didn't want to go to those schools with all the black kids in them, and of course, they were too close to where I grew up, an impetus for escape and flight. A good number of the black girls in my graduating class decided to go to South Carolina State or Claflin but not me. I didn't know what they stood for; I just knew they were all-black schools . . . but less than, not for me. I had to be different. In no way was I, only in my mind.

Black was inferior to me even despite watching *Cosby Show* and *A Different World* on TV in the late 80s. I didn't show my sons the *Static Shock* cartoon in the early 2000s because why watch a secondary DC character when there was *Justice League*, the most iconic animated series of a generation? Whiteness was my ticket to . . . something. Better.

But that theory crumbled after my failed marriage to a white woman in 2009 and the deaths of Trayvon Martin, Mike Brown, and Tamir Rice from 2012–2014. I began to educate, attempting to fill the gaps that all my textbooks in school, the TV, and the movies left behind. Black people had a whole history undocumented, uncatalogued, and unsanctified, or maybe just not by me.

Then, this past decade, something happened on the TV and movie screens. A bulletproof, shredded Michael Coulter emerged as Luke Cage. Black Lightning got his own TV show on CW apart from *Green Arrow* and *The Flash*. And a certain black cat came to life on the big screen, and the entire African diaspora had a family reunion in movie theaters. For the first time, I could remember, black was strong . . . and in numbers! Not just at the movies but in the streets and at the polls.

Little did I know while attending undergrad at the turn of the century that black was becoming perhaps its strongest ever on the page in poetry, fiction, nonfiction, theatre, and even in screenplays. Dare I say it, but I rubbed my eyes, looked around, and saw a Black Renaissance before my eyes, and I wasn't fresh out of a time machine like *Back to the Future* (which had few to no black people by the way).

Afrofuturism, at its core, is invading spaces with blackness that said black is inferior. At its nucleus, the black imagination has always been Afrofuturistic because it yearns for its roots in Africa, the place that birthed it, where communion with the supernatural originated in tribal culture. At its base, Afrofuturism is really, as Lion-O from *Thundercats* peering through his sword Excalibur would say, seeing beyond sight to find the home that many in the African diaspora lost, especially African Americans. I had a vision to track that pilgrimage with Afrofuturism and poetry back to those places that I left behind in front of the TV, in the classroom, at the library, or just trying to embody whiteness when I never should have been attempting such nonsense.

The result is the anthology *The Future of Black* (November 2021, *Blair)*, an explosion of poetry gathered over decades that speak to an Afrofuture that has existed since slaves believed they could fly away from plantations to escape the whiteness I craved. This is a moment in time that I am proud to say I chased and did not allow it to vanish.

In many ways, I am still that kid preparing a bowl of cereal after the dawn, sitting akimbo in front of that RCA floor model, trying to see in these poems where I can find myself, find my own future. *The Future of Black* includes my poetry heroes, my comics and movie superheroes, and heroes-in-waiting who are emerging poets and artists. Black is so strong in this work. Honestly, black always has been strong. I was just too weak (rather too myopic) to behold its power. Assembling my fellow editors, I am proud to offer this black power device that can be held in our palms and shared with other little Lens who may mistake whiteness for the sun despite the radiance of an Afrofuture.

> *"The Future of Black is a marvel. Some of the best Black voices out there deconstructing subjects we've all come to know intimately. But not like this.*

Superheroes and superheroism, pop-culture and genre media are transmuted into poetry that is sharp and staggering. Pick this book up and savor it. You won't regret it."—Cadwell Turnbull, The Lesson

This groundbreaking collection highlights work from poets who have written verse within this growing tradition, including Terrance Hayes, Lucille Clifton, Gill Scott-Heron, A. Van Jordan, Glenis Redmond, Tracy K. Smith, Teri Ellen Cross Davis, Joshua Bennett, Douglas Kearney, Tara Betts, Frank X. Walker, Tyree Daye, and others. In addition, the anthology also features the work of artists such as John Jennings and Najee Dorsey, showcasing their interpretations of superheroes, Black comic characters, Afrofuturistic images from the African diaspora.

REVIEWS

THE GREEN KNIGHT AND TOXIC MASCULINITY: WHERE HAVE ALL THE CHIVALROUS MEN GONE?

BY HOLLY LYN WALRATH

"And when that baron bold had Britain made, I trow,

Bold men were bred therein, who loved strife well enow,

And many a war they waged in those good days of yore

Of marvels stern and strange, in this land many more"

The latest from A24 studios, *The Green Knight* (2021), is a retelling of the fantastical chivalric romance of *Sir Gawain and the Green Knight*, a story written by an unknown author in the 14th century as part of the tales of King Arthur, medieval histories and romances of Britain.

The original manuscript was first published in its entirety in 1839 and has been dated to the 14th century, about the time of Chaucer, although the early English used is different. Despite its age, the poem's translations (including one by J.R.R. Tolkien) are quite readable and enjoyable, even for a modern audience.

As I was watching the movie, I kept thinking about how chivalry, an ancient concept of manhood, is still alive in today's values of manhood. What we know as toxic masculinity is a warped perversion of the age-old values we know as Arthurian.

In an interview with EW, Director David Lowery explained that he was asking himself, "How will history look back upon me? How will history look back on my generation? How will history reflect upon the things that

I've done?" as he worked on the film ("David Lowery on His Quest to Make the Marvelous Medieval Epic *The Green Knight*," by Devan Coggan, June 18, 2021). These are questions that until the last hundred years or so, women have not been able to ask of themselves. They are questions wrapped up in masculinity.

The Green Knight takes place at Christmas, when Sir Gawain, played by a hypersexualized (and thank you very much!) Dev Patel, is asked to sit at the side of King Arthur. Up until this point, Gawain's main strengths appear to be sleeping with women and drinking. When the King asks him to tell a tale to entertain him, Gawain replies that he has no tale. He has no past, no history, no courageous, manly-man deeds to share in boasting. Meanwhile, King Arthur is literally the stuff of legends, at the end of his life, facing death. How can Gawain compare?

Queen Guinevere (played by Kate Dickie) turns to Sir Gawain and asks, "What do you see?" referring to the crowd of knights.

"I see legends," Gawain says.

She replies, "Do not take your place among them idly."

Honestly, King Arthur and Queen Guinevere are creepy af in this movie. Dev Patel is beautiful and I want him to find my head in a spring. Can we talk about his henleys? I digress.

When a mysterious knight bedecked in wood and green arrives, he invites Sir Gawain into a "beheading game" as part of a Christmas jest.

> *"'T is Yuletide, and New Year, and here be many a guest,*
> *If any in this hall himself so hardy hold,*
> *So valiant of his hand, of blood and brains o bold,*
> *That stroke for counter-stroke with me exchange he dare,*
> *I give him of free gift this gisarme rich and fair,*
> *This axe of goodly weight, to wield as he see fit,*
> *And I will bide his blow, as bare as here I sit.*
> *If one will test my words, and be of valiant mood,*
> *Then let him swiftly come, and take this weapon good,*
> *Here I renounce my claim, the axe shall be his own —*
> *And I will stand his stroke, here on this floor of stone,*
> *That I in turn a blow may deal, that boon alone*
> *I pray,*

Yet respite shall he have
A twelvemonth, and a day.
Now quickly I thee crave —
Who now hath aught to say?
(translated by Jessie L. Weston)

The green branch the knight bears is a symbol of peace, showing he means no harm. But the court is wary, and none but Sir Gawain volunteer. Then, he is gifted with King Arthur's sword, a symbol of the King's faith in him, the famous sword in the stone.

The Green Knight is putting a challenge to the "legends" at court, questioning their manhood. Gawain's act of stepping forward both shows that he is a man of courtesy but also, in the case of Lowery's Gawain, that he has no idea what he's getting into.

But what does all this mean? Why does Gawain force himself to travel far and wide just to fulfill a silly game? Well, to understand it, we have to understand the chivalric code.

THE HISTORY OF CHIVALRY I.E., RULES FOR DUDES

For simplicity, I'll talk about The Knight's Code of Chivalry as described in The Song of Roland (which also happens to be the inspiration for Stephen King's *The Dark Tower*), an 11th-century epic poem. The rules are:

To fear God and maintain His Church
To serve the liege lord in valour and faith
To protect the weak and defenceless
To give succour to widows and orphans
To refrain from the wanton giving of offence
To live by honour and for glory
To despise pecuniary reward
To fight for the welfare of all
To obey those placed in authority
To guard the honour of fellow knights
To eschew unfairness, meanness and deceit
To keep faith
At all times to speak the truth

To persevere to the end in any enterprise begun
To respect the honour of women
Never to refuse a challenge from an equal
Never to turn the back upon a foe

Thus we see the high standard Sir Gawain was having to deal with. Becoming a knight means turning his back on everything he knew about being a man. Men fuck whores and get drunk. Knights have a higher code.

Knights in the medieval time period of the Gawain poet's writing were already a thing of legend. Living up to that ideal of manhood meant becoming such a legend. They would be expected to fight "for God" in crusades (which although not often directly mentioned in many Arthurian legends, were meant to recover Jerusalem as a "holy land" under Islamic rule, resulting in massacres of Muslim and Jewish people.)

Essentially, the main question in the movie is, "Will Sir Gawain not be a dick?" It's a standard that seems easy to achieve on the surface, but when applied to manhood, perpetually at odds with the desires of the body, it is not so easily achieved.

As Gawain's lover Essel puts it in the movie, "This is how silly men perish."

To which Gawain replies, "Or how good men become great."

Knights navigate a world of two duties—that due to God and that due to courtly love.

CHIVALRY AND MANHOOD TODAY

We can see the ideals of chivalric manhood and masculinity in the culture of the United States, dating back as far as the Civil War era and the *Gone With the Wind* tradition of men speaking out for women's honor. (This tradition often resulted in men being "trapped" by women or else dying on the sword of marriage and honor, i.e., Scarlet's tainted honor must be avenged to the injury of Dear effeminate Ashley, but I digress.) This idea of manhood emerged from British values carried over to the US, and continues on today in a hyper-idealized way. "Good men" are those that stand up for women, provide a home and living for their family, and go to church (a Christian one). It's a country song waiting to happen. God is great, beer is good, and women are crazy.

Chivalric ideals seem innocently good on the surface. But today, in the US, they have often been hijacked for the purpose of subjugation. A wing of the "Proud Boys" is called the Fraternal Order of Alt-Knights. In January 2019, a group of three men as part of a right-wing militia group were sentenced to jail for plotting the mass murder of Muslims on American soil. They called themselves "The Crusaders." In the war of twenty-first-century manhood, everything real and true gets obliterated, even the potentially useful portions of chivalry.

It's the reality *The Green Knight* shows us about manhood; these virtues are easily twisted.

Every step of Gawain's journey in the film is fraught with trauma. From having his clothing ransacked (a direct opposite to the book's repeated descriptions of his beautiful clothing), to having his dear horse stolen (don't worry, the horse doesn't get hurt), to being left for dead on the road.

When Gawain finally makes it to the home of a Lord and Lady, viewers are meant to believe he is safe. But this is just where the temptation begins.

The protection of a woman's honor comes at the cost of her freedom. The difference between Gawain's two love interests in the film (both played expertly by Alicia Vikander) is virginity. In medieval times (and in some backward societies today), virginity was a highly prized sign of a courtly lady. Her love is a method of control that results in great power. Because Essel is not a virgin, she cannot be a lady.

In a trippy scene near the end of the movie, when Gawain imagines his life if he should eschew honor and refuse to face the Green Knight, Essel is put aside when she bears Gawain's child, merely a vessel for his lineage.

St. Jerome, a Latin priest, wrote that as "long as woman is for birth and children, she is different from men as body is from the soul. But when she wishes to serve Christ more than the world, then she will cease to be a woman and will be called a man."

When examined with a modern lens, it's easy to see the chivalric knight as a mere Don Quixote, bumbling and tilting at windmills. Why go to all this trouble for a mere game of moral honor?

What sets the Gawain of David Lowery's vision apart is his complexity, married with the stellar and subtle acting of Dev Patel; this is a Gawain who struggles under the weight of the expectations of chivalry and manhood.

I particularly enjoyed the queering of The Lord that Gawain visits. In the book, Gawain's kiss with The Lord occurs three times. On the third, the kiss is described by translator Jessie L. Weston as "setting them on his lips with all solemnity." J.R.R. Tolkien's translation of the kiss is far juicier, "He clasps then the knight and kisses him thrice, as long and deliciously as he could lay them upon him" (2021, 89).

In the original tale, Gawain spends most of his time at The Lord and Lady's home with the ladies in feast or attempting to avoid the advances of The Lady as she tempts him. In contrast to these romantic scenes in Gawain's bed (with the curtains closed about him) are long, violent descriptions of The Lord's hunt for the fox. While some have cast aside this scene of male kissing as being a part of the film's horror elements (and even poorly chosen to call it "gay panic"), I felt that this section captured the strangeness of relating a medieval story to a modern audience.

Leann Stuber explains in "The Contradiction of Masculinity in the Middle Ages" (The Delta, V.3, Issue 1) that as urbanization and an expanding population meant men and women often worked together in professions, traditional male gender roles based on dominance over women became far more complicated. Originally, "concepts of male superiority from classical literature were incorporated into Christian doctrine, creating a definition of masculinity based purely on male dominance and virility."

But, as Stuber goes on to explain, gender began to be defined by profession, and "The varying definitions of masculinity created numerous contradictions for men in medieval society." In the medieval time period, gender was far less tied to sex differences than it was to actions. A man acting in a way that was "feminine" or "womanly" would be far more dangerous than his body being unfeminine in some way. Kissing was common between men and often described as a part of the chivalric knight's "free and gay" persona. But the queering of the text is necessary and important to translating the work for a modern audience. What IS with all this jousting and swordplay and penis metaphors? Was the kiss merely between two men chaste, or was it something more?

Romantic chivalry was far more a literary concept than a true concept in the age of chivalry in the absence of useful evidence. The truth is, what we know about medieval masculinity comes from literature—not from first-hand accounts.

The film engages with these themes in a nuanced way. Even the green girdle wrapped around Gawain by multiple women is a sign of the feminine—to be shunned at the last moment for the purpose of gallantry. The introduction of Gawain's mother (a character not present in the text but who plays a large figure in the larger Arthur mythos) as a witch-like schemer whose actions are ultimately mysterious to the viewer, places women at the forefront of the fate of the male lead. Gawain's mother is the one who summons the Green Knight, to test her son or else force him to take his place in the world, "to test [his] knightly pride." (By the way, the whole scene with the green girdle at the end totally gave me Carmen Maria Machado Husband Stitch vibes.)

David Lowery's Gawain receives his due in the end and rightly place at Arthur's side. It's a film worth watching over and over again for its cinematography, exploration of surrealism, and excellent rendition of a centuries-old tale that deserves reading through a feminist lens.

THE FALCON AND THE WINTER SOLDIER ALMOST CRITIQUES AMERICA: MARVEL'S LATEST ON DISNEY+ EXPLORES METAPHORS FOR US FOREIGN POLICY

BY A.A. VOIGT

At the end of Episode four of *The Falcon and the Winter Soldier* (*Marvel Studios,* 2021), John Walker, the hotheaded replacement for Steve Rogers' Captain America, murders a man in broad daylight. The iconic shield comes up and down, over and over again, until its pristine edge is stained with gore.

While watching this jarring sequence play out, I could not help but wonder, "Is Marvel trying to say something about America?"

It would be the first time. The United States military has been deeply involved in the production of the MCU, from editing the *Iron Man* script to actually filming commercials timed with the release of *Captain Marvel*. The entire plot of *Captain America: Civil War* revolves around the idea that it's somehow a miscarriage of justice for the Avengers (and by proxy, the United States) to face international oversight. Hell, *TFATWS* opens with Sam Wilson flying missions for the Air Force. So when I saw John Walker carry out an act of violence that is more consistent with the rest of the world's understanding of America, I was genuinely surprised.

Walker is presented as an antagonist from his introduction, a pretender who could never fill the boots of that Nazi-fighting kid from Brooklyn we all know and love. Despite the fact that the audience is supposed to view him with skepticism, I found many aspects of his character to be fitting metaphors for actual US foreign policy.

In his introduction, we learn Walker is a high school football star and three-time Medal of Honor winner, MIT-certified as genetically superior to the average Joe. He talks about being a regular guy without superpowers but a lot of "guts," who just wants to make people feel safe.

That facade of respectability, courage, and love of whatever American family values belies Walker's actual character. As we see in his interactions with Sam Wilson and Bucky Barnes, Walker cannot hold up the mask of civility for any extended period of time before he becomes brash, cocky, and single-minded in pursuit of his agenda. Walker would rather punch first and ask questions later and becomes so consumed with the hunt for anarchist straw-villain Karli Morgenthau that he'd rather pick a fight with a squad of super-soldiers than let Wilson talk the girl down for ten minutes. This fight results in the aforementioned shield-murdering, which is a pretty accurate representation of what happens when America doesn't get its way overseas.

The United States has a long history of intervention in foreign conflicts for reasons ranging from resisting communism to baldfaced opportunism. Whether it is suppressing Philippine revolutionaries, propping up a colonial state in Vietnam, or selling cluster bombs to Saudi Arabia, America never misses an opportunity to dip its red, white, and blue fingers into popular uprisings or rebellions. There is no shortage of atrocities to compare: the fact of the matter is that Walker's heinous attack is just a microcosm of the instances in which the United States has openly slaughtered thousands without remorse (Fact Sheet: United States Policy on the International Criminal Court).

Contrasted with Walker's brutality are characters who represent the people whom America has harmed over the years. The Flag Smashers, a group of anti-border refugees who have taken up arms against the fascist Global Repatriation Council, can cleanly map onto any group of immigrants being forcibly relocated by state actors. The show does have them bomb a building full of GRC stormtroopers just so the audience knows they're not too sympathetic, but they are generally portrayed as a team of young people just trying to survive against a highly militarized police force backed up by ultra-commandos with cool names.

Furthermore, the introduction of Isaiah Bradley, a Korean War veteran who received an untested variation of the super-soldier serum given to Steve Rogers, very nearly addressed America's exploitation of its Black citizens, especially in the military.

From the horrendous casualties of the 54th Massachusetts, to the nonconsensual harvesting of Henrietta Lacks' cells, to the purposeful neglect of the subjects of the Tuskegee Syphilis Study (an image specifically evoked by Bradley's retelling of the experiment that gave him his powers), Black Americans have suffered and died for centuries in exchange for some nebulous greater good of the nation that systematically abuses them. And as I watched Isaiah Bradley say that bringing his torture to light would get him assassinated, because if there's one thing white supremacy is good at, it's mopping up the blood it has spilled, I was pleased and impressed that Marvel had the guts (as Walker would call it) to put America's atrocities on display.

Then the final episode dropped.

I'd never felt my opinion of a media property curdle faster than when the orchestra swelled to reveal John Walker saving a bunch of government types from falling to their deaths. **What's the purpose of giving an unrepentant murderer a redemption scene?** God forbid a Medal of Honor winner be a bad guy. And after Morgenthau is shot to death by a former CIA agent, we hear Sam Wilson's well-intentioned but substantively empty call for governments to do better by those they disenfranchise, dressing down a senator as if we haven't already seen that the heart of the American authoritarian movement is entirely built on bad faith and false promises.

Lastly, the most embarrassing slap in the face of the interesting narrative the show worked to build, we see Wilson take Isaiah Bradley and his grandson to the Captain America exhibit seen in *The Winter Soldier*, where he proudly reveals a bronze statue and informational plaque honoring Bradley's decades of suffering. It is borderline comical that a program daring to criticize America's historical abuses against both the marginalized across the globe and within its own borders ends with a statue and a speech. Sadly, considering the United States' track record on actual, material reparations, it is the most realistic conclusion.

It was foolish of me to expect a radical narrative out of a company whose success is so deeply entrenched in the American status quo as Marvel. But I couldn't help myself. It is clear that the writers of *TFATWS* are interested in at least asking why America has so many enemies and giving a sympathetic voice to the people using violence to resist its influence. Those glimmers of substance, of pointed critiques with no easy answers, they gave me hope that our current monopoly-dominated media sphere could still produce the imaginative and difficult stories our current moment calls for.

Maybe in another decade, we'll get a movie about a group of supervillains trying to strengthen antitrust laws. I can only hope they don't get their skulls caved in.

GRIEF AND THE HOUSEWIFE: WANDAVISION'S BOLD TAKE ON LOVE

BY ANNIKA BARRANTI KLEIN

> *"Grief: n. deep sorrow, especially that caused by someone's death." — Oxford English Dictionary*
>
> *"Grief is the response to loss, particularly to the loss of someone or some living thing that has died, to which a bond or affection was formed. Although conventionally focused on the emotional response to loss, grief also has physical, cognitive, behavioral, social, cultural, spiritual and philosophical dimensions. While the terms are often used interchangeably, bereavement refers to the state of loss, while grief is the reaction to that loss."— Wikipedia*

Content warning: in addition to the fictional deaths in the Marvel Cinematic Universe (MCU), this essay discusses the loss of a parent to ischemic stroke.

Spoiler warning: contains mention of events throughout the MCU and in WandaVision in particular.

Wanda Maximoff's loss is incalculable. Certainly, it would be possible to list the people she has lost—both of her parents, her brother, Vision—but loss is not counted in numbers. No mathematics can measure the love that no longer has a place to go when someone you love dies. As Vision (Paul Bettany) said to Wanda (Elizabeth Olsen) in a post–Age of Ultron (2015, in which Wanda's brother Pietro was killed by Ultron) flashback in Episode 8, **"But what is grief if not love, persevering?"**

The internet has lost its collective mind over that line, split between people finding it beautiful and profound and those who find it trite, corny, or . . .

honestly, I am not sure what people object to. I found it achingly familiar: I wrote a very similar line in a story I wrote not long after my father died. Describing grief as love is an honest and powerful way of describing the pain of loss.

WandaVision is a story told out of order. We learn of Wanda's bereavement only after we see the manifestation of her grief: a perfect television nuclear family, with Vision alive and a whole town in on the lie. But why does Wanda choose—even subconsciously—to model her ideal life after sitcom families? Why is the housewife the most comforting role for a powerful witch to cast herself in? The series shows us that she grew up in war-torn Sokovia (a fictional eastern European country) watching sit-coms that gave her a peek at "normal" (white middle-class American) life, but I believe there is more to it.

> *"Housewife: n. A woman whose main occupation is caring for her family, managing household affairs, and doing housework, while her husband or partner goes out to work." — Oxford English*

> *"A woman whose work is running or managing her family's home and who is not employed outside the home (a career woman)." — Wikipedia*

My father had two strokes, the first on Christmas 2018. He was living in Mexico and I could not reasonably travel to see him—I had no passport, among other reasons. While I waited for news, then waited for his condition to improve, I focused on two things: I cooked a lot of beans (one of my favorite foods), and I knitted gnomes. I got the beans from Rancho Gordo and the gnome patterns from Imagined Landscapes.

Why did I choose these domestic arts to channel my fears into? Why does Wanda choose to be a housewife instead of facing reality? Because there is comfort in the domestic. The mid-century image of the housewife is absolutely, positively post-WWII propaganda designed to keep women in the domestic sphere in support of capitalism and the patriarchy, but the domestic sphere is based entirely on things that are both necessary and comforting.

The home is the place of safety. It is the place of sustenance (food), of warmth (clothing, bedding, window coverings), and of comfort and love (family). It is a place of stability. Wanda has only ever had that in Vision, so when he is taken away from her by Thanos, her grief is the size of the universe (as all grief is).

Without meaning to or knowing how she accomplished it, Wanda creates the safety of home for herself, and places herself in the domestic role western society assigned to her: that of the housewife. Taking this role recreates the home she had found in Vision, as well as recreating the sitcoms she has found comfort in her entire life.

Monica Rambeau (Teyonah Parris) creates an interesting juxtaposition to Wanda. Where Agatha Harkness (Kathryn Hahn) is her antagonist, Monica is her mirror. Returning to life after being taken by "the snap" (*Avengers: Infinity War*, 2018) she finds a changed world (*Avengers: Endgame,* 2019) and her mother, Maria Rambeau, dead. Monica does not have time to grieve Maria or the five years she lost—she is almost immediately called to New Jersey to assist FBI Agent Jimmy Woo (Randall Park) as he investigates the strange disappearance of the town of Westview.

Of course, by the time the audience learns all of this, we've already met Monica—as Geraldine, Wanda's neighbor in Westview. When Monica goes through the magical barrier into Westview and becomes Geraldine, Dr. Darcy Lewis (Kat Dennings) is brought in to work with Agent Woo. She is the one who figures out a way into Wanda's creation via the television signal.

Over the course of WandaVision, Monica connects with Wanda and refuses S.W.O.R.D. director Tyler Hayward's (Josh Stamberg) orders to stay out of Westview; instead, she tries to reach Wanda through the barrier, to help her. It is very important to note that Rambeau is a Black woman and Hayward is a white man. Hayward's goal is not to help Wanda; it is to use what remains of Vision—the real one, not the one created by Wanda's grief—as a weapon and make Wanda's Scarlet Witch powers a scapegoat.

Monica defies Hayward and goes through Wanda's magical barrier for a third time, rewriting her own DNA and developing superpowers. Wanda's powers were there from birth, but Monica's are a choice she makes in an effort to help Wanda in her grief and to save Westview from it. This is a powerful choice, especially given Darcy's warning that the act could kill her. In what is perhaps my favorite moment in recent TV history, Darcy lays out the danger for Monica and then supports Monica's choice to ignore it.

This is not a show specifically about women supporting women; Agatha wants to take Wanda's power; Vision and Agent Woo, both men, support Wanda, albeit in different ways. But it is worth noting that women supporting women, as Darcy supports Monica and Monica supports Wanda, is still noteworthy.

My father's second stroke killed him. I do not remember how I channeled my grief after that. It was too big to be compatible with memory. Like Wanda, my grief was (and is) the size of the universe. I do know that I have not knitted a single gnome since. When I dream of my father—which is not often—we are usually in a kitchen, cooking or eating or just sitting together, talking. If I was "a being capable of spontaneous creation," as Agatha describes Wanda, it seems very likely that I would find myself in an imagined kitchen with him.

DUNE: THE GOOD, THE BAD, AND THE CONTRADICTORY: VILLENEUVE'S 2021 DUNE AND BIG BUDGET SCI-FI CINEMA

BY COREY J. WHITE

> *"The film is both a lavish and lovingly-realized adaptation of the classic novel and a somewhat hollow blockbuster that still can't capture all the nuance of the book."*

I first read *Dune* (1965) when I was eleven years old. I remember it distinctly, not for the epic scale of the book or the highly detailed universe Frank Herbert had created, but because of the word 'sensuousness'. Used to describe some of the female guests at a dinner party, I had to ask my mum what the word meant and—perhaps checking the tome her son was reading wasn't too *adult* for the youngest member of our Christian family—she quickly read the passage before giving me an explanation.

The aforementioned dinner party is one of the few noteworthy scenes from the first half of Herbert's 1965 novel that is entirely excised from Denis Villeneuve's 2021 film *Dune* (also known as *Dune, Part One*). I mention its absence only because the film is both a lavish and lovingly-realized adaptation of the classic novel and a somewhat hollow blockbuster that still can't capture all the nuance of the book, even with its long run time and slow-and-steady pace. After finally seeing *Dune,* it seems like everything I read about the movie is true—the good and the bad, even the contradictory bits.

For anyone who is reading this review with no idea of what *Dune* is about, a summary. The planet Arrakis is the sole source of spice, a substance that is extremely valuable for its use in enabling navigators of the spacing guild to plot safe routes throughout the stars—it forms the bedrock that the entire galactic imperium is built upon. The movie opens with the Emperor taking authority over Arrakis away from House Harkonnen and handing it over to House Atreides. Arrakis has made the Harkonnen extremely wealthy, and they don't plan to make the handover easy for their greatest rivals in the Landsraad Council. Not only that, but the Emperor himself grows wary of Duke Leto Atreides' growing influence, and together, the imperial house and the Harkonnen plan to destroy the Atreides as they take over Arrakis. (That's not a spoiler—it's all revealed in the first twenty minutes of the film.)

But the Emperor and the Great Houses are not the only powerful forces at work. The secretive Bene Gesserit have spent millennia selectively cross-breeding amongst the great houses in their efforts to create a male messianic figure for their otherwise matriarchal order. Their plans were put at risk when Lady Jessica (played here by Rebecca Ferguson) failed to give birth to a daughter—she loved her Duke Leto (Oscar Isaac) so much she instead provided him a male heir. When the movie begins this male heir, Paul Atreides (Timothée Chalamet), is already seeing visions of Arrakis; visions of death and carnage that he wants to avoid even as he feels fate pushing him toward them.

It is Paul and his grand fate that drives the narrative of *Dune* the novel, and so the movie is duly focused on Paul, with Timothée Chalamet perfectly cast in the role. It's not that I am particularly fond of Chalamet, in fact, this might be the first time I've seen him on screen, but with his stick-thin build, floppy hair, and big wet eyes, he perfectly captures the essence of uncertainty and self-doubt that define the young Atreides at the start of his journey. Sure, there is strength, training, privilege, and a strong drive behind him, but these qualities must be coaxed out from beneath the uncertainty.

I found the casting of the film exceptional, but it's still worth noting that in their portrayal of the Fremen there is a distinct lack of MENA representation. Frank Herbert was upfront about the influence he took from MENA cultures in creating the Fremen, so it's disappointing (but perhaps not surprising considering the anti-Muslim bigotry propagated by Western governments in their failed "War on Terror") that more than sixty years later those influences are still being downplayed and erased.

Jason Momoa's Duncan Idaho and Josh Brolin's Gurney Halleck in particular made me hope we get a long, multi-part franchise covering at least the first three *Dune* novels if only to see what happens to those characters. Zendaya's Chani haunts this film, and Javier Bardem embodies Stilgar so well that it's a shame the film ends when Paul's journey with the Fremen is only just beginning. We need far more of the Fremen, but we'll have to wait for Part Two before we see that.

Stellan Skarsgård and Dave Bautista as the pale goth Harkonnen's are suitably unsettling, with production design on the Harkonnen planet and their equipment falling somewhere between H.R. Geiger and the Empire from Star Wars. It might not be inspired, but it is effective.

Uninspired but effective is probably the best way to describe the production design of the film, and if you've played any of the canonical sci-fi video franchises of the past decade or so (I'm mostly thinking of *Mass Effect* and *Halo*), you'll find plenty that is familiar on screen here.

It's incredibly well-realized, highly detailed, and often beautiful, with first-class CGI, effects (and only one shot that looked like it came out of a Dune RTS game), and actual physical and sometimes gorgeous sets (no cheap Disneyfication happening here), but all in service of design work that is never truly unique or particularly interesting. It looks like an empire under austerity.

The ship designs look as though the artists were attempting to make something recognizable to generations raised on Star Wars, but lacking any color or flourishes that might make the movie appear anything less than a mature and staid affair. Heaven forbid they used color and cause anyone to think this is a movie for children . . . (I'm being facetious—with a PG-13 rating, they're obviously hoping this appeals to a broad audience.)

The film looks both beautiful and boring at the same time, but I'm holding out hope that these decisions were made deliberately with an eye toward the full story being told here. If *Dune* (*Part One*) is often dominated by a color palette of flat grays and browns, it could be to serve to make the second part of the story more vibrant and alive. I won't spoil anything, but there is reason to hope they might present us with a brighter and more varied design in the sequel (though, admittedly, I won't hold my breath).

It's a shame that I could never have the experience of seeing this film without the foreknowledge of the book resting in the back of my head. As impressed as I am by what made it on screen, I can't help but worry that viewers are missing, if not important elements of the book, then details that bring the universe of *Dune* to life. Rather than being a replacement for the book, the movie feels like a big-budget, cross-media experience designed to be supported *by* the book. Just about the entire story is there on screen, but for the viewer who wants more—more detail, more context, more intrigue—the book is waiting, better than any IMDB trivia page, better than any fan wiki. We've seen film adaptations that can stand in place of the book (*American Psycho, Trainspotting,* and *Fight Club* come to mind), and film adaptations that are barely a pale shadow of the book and everything that made it a compelling story in the first place. But this is a film that is both an accurate enough adaptation to please fans (not all, but some), and compelling enough on its own to bring readers to the books . . . Though let's just hope they know they can stop after the original three books, and that they *certainly* don't need to bother with Junior's additions to the canon.

Dune is the first science-fiction film in a long time that feels truly epic in scope, supported by a fantastic cast, and featuring some of the best quality work in effects and production (but sadly not design) to come out of Hollywood in recent years. It is, however, only part of the story—just the beginning of what could be a long and interesting journey through the universe that Frank Herbert created decades ago.

SOUTH KOREAN "QUIET PLACE" THRILLS: NEW THRILLER MIDNIGHT IS A HEART-POUNDING EXPLORATION OF DEAFNESS

BY HOLLY LYN WALRATH

> *"After all, horror loves nothing if not capitalizing on putting women in danger."*

If you loved *A Quiet Place* (2018) and K-dramas, *Midnight* (*Tving*, 2021) is the thriller for you. The film follows the story of Kyung Mi (played by Ki-Joo Jin), a deaf woman working at a call center where her coworkers constantly ridicule her. When Kyung Mi finds an injured woman on her way home, she is forced into the path of a serial killer (played by the creepily swoon-worthy Wi Ha-Joon). What results is a horrific chase through the city to save both the young woman and her own mother.

The fear here is not just a young woman having to try and protect herself and others from an ax-wielding killer, but the added tension of her inability to communicate or hear potential threats.

It's important to note that Ki-Joo Jin is not a deaf actress, and neither is Hae-Yeon Ki, who plays the main character's deaf mother. The lack of representation of deaf actors limits the movie somewhat for those who are familiar with deaf culture, as there are a few stereotypes that play out such as the character's speech being overly stunted (while some deaf people cannot speak, there are some who learn to or developed deafness later in life) or the disregard that while cell phones play a major role in the movie, many deaf people use text-to-speech apps which would prevent some of the misunderstandings the characters encounter. And to me, the signing seemed far too dramatic, but I'm not an expert on how Korean Sign Language is different than American Sign Language (and I am not deaf).

That being said, the movie delivers satisfying thrills and intense chases. The film draws on the concept of silence to create fear in the viewer as we watch the protagonist unaware that she is being stalked by the killer. There are many night scenes that utilize the city setting to great effect, with jump-scares like the leading lady nearly running into traffic or not hearing oncoming bikes. Lots and lots of running.

The scene where Kyung Mi finds the injured woman is particularly effective. A white-heeled shoe is thrown into the street, and Kyung Mi turns to look into a pitch-black alleyway. An injured woman is breathing heavily and crying for help, but Kyung Mi can't hear her.

Midnight casts light on the issue of both representation and awareness of deafness in South Korea. The debut director Kwon Oh-Seung stated in an interview that he got the idea when he was at a cafe and he witnessed a deaf woman struggling to communicate and someone touched her and she jumped in fear *(Korea Times,* "Jin Ki-joo plays deaf person who confronts serial killer in thriller film 'Midnight'"). Kwon Oh-Seung also wrote the tightly scripted screenplay, which mixes horror and humor.

The film has many clever uses of deaf assistive devices to invoke terror. The lights that deaf people use in their homes to indicate sound (such as a doorbell) or in their cars to alert for sirens become instruments of fear when utilized by a serial killer.

In South Korea, deafness is rare and is estimated at .46% of the population or about 255,000 people, according to a 2018 report in *Nature* ("Prevalence of Severe-Profound Hearing Loss in South Korea: A Nationwide Population-Based Study to Analyze a 10-Year Trend (2006-2015)". In 2014, protestors held a sit-in at the National Assembly in Seoul's Yeouido neighborhood, where one protestor reported not having necessary access to an interpreter during surgery at a hospital. Sueo, or hand language, is the term used for Korean Sign Language. Services such as interpreters are limited, with only 1,134 interpreters in the entire country according to one source ("In South Korea, Hearing Impaired Live in a Different World," in Hankyoreh, November 25, 2014).

There were several moments in the film that also capitalize on the fear of being a young woman in a teeming city. Women will recognize the anxiety of walking down a deserted hallway, or deciding to trust an unknown man, or running from a would-be assailant. The film also seems to comment on the inaccessibility of CCTV stations—as when the woman uses one to alert the police, she is unable to communicate with them.

There is also a deeper cultural discussion to be had here regarding assaults on women in South Korea. According to one article, "in 2019 women accounted for 98 percent of victims in the nearly 10,000 cases of crimes against intimate partners, and the Korea Women's Hotline estimated that a woman was killed or nearly killed every 1.8 days that year. Korean women account for more than half of all homicide victims, making it one of the highest rates of female murder in the world" ("South Korea Needs to Contend with Sexual Violence," by Olivia Schieber in *Foreign Policy*, August 10, 2020).

Overall, *Midnight* is an interesting and empathetic exploration of deafness and womanhood in South Korea. The writing is clever and forces the viewer to think through what the heroine's next actions will be, and the women in the movie shine as intelligent and fierce. After all, horror loves nothing if not capitalizing on putting women in danger. The sound direction in the movie seems particularly clever, utilizing silence and sudden onslaughts of sound as well as lip-reading to invoke fear in the audience.

One of the most compelling moments in the movie is when Kyung Mi is pleading with her assailant, explaining how she wants to get married, have children, and live out the rest of her life. It struck me that this was the director's way of building empathy for deaf people—by saying that, like everyone, they just want to live their lives and be happy. It's a moment that's well-acted and honest, heart-warming, but not in a way that minimizes the reality of the situation.

All in all, I enjoyed this one and was glad for the ending. Everyone in the screening I saw clapped when the baddie got his, and it was fun to root for the main character. *Midnight* is not yet out on streaming networks, but I'd bet it gets picked up soon. It would be a shoo-in for Netflix.

Now if you excuse me, I'm going to go on a run, just in case.

This film is reviewed as part of Interstellar Flight Press' coverage of the Alamo Drafthouse Fantastic Fest 2021. We thank Alamo Drafthouse for providing a free screening of this film.

WHY SPACE SWEEPERS IS THE FUTURE OF THE FUTURE: THE KOREAN SCI-FI FILM THAT WON 2021

BY HESPER LEVERET

"This is the future of science fiction we deserve."

The Korean science-fiction movie *Space Sweepers*, directed by Jo Sung-hee, was released on Netflix on 5th February 2021. It's a fast-paced two-hour movie that feels no need to be a mini-series, still less several seasons of self-indulgence. It shows us a vision of the future that's bang-up-to-date with the present. It's multi-lingual and multi-cultural, extremely class-aware, and whip-crackingly smart on climate change while keeping up the popcorn quotient with plenty of action and heart-wrenching character moments. Also, there's an adorable kid and a transgender robot. This is the future of science fiction we deserve.

Set in 2092, *Space Sweepers* is about that most beloved of science fiction tropes; the bashed-about spaceship with a motley crew of plucky under-dogs. There are several other tried-and-tested tropes here, from Tae-ho, the embittered former soldier (played by Song Joong-ki), to 'Dorothy', the cute kid who's more than she seems (played by Ye-Rin Park). What makes it feel modern and refreshing are two things: the sheer visual verve of the filmmaking and the diversity on display. Jang, our hard-drinking, hard-gambling captain, is a Korean woman (played by Kim Tae-ri), while Bubs the snarky robot loves doing makeup.

Another thing I loved is that, rather than English being assumed to be the Language of the Future, all the characters speak in their own language; in-universe translation gadgets (and subtitles) do the rest. There's English,

Korean, French, Filipino, Nigerian pidgin—this future is multi-lingual. There's no sense of the current multitude of Earth cultures being erased by a dominant, non-descript "Earth Human Culture" that many sci-fi flicks default to.

And while you can easily watch it as simply a fun space adventure movie, there's definitely some strong political commentary here, just below the surface. The antagonist is a billionaire inventor who's obsessed with saving humanity from a dying planet. But only certain parts of humanity—the ones he considers worthy. Probably the hardest-hitting scene in the movie is his confrontation with a journalist who questions the ethics of his decision to create a space refuge for the chosen few—only to face a test of his own moral purity.

Meanwhile, the main characters are literally picking up trash from space, struggling to survive. The main character, Tae-ho, is someone who used to be relatively well-off and has now—thanks to events viewed in gut-wrenching flashbacks—lost everything, showing how easy it is to tumble from one of the Chosen Few to piloting a space ship in his socks because he's had to sell his shoes. Of course, the characters pull together to save each other and the day, because that's how stories work. That's how humanity works.

Space Sweepers, while being entertaining at every moment, poses some uncomfortable questions about our collective future, especially around climate change. Is the planet doomed? Can we save ourselves? Can we save everyone or only a few of us? Can we create a better world from the ashes of this one? While you eat your popcorn and enjoy the explosions, you can think about the future of humanity, and decide how you want to fit into it.

This kind of hard-hitting, class-conscious, thoughtful-but-action-packed filmmaking feels only too rare in Hollywood, but there's analogous work from other Korean filmmakers—like the zombie film *Train to Busan* from Yeon Sang-ho, *Snowpiercer* and *Parasite* from Bong Joon-ho, and of course the new Netflix smash hit *Squid Game* from Hwang Dong-hyuk. I'm hoping the success of these films and TV shows will prompt more Western filmmakers to follow suit, and more Korean (and other international) films to get wide releases overseas. This, my friends, is the future of the future.

SCIENCE FICTION HAS ALWAYS BEEN ABOUT REVOLUTION: AELITA, A 1920S RUSSIAN SILENT FILM ABOUT SOVIET UTOPIAS, FREE SPEECH, AND SEX QUEENS FROM MARS

BY HOLLY LYN WALRATH

Not to be dramatic, but I would build a spaceship and fly to Mars and start a proletariat revolution for Aelita Queen of Mars. If you haven't seen this silent film that is considered the first Russian sci-fi film, you're missing out on an absolutely bananas mashup of romance, Russian civil war history, and of course, sexy space queens from Mars.

But let me step back a moment because *Aelita* (1924) requires a lot of context to talk about. When I first saw it, I was immediately reminded of the recent discourse regarding science fiction's so-called "social justice warriors" and the case against politics in books. There's a common argument among the American conservatives that politics don't have a place in science fiction—which should just be fun space lasers, pew pew pew.

"Authors can either cheerlead for left-wing causes, or they can keep their mouth shut. Open disagreement is not tolerated and will result in being sabotaged and slandered. Message or identity politics has become far more important than entertainment or quality," says Larry Correia, who was embroiled in 2014 in the Hugos controversy (original quote from

Correia's blog, more on his views at USA Today, for a full run-down of the events of that year, check out this great article at Lit Reactor – "The Great Hugo Controversy of 2014," by Rajan Khanna, August 13, 2014.)

Anywho, the movie *Aelita* is deeply "political." Set in 1921 and based on a 1923 novella by Aleksey N. Tolstoy, cousin of *War and Peace* author Leo Tolstoy, the film follows Los—an engineer who fantasizes about going to Mars after receiving a mysterious message on the radio.

Los and his wife are members of the working class in Russia living through the Russian Civil War and Bolshevik revolution. In 1917, Lenin was established as the leader of Russia in the October Revolution as leftist revolutionaries overthrew the provisional government, ending the Romanov dynasty.

In a series of events following, the Bolsheviks introduced food rationing and Lenin made farms and factories collectives, as well as outlawing the church. There was an economic collapse, famine, and five million people died. This all occurred in 1918–1921. Ultimately, Lenin prevailed, only to be replaced by Stalin. By 1929, Stalin deported 15 million peasants to Artic reasons, a huge portion of whom died.

Aelita is a movie that takes place at the intersection of the 1920s Russian space craze and the uprisings of revolutionaries. In 1903, Soviet rocket scientist Konstantin E. Tsiolkovsky first determined that it was possible to send a rocket to space when he came up with the mathematical formula for the escape velocity from Earth ("Konstantin Tsiolkovsky" at European Space Agency). His drawing for the first spaceship resembles the spaceship in Aelita.

The fans of space travel at the time were amateur scientists with little formal education who embraced pop culture at the time. Space exploration became a part of Lenin's New Economic Policy (NEP) plan with a desire to find a more utopian society, which makes sense if you consider that at this point in time, society was undergoing extreme changes. For a brief moment, the NEP represented a utopian dream, one that combined a free market and capitalism after the Russian Civil War and the nationalization of industry. This period was short-lived, as Stalin came to power, the NEP was removed in 1928 in favor of the Great Bank.

"Notwithstanding harsh conditions in the cities, the urban population continued to grow through the 1920s due to peasant migration into the cities and massive demobilization following the end of the civil war. Despite one million unemployed in 1924, wages finally began to rise the same year, and the standard of living for the average factory worker—someone like the tireless space crusader Fridrikh Tsander—began to improve noticeably. With urban renewal accelerating and the first fruits of the revolution appearing, people conjured up old dreams of utopia in new and experimental ways." *—Asif A. Siddiqi ("Imagining the Cosmos: Utopians, Mystics, and the Popular Culture of Spaceflight in Revolutionary Russia." Osiris 23, no. 1 (2008): 260–88.)*

Science and technology were seen as a way to aspire to this utopian dream. In *Aelita*, Los' wife Natasha works at an evacuation center. The film intercuts dreamily bizarre scenes of Mars with real-life footage of starving refugees on trains and orphans tied in high chairs. This juxtaposition of footage conveys the message that space travel is a solution to—and escape from—social ills. This "fantasy of liberation" as Asif A. Siddiqi refers to it in the above-quoted article, shows that science fiction has always been about escaping the dominant paradigm in an oppressive society.

The result is a kind of alternate reality utopia that, in *Aelita*, takes place in the scenes on Mars. Los is a kind of Dorothy in Oz character. He imagines Aelita as this perfect sex symbol who needs his help to overt row the repressive "elders" who refuse to let her communicate with Earth. When Aelita sees Los through a device meant to show her earth, she falls in love with Los. She is in direct contrast to Los' plain, working-class wife Natasha. In this way, Los desires to be a member of a higher class of elite royalty—or rather, to remake the world through his fantasies.

Los becomes jealous when Natasha gets involved with a scheme to steal sugar with their tenant, a member of the NEP, and when she starts becoming involved in the parties that deeply contrast the poverty at the time. Los ends up killing Natasha and escaping on a rocket to Mars, where he helps the slave class of Mars overthrow the elders. An impassioned speech promotes the revolution that overthrew the House of Romanov and established the Soviet Union:

"The free speech of free men has beat the Elders thousand years of hypnosis."

Of course, Aelita ultimately betrays Los and sides with the elders—because she is a symbol of the elite. At the last moment, Aelita is transformed into Los' wife Natasha, right before he pushes her to her death once more.

The next cut scene reveals that the original message from the beginning of the movie is actually a publicity stunt. Los, like Dorothy returning from Oz, awakens and realizes it was all a dream. Nathasha is safe and Los vows to stay and fight for a better world.

When it came out, the film was widely popular but panned by critics for years to come for not being Soviet enough. The film was marketed by adverts put in the newspaper that mimicked the message from the film. They even released leaflets from planes that contained the mysterious message. Ars Cinema, where the movie premiered, was reportedly decorated with giant figures of Aelita and art deco Martian decor.

Aelita is ultimately a pro-Soviet film, but at the time, its utopian leanings represented a hope for a different future, one that would not come to bear. *Aelita* is an example of a film that expresses the complex political and social mores of its time. While Los ends up rejecting Aelita and the elite, backstabbing, ruling class she represents, the film's controversial representation of the gray area of a revolution seems subversive when viewed some 97 years later. I found myself rooting for Aelita, the lonely space queen who just wants a good snogging.

Los buries his dreams of traveling to Mars—but not because those utopian ideals are bad, per se, but because he wants to build that ideal here on Earth. Without words, *Aelita* shows how the political-cultural moment of a time will always make its way into representations of that time, even when the goal is short-lived.

I was lucky enough to catch a screening of *Aelita: Queen of Mars* at Fantastic Fest 2021, where the film got a new score. In partnership with GroundUp Music, Fantastic Fest and Alamo Drafthouse Cinema partnered to introduce a new score by Chris Bullock. Bullock is a member of the band Snarky Puppy.

Chris Bullock brings a beautiful quality to the music added to the film which elevates and entrances. Mixing synth and organic qualities, the music is simply magical. You can watch an excerpt on YouTube. I am really hoping that this version of the film gets a wider distribution at some point in the future.

This film is reviewed as part of Interstellar Flight Press' coverage of the Alamo Drafthouse Fantastic Fest 2021. We thank Alamo Drafthouse for providing a free screening of this film.

WHAT IT MEANS TO BE A FAMILY IN A TECHNOLOGICAL DYSTOPIA: REVIEW OF THE MITCHELLS VS. THE MACHINES

BY PRESLEY THOMAS

"The dystopian element is just a way to amplify and expand the complexity of the characters and their growth in the process."

I first started hearing about *The Mitchells Vs. The Machines* (Netflix, 2021) on Twitter from parents who watched movies with their children. They were surprised to find that both kids and adults were entertained. Parents and kids were both laughing and enjoying their time watching the movie. This is an outlier experience for much of family-oriented movies outside of Pixar blockbusters.

When I went to my dad's 65th birthday party, I talked to my older brother and his wife and kids, and they expressed the same feelings I heard online, "It's great, but it's about twenty minutes too long," he said. Which I tend to agree with after viewing it with my husband on a Saturday night. There were also some surprises though . . .

My husband kept telling me one of the lead protagonists was a lesbian, that she mentioned a girl crush and wore a rainbow pin. I was squinting to see when there were shots of her jacket. There wasn't a lot of talk outside of that one incident, which I didn't remember, and the jacket where I did see a rainbow pin. In my mind, I guess, I assumed when she said she was looking forward to meeting someone it was just a future college friend, not a girlfriend.

You see, the Mitchells are in the middle of a transition as their oldest daughter, Katie, has applied and gotten into film school after graduating and is moving to LA for college. She is spirited and passionate about film and has a whole youtube series featuring their hapless family dog, Monchi, as a canine police officer who we find later voicing Katie's own frustration with her family when her father finally watches one of her movies through the transparent pod of a ship meant to blast all humanity into space forever.

Unlike other dystopian fantasies that separate families and children who then have to create new ones the robot takeover of humanity instigated by a tech monopoly stand-in (think Apple, Amazon, or Microsoft), actually brings the family closer together. The dystopian element is just a way to amplify and expand the complexity of the characters and their growth in the process.

When Rick Mitchell realizes the distance from his daughter will only increase when she's gone to school, he cancels her plane ticket and plans a family road trip to LA instead. It seems a little cloying at first, but if you put it in the context of a robot takeover it puts Katie and her family in a much better place for support—if they can get through their own insecurities as mom, dad, daughter, and son to find it.

As this calamity happens, the Mitchell family has to find themselves and a unique bond that is all their own. Their perfect neighbors act as a foil at parts of the movie, but it doesn't overshadow or dim any of The Mitchells' shine as they learn and grow together.

Just like my brother's earlier critique, I do think some of the action elements cover the same emotional ground more than once, and it could be about twenty minutes shorter and be just as strong. If you fire this movie up you are in for some laughs and some feels.

You will also get softly affirming vibes from The Mitchells as they ask, "Is Jade coming home for Thanksgiving?" at the end, lightly demonstrating how different sexualities don't have to break families (it's not even an issue for them, really) but can complement them and create more opportunity for growth.

If The Mitchells can make it through a robot apocalypse, I think anything is possible.

NORSEMEN: THE BEST NETFLIX SERIES YOU HAVEN'T SEEN

BY HENRY L. HERZ

Norsemen (2016) may well be the best Netflix series you haven't seen. Flashback to how I imagine the creators devised their adult comedy:

Jonas Torgersen: "Let's write a show about Vikings. We're Norwegian, after all."

Jon Iver Helgaker: "True, but History Channel's already got a Vikings series. Hey, what if we mash up Vikings with something completely the opposite, like NBC's The Office?"

Jonas Torgersen: "Yes! Our Vikings could be hilariously inept and self-deluded."

Jon Iver Helgaker: "And it should have sex-, violence-, and anatomical-based humor."

Jonas Torgersen: "Testicles are never not funny. Totally worth an R rating."

Norsemen's (*Vikingane* in the Norwegian version) first episode opens with a perfect example of the show's trademark dialogue, blending medieval and contemporary sensibilities with deadpan delivery. As the Vikings return from a raid, one of their captives has difficulty appreciating his dire situation. He's like a disgruntled airline passenger. Or perhaps a medieval Karen who wants to speak with the manager.

Rufus: "Before you say anything, let me alert you to the fact that we haven't been served water for over twelve hours. That's ridiculous."

(later)

Rufus: "Not to complain, but I think the flow of information here on this boat is extremely arbitrary. And that's totally uncalled for when we're so crammed together in such a small craft. I didn't know until yesterday that we were even going to Norway."

Olav punches Rufus in the face.

Olav: "Was that too much?"

Arvid: "No. You're the chieftain. Aren't you supposed to be a little like that when you're in charge? A little crazy?"

Olav: "Hmm. It's not really me, that fear-based leadership style stuff. It doesn't feel right."

Just like *The Office,* Norsemen's appeal derives from a winning combination of hilarious dialogue, absurd/slapstick situations, a large quirky cast with a shared fate, and surprisingly nuanced character development. The Viking villagers are a sword-wielding version of the hapless Dunder-Mifflin crew, and you'll fall in love with them too. *Side note: Scranton, PA is just as cold as Norheim in the winter.* Let's meet some of the inhabitants of Norheim, shall we?

Orm (Kåre Conradi)—The dim-witted, cowardly protagonist channels The Office's Michael Scott. Orm is shunned because he's more interested in poetry, art, and crochet than raiding. His lack of martial (and marital) skills is frequently the source of both mocking and hilarity. In one of my favorite scenes, he fails to set alight his brother's funeral barge.

"Who dares to boo their own chieftain? I'm really, really disappointed. You shouldn't boo your own chieftain. That's just child's knowledge. Try firing an arrow with really cold fingers yourself before you start booing."

Orm's far and away the most nuanced character—simultaneously empathetic and despicable, sad and funny, "humble and proud," power-hungry and desperate for friendship. I want to root for and against him at the same time. Orm's overwhelming need to fit in and find physical intimacy takes him to ridiculous extremes, including consenting to being raped and stalking others when they're using the "shitting log" (latrine). *Side note:*

even in 790 AD, people like to read when on the toilet, except that in Norheim, they read rune sticks.

Orm seems gentle, but we learn he has a dark side. Very dark. He kills his brother to become chieftain. When a woman is about to unmask Orm as the shitting log stalker, he stabs her. The outcast Orm murders the Law Keeper to become chieftain again. Maybe Orm is less Michael Scott and more Dexter Morgan.

Arvid (Nils Jørgen Kaalstad)—Big, selfish, and good at his job, Arvid reminds me of Stanley from The Office. As we might expect of a Viking, he's all about "pillaging and ravaging and things like that." And true to trope, this fighter is no philosopher. When he sits to contemplate big things, he thinks about mountains and whales. The thickset Arvid maintains he's not fat, but rather has a curved spine that makes his stomach protrude. *Note to self: remember that line.* His easygoing simplicity makes him likable, but just like Stanley, he has a dark side. He kills a merchant to seize his property and has no qualms about sleeping with other people's wives. *Norsemen trivia: he's married in real life to Hildur (Marian Saastad Ottesen), taking method acting to its logical extreme.*

Jarl Varg (Jon Øigarden)—When this ruthless jarl (earl) rules loses his cherished full head of long blonde hair, he literally goes insane. He wages a war of vengeance against another jarl for mocking his baldness. When one of his warriors organizes a modern brainstorming session to offer feedback on earl's leadership, Varg encourages the process, listens politely, and then has the warrior impaled. After Varg's hands are severed in combat, viewers are treated to a hilarious sequence of medieval smiths attempting to craft primitive prosthetic hands. His close-cropped head and utter lack of scruples reminds me of The Office's Creed. *Office trivia: the character Creed Bratton is played by the actor Creed Bratton.*

Despite having less screen time, these supporting characters steal the show with their hilarious quirks and dialogue:

Kark (Øystein Martinsen)—I loved how he portrays a mashup of two diametrically opposed concepts: cheerfulness and servitude. The invariably optimistic Kark is so habituated to slavery that he works for the Vikings even after being granted freedom. He is the most zen slave of the Middle Ages, a constant island of calm in a swirling sea of chaos and violence.

Ragnar (Mikkel Bratt Silset)—Ragnar's anachronistic beliefs make me laugh out loud. He prefers to be truthful because being caught in a web of lies is "really stressful." He's a strong advocate of the saved-seats policy on their longboat. But Ragnar is best known for being a fashion-conscious Viking. Despite the ribbing from other warriors, he espouses the aesthetic appeal of horns in this fan-favorite scene.

> *"The helmet is a basic head cover, right? But when you add some other material, like horns, it becomes something else. It's no longer just a helmet. It is something bigger. It tells a story. And that is what fashion is all about."*

Torstein (Bjørn Myrene)—The quirky, easily confused, and unswervingly loyal second in command to the maniacal Jarl Varg is the Dwight Schrute of Norsemen. *Office trivia: no actor appeared in more Office episodes than Rainn Wilson*. We feel sorry for Torstein when he invariably follows Varg's orders, whether having his family killed for no good reason or peeing in his pants. Warning: you too may pee your pants in laughter at the squishing sounds Torstein subsequently makes on the field of battle. He's incapable of making small talk, even after devising the tactic of talking about the weather. Torstein's attempts at party chit-chat are hilariously painful to watch. But, we've all been there, amirite? In my absolute favorite scene, he reveals another odd handicap.

> *Torstein: "Is that an important message you have there, little raven?"*
>
> *Ragnar: "That's a chicken."*
>
> *Torstein: "Chicken? Right. Of course. I've never been very good with birds. I see beaks and wings, but aside from that, they look all the same to me. Totally identical."*
>
> *Ragnar: "So, you can't tell the difference between a sparrow and an eagle?"*
>
> *Torstein: "Not a chance. Totally bird-blind. Always been."*

Since hearing that line, I'm Norsemen-bound and always will be. The series contains far more R-rated humor than The Office, but it's equally clever and entertaining. Don't believe just me. The New York Times called *Norsemen* one of the ten best international TV series in 2017 and one of the best international TV shows of the decade.

In these challenging times, don't you deserve a vacation in Norheim? Of course you do. Go watch *Norsemen!*

APOCALYPSE MEOW: THE GRUDGE AT THE END OF THE WORLD

BY SYDNEY RICHARDSON

A short glimpse into the Grudge franchise, nihilism, and why Kayako Saeki is much more terrifying than any other ghost that has ever existed.

There's a comment that can be found underneath the Youtube video "JuOn The Grudge with English Subs," which, is exactly what the title suggests; the Japanese 2002 smash-hit *Ju-On*, plastered onto the website almost nine years ago by some kind citizen. As of writing this, the movie has yet to be removed.

Posted by Youtube user Rylosalex two years ago, the comment is simple, but haunting:

"The ending scene with empty streets and all of those missing persons posters . . . creepy."

Creepy is a word for it.

The moment in question comes at the very end of the film after the curse has run its course, leaving nothing behind in its wake. It lasts for no longer than thirty seconds, but the effect is haunting.

Six shots of Nerima, Tokyo. The streets are completely devoid of life. Missing person posters, their edges curled yellow by the passage of time, flutter in the wind and fall to the ground, no one left to heed their warning. There are no children playing on the sidewalk. No passersby with groceries in hand, headed home for the day, no ambient noise of traffic, because there's no one left to drive the cars. There is no sign of the everyday hustle and bustle of life in Tokyo, Japan, as there is no life left.

The curse has taken everything.

The Grudge, or *Ju-On* Series, is an absolute must for any horror fan; it is the pinnacle, the piece-de-resistance, if you will, of the dead wet girl, the beginning of the stringy, black-haired ghost woman we fear, the one that creeps and crawls into our nightmares. The series of films, starting in 1998 and boasting a lineup of ten movies, all center around a single plot thread; housewife Kayako Saeki is murdered by her jealous husband after she shows interest towards another man. In his rage, Takeo Saeki murders the family cat, and it is implied that he kills his son, Toshio.

Anyone that enters the Saeki house is then pursued by Kayako, now transformed into a terrifying Onryō. In Japanese literature, the Onryō (怨霊) is a wrathful ghost, a spirit wronged in life now looking to get even with the living. Once an unsuspecting victim steps foot into the property, they are doomed to die, and the allure of experiencing an actual haunted house keeps the citizens of Tokyo flocking to the Saeki house, giving Kayako and Toshi, now a vengeful spirit himself, a steady diet of victims.

This isn't the isolated haunting that most of us are used to. The typical ghost story plays out as: victim ventures into a haunted house, and the victim is terrorized and or killed by the spirit that inhabits said haunted property. Or perhaps you can replace the house with some other haunted item. The victim comes into contact with haunted tape/haunted box/haunted doll, the victim is terrorized and or killed by the spirit that haunts the cursed item. Rinse and repeat.

But what makes *The Grudge* especially haunting, is that it—it being the curse, Kayako Saeki, the Grudge herself, etcetera—seems to function dually. It is a ghost story with an apocalyptic end, what happens when you cross something like *Contagion* and *The Woman in Black*.

The Ju-On/Grudge series is told in segments, each focusing on a seemingly random person that somehow comes into contact with the house; let's refer to the structure as Patient Zero. Dare to enter the property, and you're immediately infected, with a zero percent survival rate. Hysteria, hallucinations, fever, and visions of a ghostly white naked cat-boy are just some of the symptoms that the infected experience before death. And, just like a bad cold, the Onryō can be passed on to the poor unfortunate souls who just happen to be in the vicinity.

In the first film, doting sister Hitomi becomes infected after visiting her brother Katsuya, when he unknowingly moves into the Saeki house. She inevitably dies, but it gets worse; when the spirit follows her from the house to her office like that cough you just can't get rid of. A security guard with zero ties to Hitomi, the Saeki family, or that infected house, "falls ill" with Kayako, and the spirit eats him alive.

In fact, the much-maligned *Grudge 3* expands on this idea when an American girl living in Japan moves back to Chicago, Illinois, only to infect her entire apartment building. Even after she dies, residents get passing glimpses of Toshio, of black cats running just past their field of vision, until it's time for Kayako to take what is hers. The curse runs rampant in the building, forcing residents to move out, and the unspoken idea here is that, since there's no escape from the curse, the only thing they're doing is spreading the infection further, prolonging the inevitable. The residents that stay end up dying. The residents that leave will likely die.

Think back to the empty streets of Tokyo from the first *Ju-On*, and that's how every place visited by the Onryō will end up; empty, lifeless, forgotten.

Like a bad case of HPV, Kayako Saeki cannot be cured. There is no antidote for an Onryō, and your efforts of resistance—be it moving away, visiting shamanic matriarchs, or trying to tape the windows up with newspaper, so your dead friends don't look in through the windows at night—are all futile.

In the end, the infection—the curse—will run its course, and everyone will die. And, in my opinion, that's part of the allure. *The Grudge* is a fantastic series in that it really tests and pulls at the restraints we put on hauntings. It forces us to confront the unfairness of being mortal, to come to the understanding that sometimes bad things happen to people who don't deserve it. And there's nothing we can really do about that.

There's a special sort of nihilism in those shots of empty Tokyo that is much more terrifying than the croaking apparition of Kayako; it's the thought that, given time, each of us will fall victim to the infection that is time, and the only thing to prove that we ever existed will be a piece of yellowing paper fluttering in the empty street.

PHIL TIPPETT IS A MAD GOD: THE NSFW PASSION PROJECT OF A STOP-MOTION ARTIST WHO NEVER GAVE UP ON HIS ART IS THE PERFECT REFLECTION OF TODAY'S BIZARRO ALTERNATE TIMELINE

BY HOLLY LYN WALRATH

> *"The final form of Mad God isn't the film itself, but the memory after you watch it. It's bringing you to that moment just after waking up from a dream, frozen, exploring fragments of your feral mind before they fade back into the shadows. That's the moment. Mad God is just a way to get you there." —Phil Tippett in Fangoria ("Phil Tippett on Experimental Stop Motion Passion Mad God)*

2021 is the year that stop-motion animation evolves once more with the debut of Phil Tippett's *Mad God* (Tippett Studio). The phantasmagoric passion project of the genius who is responsible for how much we love and cling to the "old-school" methods of films like *Star Wars*, *Starship Troopers,* and *Robocop* finally brings his opus to the screen in a jaw-droppingly freakish feature film.

Mad God is a fully practical stop-motion film that is unlike any you've seen before and yet will feel completely familiar to a certain generation of audiences. As I was watching it, I found myself thinking, "What did I just watch?" along with "How did they DO that?" and when I was done, I had to go watch every YouTube video about its making that I could find, longing for a feature-length documentary about the film.

It's not that the film doesn't stand alone. It does, in infinite detail. Set in a steampunk-esque post-apocalyptic nightmare, the story (or non-narrative, as Phil Tippett refers to it) follows an assassin from a long line of assassins sent to destroy the world, or save it, depending on your viewpoint. The film opens with a long shot of a space-pod-like diving bell descending into a hellscape of dystopian madness that is far too entertaining for me to describe here without giving away the surprises; you're going to have to watch it yourself.

That is if you think you're up for a film steeped in imagery that is dark, sticky, monstrous, horrifying, and yet somehow recognizable at 24 frames per second.

THE HISTORY OF MAD GOD

The project began in 1987. Phil Tippett at this point was a huge artist in the stop motion animation scene. Tippett got his start in animation when first inspired as a child watching the 1955 airing of *King Kong* (1933). He says in the 2019 documentary, *Phil Tippett: Mad Dreams and Monsters*, "I got amazed by the concept that there was another world before our world where monsters without men lived." Tippett started in his garage, cooking up small stop-motion films of dinosaurs and other monsters. "No one was interested in what I was interested in."

Prior to this point, stop-motion animation was a common feature of genre films in the 1920s-1950s. Its history is inexorably tied to the creature feature. One of the early pioneers was Willis O'Brien, who worked on *Lost World* (1925) and *King Kong* (1933). O'Brien went on to mentor another great, Ray Harryhausen, whose filmography includes most of the popular genre films of the time, from *The Golden Voyage of Sinbad* (1974) to *Clash of the Titans* (1981).

By the 1970s, stop motion was a well-known technique, which explains why there is a huge amount of nostalgia built around the style. I remember watching old reruns of *The Gumby Show* (1955) and the iconic California

Raisins commercials. But probably the most iconic stop-motion comes from *Star Wars*, which was one of Phil Tippett's early films. Tippett was working alongside Bill Stromberg at Cascade Studios, which made stop-motion commercials (including the Pillsbury Doughboy). George Lucas actually set up Industrial Light and Magic (ILM) as a way of being able to incorporate stop-motion animation into *Star Wars*, because there were no unions for them at the time, and unions were a huge part of Hollywood filmmaking (*Phil Tippett: Mad Dreams and Monsters*).

You can see Phil Tippett's (literal) touch in the cantina scenes, where Tippett helped create the iconic blue keyboard playing alien (which was acted by Tippett himself in the costume) and other costumes, as well as the AT-AT walkers, the classic chess scene in the Millenium Falcon (which Tippett helped recreate in the new films), the monster in the trash compactor, the taun-tauns, and various other monsters in the original Star Wars films such as the Rancor (one of the most beloved movie monsters of all time) and Jabba the Hutt. Tippett was the primary designer for the puppet for Jabba the Hutt, which once conceived, managed to fit three people inside of it.

It is this iconic hand-craftsmanship that *Star Wars* fans still obsess over today. It's also seen as one of the major reasons that the prequels failed so spectacularly. As Jordan Maison puts it in the fantastic article "Why People Can't Enjoy the VFX in The Star Wars Prequels," "The biggest issue with the clone troopers came from the Uncanny Valley effect (Cinelinx). If you're not familiar with the term, it's a theory that holds when something looks and moves almost, but not exactly, like humans do, it causes viewers to be repulsed. Basically, you know something is off, even if you can't pinpoint it, and it throws the entire scene out of whack for you. Instead of investing you in what's happening, it's causing a sense of revulsion."

Stop motion creations are a kind of golem, requiring delicate work to create as they must be first built on a skeleton and then sculpted with clay. And the act of filming them is like sculping too. Capturing stop motion relies heavily on the animator's natural understanding of movement and organic beauty. What results is often a more believable animation, which explains why audiences are still captivated by the art form today.

HOW MANY ADJECTIVES CAN I USE TO DESCRIBE THIS MOVIE?

Mad God began as a way for Tippett to do his own work outside of the studios in the 80s. It seems that part of what stalled the project for so long was his emotional reaction to the advent of computer animation and the fear that stop-motion was a dying art.

There's a sense that Tippett is the kind of artist who's happier working behind the scenes. "Once one puts on a mask or changes your physicality, you can become something else that you're not. You can inhabit what that character is," he says of his work on *Star Wars* in costuming in *Phil Tippett: Mad Dreams and Monsters.*

Audiences are familiar with the digital-organic divide in filmmaking. Despite the fact that we can recognize that digital animation is in fact, just as intensive of an art form as something like stop-motion, and in all honesty, a technique that doesn't have the limitations of the latter, we still appreciate and miss these organic techniques, imbuing them with a kind of nostalgia that makes me wonder if today's generations of viewers will understand the significance of this history.

Mad God proves that the future for stop-motion animation is not dead. It is alive and thriving and perhaps more than a little bit pissed off. Over the next thirty years, Phil Tippett would work on *Mad God* in pieces, sketching out ideas in notebooks, storyboarding scenes, and crafting prop upon prop in his studio like a slightly unhinged but loveable hoarder.

The project found new life when a group of animators found boxes of props and puppets from the original footage and helped Tippett complete his vision. The fact that over sixty people spent most of their free time and weekends volunteering to help bring the project to fruition proves how although Tippett may not have seen it as viable, the people around him did.

In 2012, Tippett Studios launched a Kickstarter to fund the film that was quickly funded and grew to $125,000. This allowed the release of the film in three parts in 2014, 2015, and 2018. The 2021 feature includes these three films plus thirty minutes of additional footage, combining them into a film that somehow manages to work despite being a Frankenstein's monster, which feels fitting.

Audiences will not be prepared for this kaleidoscopic experience, even those who, like myself, grew up loving stop-motion animation in the form of *The Nightmare Before Christmas*, or are hardcore fans of the genre. We are simply not used to seeing a full-length feature film that is stop motion treated like this, let alone one that is unflinchingly NSFW and aesthetically obsessed with perfection.

There have been amazing stop-motion films before but rarely do filmmakers apply the kind of camera styles like the zooms, moving cameras, long-shots, and intense focus that Tippett uses. The movements are recognizable and deeply realistic, almost hyperrealistic. The music, scored by Richard Beggs (*Apocalypse Now, Harry Potter, Ghostbusters*), is haunting and at times charming. And the film utilizes animation and live-action, weaving together all of the schools of filmmaking in a way that is relatively unheard of in today's cinema.

It's worth noting that the film is extremely dark and deeply disturbed. I'm talking "female mannequins masturbating on screen" and "vomi -guzzling gore" and "surgeons rooting in bodies for tentacle monsters" kind of disturbing. But I don't think this makes the film one that can't be enjoyed and appreciated.

After watching a million behind the scenes on YouTube, I was sort of enchanted by how Tippett has done so much with his career but sweetly, buys a lot of his models at Ace Hardware. I think I missed the uncanny valley naked masturbating doll aisle on my last trip to get paint. But somehow, I don't feel weirded out by this. It makes sense to me that 2021 would be the year this kind of film gets to debut.

As Tippett's wife (who has run Tippett Studios from the beginning and is the "business side" of the venture) lovingly puts it from her role as the keeper of the mad god, "*Mad God* is a very unique kind of experiment."

Mad God is a lush, exhausting, entrancing deep-dive that requires either full commitment to geekery or some hardcore drugs to witness. It's a sequence of dreams tied up in a nightmare. It's abstract, weird, obsessive, absurd, eccentric, visionary, and dark. It's *Fraggle Rock* meets *Doom* meets *Beetlejuice* meets *Bioshock* meets WWII historicals meets M. Night Shyamalan's *The Village* meets *Spirited Away* meets *The Matrix.*

Mad God is a new cult classic.

This film is reviewed as part of Interstellar Flight Press' coverage of the Alamo Drafthouse Fantastic Fest 2021. We thank Alamo Drafthouse for providing a free screening of this film.

COME AND SEE: FASCISM AS COSMIC HORROR: HOW A 1985 SOVIET FILM TAPS INTO THE INCOMPREHENSIBLE HORROR OF GENOCIDE

BY COREY J. WHITE

> *"And when he had opened the fourth seal, I heard the voice of the fourth beast say, 'Come and see.' And I looked, and behold a pale horse: and his name that sat on him was Death, and Hell followed with him. And power was given unto them over the fourth part of the earth, to kill with sword, and with hunger, and with death, and with the beasts of the earth." (The Book of Revolution, inspiration for the title of Come and See, 1985).*

It's there from the opening minutes of the film: a Nazi reconnaissance plane circling overhead.

But is it just a plane, or could it be an artifact created by a higher-dimensional entity intersecting our reality—the entity of war?

Come and See is a 1985 Soviet film directed by Elem Klimov—a cinematic masterpiece and possibly the most harrowing war movie ever put to film. It opens with Flyora digging for weapons in an old trench so he can join the Belarusian partisans to fight against the invading Nazi forces. He is so gleefully eager to fight, it's obvious he never learned the lessons of the First World War—there is no glory or adventure in war despite the propaganda, just death and misery.

Left behind at the partisan camp while the others go to fight, Flyora bonds with a young nurse named Glasha. Again, the reconnaissance plane appears, signaling the arrival of war (Flyora: "That's the one that's always flying."), and Flyora and Glasha barely survive an attack by Nazi forces, with the entire encampment bombed prior to the arrival of paratroopers.

Now war has completely broken through into Flyora's reality and, deafened by the bombing and shellshocked by his brush with death, the young boy will find his mind shattered, his life destroyed, and his fellow Belarusians slaughtered by genocidal SS forces. *Come and See* is unflinching in its portrayal of war and carnage, and is a far more important and *true* war film than Hollywood has ever produced or likely *could* produce. There are no heroes in this film. There is no adventure. The action on screen is not entertainment, it is pure kinetic terror (1).

Cosmic horror is, of course, strongly associated with the fiction of H.P. Lovecraft (2). In recent years, however, we've seen a diverse set of creators picking up the torch of cosmic horror and taking it far beyond the boundaries established in Lovecraft's work (3). The basic tenets of cosmic horror suggest that there is something incomprehensibly horrifying beneath our current reality and that learning about this horror is enough to drive a person insane. Within the stories, there is also a belief, or perhaps the *knowledge*, that a person's life—and indeed all human life—is utterly insignificant, that if the horrifying beings waiting beyond the veil of consensus reality killed us, it would be as an afterthought or a byproduct of their actions. We are so far beneath them that our extinction would completely escape their notice.

It's fitting that in *Come and See* it's a reconnaissance plane that is constantly circling overhead—it's the forward scout for the war entity, the higher dimensional being appearing as a 3D object as it intersects the barrier of our reality. Where it appears, death and carnage are close behind, incomprehensible horrors that seem cosmic in scope, but which are sadly all too human.

If war really is a cosmic entity breaking through into our reality, it has no shortage of disciples here.

After returning home, Flyora finds the badly burned mayor of his village —the sole survivor of an attack—the dying man says "Didn't I tell you not to go digging?" The inference here is that the attack only happened because the Germans saw the locals arming themselves. But this completely ignores the scale of the bloodshed happening across the Belarusian countryside. The Nazi forces did not attack Flyora's town because they were provoked by the actions of children who wanted to play soldier, they attacked because the engine of fascism runs on the blood of the other, enabled by the sort of xenophobia familiar to Lovecraft and his writings.

Though *Come and See* is a piece of realist cinema, its depiction of war perfectly aligns with the themes of cosmic horror. Not only that, but the genocidal projects of the Nazis, while all too real, share the incomprehensibility of cosmic horror in their sheer scale. No individual mattered compared to their massive works of extermination, and pain, death, and insanity, even on an industrial scale, were inconsequential contrasted with the anti-human Reich they wished to spread across the world.

China Miéville, author of weird fiction (as well as leftist historical fiction), has said: "Lovecraft's horror is not one of intrusion but of realization. The world has always been implacably bleak; the horror lies in our acknowledging that fact." Indeed, the true cosmic horror of *Come and See* is not the incursion of an outer entity of war, it's the all too human faces of the genocidaires and their celebratory tone as they commit the atrocities of the film's climactic scenes.

Fascism is not an intruding force, it is ever-present, ready to emerge when those in power conspire to turn us against ourselves, to split us into groups so that one or more of those groups can be othered and eventually destroyed.

NOTES

(1) That all said, the film is not without lighter moments, underpinned by surrealism, like with the crane that befriends Flyora and Glasha after the bombing, or absurdism, best exemplified by the life-size Hitler effigy the Belarusian men build using human bones and a pilfered SS uniform and then proceed to shower with insults.

(2) Many have argued that Lovecraft's xenophobia led directly to his invention of cosmic horror—fear of the unknown serving as the foundation of both his bigotry and his fiction.

(3) Including Victor LaValle's *The Ballad of Black Tom*, Cassandra Khaw's Persons Non Grata books, and Kij Johnson's *The Dream-Quest of Vellit Boe*.

MANJULA PADMANABHAN'S FEMINIST DYSTOPIAN SCIENCE FICTION: HOW CONTEMPORARY INDIAN SFF TACKLES COMPLEX ISSUES

BY ANUSHMITA MOHANTY

"These novels are at their best when they make readers think about the relationship between selfhood and gender—if being a person is a delicate balance of internal and external influences, then to what extent does gender influence identities?"

TW: This article contains mentions of transphobia, transmisogyny, sexual assault, and gender-based violence.

As a child in late-1990s India, my approach to literature was simple. I read whatever I could find and the idea of genre was mostly immaterial. This included Enid Blyton's works (the original cottagecore!), Tintin comics ("Kya? Phir wahi??!!"), and then, when Harry Potter happened, entire archives of fanfiction. Like many other upper-class, privileged child readers, my knowledge of the English language provided me a whole new world to base my identity on. The only issue—spending part of my childhood unconsciously imagining myself as white. Little science fiction came my way, perhaps some HG Wells and some Isaac Asimov. It would be a long time before I discovered Octavia Butler and Ursula LeGuin, and thus for a large part of my reading life, science fiction passed under the radar.

A SHORT HISTORY OF INDIAN SCIENCE FICTION

I begin this essay on Manjula Padmanabhan with a personal reading history to illustrate that generic definitions like "science fiction" can often hold little meaning in Non-western cultures. They can be as arbitrary as national formulations like "India", an identity resisted by several writers from the subcontinent. Indian science fiction, the context in which Manjula Padmanabhan is often read, is therefore slippery; this is important to keep in mind while understanding the history of SFF from South Asia.

Literature in South Asia before British colonialism included orature, non-fiction, theatre, and poetry. Colonial binaries, like 'realism versus fantasy' and 'the novel versus oral literature' are inapplicable to most pre-colonial South Asian fiction. Nonetheless, fiction that can be loosely categorized as SFF was initially published in Urdu, Bengali, Tamil, and other regional languages. These were in the oral traditions of Urdu dastans and Indigenous folklore, and some examples are *Chandrakanta* (1888) by Devaki Nandan Khatri, a Hindi dastan from 1888, and *Sultana's Dream* (1905), a feminist-utopian short story by Begum Rokeya Sakhawat Hossain.

After India's Independence (1947), science fiction began to be written in English, in conjunction with the increase in English-language publishing. Contemporary Indian authors who have self-identified their writing as within the generic umbrella of science fiction include Samit Basu, author of the *Gameworld* trilogy, Anil Menon, who wrote *The Beast with Nine Billion Feet*, Vandana Singh, writer of *The Woman Who Thought She Was A Planet*, and Mainak Dhar, author of popular zombie literature.

Does Indian science fiction have any defining characteristics? Perhaps no more than "Indian" or "science fiction" do.

Science fiction based in the Indian subcontinent, imbued with certain South Asian flavors, tropes, or ways of being are some possible contenders. Science fiction based on Indian folklore characters that incorporate mythological aspects and traditions into stories is also popular. Given that science fiction is inherently political, it is natural that issues of Hindu nationalism, misogyny, and casteism are fundamental to several works. However, it is entirely possible for Indian science fiction to possess some (or neither) of these features—I am thinking here of *Insects Are Just Like You and Me Except Some of Them Have Wings* (2008) by Kuzhali

Manickavel, an anthology of unsettling fiction that deliberately eludes categorization.

MANJULA PADMANABHAN'S DYSTOPIAN WORLDBUILDING

While science fiction has effectively pushed back at constructs of gender and imagined fluidity of both gender and genres, it is also true that a large canon of science fiction was imagined for a primarily male audience. The male gaze baked into this science fiction often produces a rather dry cake of primarily male characters, harsh clinical environments, or a tendency to prioritize facts and rationality over lived experience. Manjula Padmanabhan, a contemporary Indian playwright, comic artist, and novelist, situates her fiction solidly within these gendered tensions in the science fiction genre. Both her play *Harvest* (1997), and novel *The Island of Lost Girls* (2015), turn the genre against itself to imagine a future in which the reigning beliefs of our time are pushed to the extremes of their logical conclusions. *Harvest,* a play written in 1997, imagines a future now long-gone: it is set in 2010. At the time it was written, India was in the process of economic liberalization, and "globalization" was a word that would soon ossify in our shared cultural lexicon. Despite its promises of international networks of sharing, globalization was only to reproduce existing inequalities between countries, and Padmanabhan's play is prescient to this eventuality. She says, in an interview, "I think the golden age is over—perhaps because a lot of SF no longer seems adequately fictional any more. Even HARVEST—it's hardly fiction—it's almost yesterday's news bite".

In the play, Om Prakash, who has just lost his job, applies to *InterPlanta* services as a donor of unspecified organs to a "receiver" based in a version of North America, who has chillingly promised to leave one-third of him intact. Composed after Padmanabhan read a newspaper article on organ trade, this play underscores the exploitative relationship between developed and developing nations. Colonial and neo-imperial countries continue to extract "raw material" from "third-world countries" and interfere within their internal working—the company in *Harvest* refurbishes Om's house, replaces his food with pellets, and sets up a surveillance camera. In this situation, it is only Om's wife Jaya who is deeply suspicious of the consequences of these events: Om and his mother have been literally lulled to sleep through a TV, symbolic of consumerist practices. Eventually, Om's brother Jeetu is taken in his place, and the receiver—revealed to be a white man named Virgil—plans to artificially inseminate Jaya from across the world. Virgil's attitude of not wanting to physically touch Jaya on grounds of "infection", is intended to mirror white prejudices against women of color. The play ends on a note of resistance and hope, as Jaya refuses to bear his child until he touches her himself and locks herself into her home with a lifetime's supply of food, electricity, and comfort.

If *Harvest* exposes fault lines in global power relations, Padmanabhan's novel *The Island of Lost Girls* and its precursor *Escape* (2015) deal directly with feminist dystopian themes. These novels are about Meiji, who is born in and eventually escapes from a version of the Indian subcontinent in which all women have been murdered by a group of men known as the Generals. With the help of her father, Youngest, she must now survive in the outside world, particularly on the Island of Lost Girls.

As an Indian reader, Padmanabhan's inspirations for these novels are clear: Khap Panchayats, a quasi-judicial body, usually of older village men, who proclaim and uphold conservative customs. Like the Generals in the novel, they cast inescapable decrees on women, especially in rural settings, and "honor killings", where in the novel, men volunteer the women in their family in order to survive, is witness to events of the Partition of India and beyond.

Padmanabhan is incisive in her depiction of how women are only valued for their ability to reproduce—the Generals, refer to them constantly as "vermin". When this version of Indian society is able to create reproductive technology, women are killed altogether, hunted down one by one. Less evident in these stories, however, is the casteism through which these bodies operate. "Drones", an entire servant class of technologically modified clones, are a satirical description of the caste system propagated by Brahmanical supremacy. This is intended to make the upper-caste Indian reader uncomfortable and question the extent to which these systems are reflected in our everyday lives.

And yet, because these drones are the *only* way that caste is depicted, as Shashi Mike asks, "The genocide of women at least offers the survivors a voice and a chance of resistance with Meiji, which is something a female reader can at least hold on to. But what hope is given to a Dalit or Bahujan reader in either *Escape* or *The Island of Lost Girls*? Were we intended to read these books at all?"

A NOTE ON GENDER

These novels are at their best when they make readers think about the relationship between selfhood and gender—if being a person is a delicate balance of internal and external influences, then to what extent does gender influence identities? Padmanabhan constantly needles ideas of girlhood and womanhood. Meiji, who has spent much of her life with a prosthetic penis, is suddenly asked to identify as a woman, and shouts back, claiming that she is just a person. The Island of Lost Girls she is rescued by is supposed to serve as her refuge from the broken patriarchal system of her homeland but is fraught with its own problems. The island, which represents white feminism, insists on its inhabitants being naked and identifying as women, and Meiji's memories are wiped without her consent. The island's inhabitants thus have a problematic attitude towards trauma survivors, and this causes immense dissonance for Meiji—even though the island only has cisgender women, she is naturally unwilling to forego bodily and mental privacy and autonomy. Tellingly, the Island cannot repair the problems of Meiji's home country: only Meiji can.

Unfortunately, though these books radically prod at what it means to be an Indian woman, they are heavily let down by Padmanabhan's depiction of trans experiences. The premise of a world in which men commit genocide on female populations creates a gender binary that leaves no room for trans and non-binary experiences. In the story, Youngest, Meiji's uncle, is forced by a General to undergo sex reassignment surgery. His purpose: to maintain a masculine world order that nonetheless contains elements of heterosexuality is a cruel, deliberate mockery of gender identity. It is essential to note here that genitals are not linked to being a woman, though the novel never does. Crucially, there are continuous subplots of trans people being sexually assaulted, unsatisfied, or solitary which definitely reproduces transphobic narratives of one-dimensional lives marked with violence.

While it can be argued that Padmanabhan is simply imagining a future in which the current transmisogyny circulating in India is taken to its conclusion, it is nonetheless problematic that she does not provide a single hopeful counter-narrative or multi-dimensional trans characters. It remains to be seen how Padmanabhan engages with these questions in future sequels, and where India's current socio-political scenario takes its science fiction writers.

INTRIGUE, SECRETS, AND A FORBIDDEN ROMANCE: REVIEW OF MASK OF THE NOBLEMAN BY LAURA DIAZ DE ARCE

BY ARCHITA MITTRA

". . . a lighthearted and enjoyable read, with a familiar plot, engaging characters, a classic fairytale charm, and a fair share of steamy scenes."

Mask of the Nobleman (2020)—the debut novel by Laura Diaz De Arce and the first of a series—is a quaint fantasy retelling of the *East of the Sun, West of the Moon* fairytale (a *Beauty and the Beast* variant), brimming with intrigue, secrets, and a forbidden romance.

Peytra Silke is a young and talented sculptor who works in her father's shop. Since women in that profession are frowned upon, Peytra never receives the due credit for her exquisite carvings or her bold reinterpretations of the gods, until a mysterious Duke stumbles upon her work and hires her to work at his palace. Delighted to escape her sexist society and at the prospect of creative freedom, Peytra leaves her home to focus on the Duke's commissions. A cast of funny and charming side-characters quickly helps her settle in, and gradually Peytra and the Duke, despite belonging to different classes, strike a companionship, based on mutual respect and fascination, that soon blooms into love.

But of course, the Duke Jors is promised to another, so naturally, their romance must be kept hidden from the other nobles and servants. Meanwhile, Peytra is ever curious to catch a glimpse of the Duke's seemingly scarred face, always hidden behind an intricately carved mask.

Thus, much of the story is concerned with masks and unmasking. In a world where women are not recognized for their artistic achievements in the same league as men, the masked nobleman Jors is the first to truly see Peytra and appreciate her creative skills and eye for detail. And while Peytra remains blindfolded in all of their intimate encounters, her maturity and tenderness allow Jors to show a side of himself that court machinations compel him to keep repressed. They meet up in the middle of the night, for conversation and more, and when they cannot, they exchange cutesy love letters. In short, their love for each other sets them free.

However, although their romance is quite believable, it feels deliberate and forced, as though Peytra and Jors take up their respective roles in a fairytale rather than shine forth as complex individual characters. This isn't necessarily the author's fault. Given that it's a retelling, she has adopted a lucid and simple writing style to better evoke a "classic fairytale" feel—one that relies on more telling and less showing.

The tale is also rather slow-paced, without much conflict or tension. The plot moves in a straightforward fashion, quickly resolving the problems as they come up, with former threats (such as the Baroness) later becoming aides. The story could've been more condensed, or have had a greater focus on court intrigue. Yet towards the end, things pick up as the narrative builds to a devastating climax that simply begs for a sequel, suddenly reminding the readers that curiosity isn't without its consequences.

Also, interspersed throughout the tale, are little stories and myths, usually narrated by one of the characters, that give the readers a greater sense of the fantastical world, and its history and culture. Peytra's own point-of-view is rather sharply rendered, and it is a delight to glimpse the settings through her painter's eyes which notice the colors and small details. There are minor queer romance subplots with the rather wholesome secondary characters, and it is hoped that they will be explored in proper detail, in the sequels. And finally, a fantasy fairytale retelling is incomplete without a customary masquerade—this book, fortunately, has one, a rather lavish masked ball that is used as a thematic marker to dwell on the natures of the masked nobility that Peytra is surrounded by, and the physical (and metaphorical) masks that we wear, often even unconsciously, to get on with our daily lives.

Overall, *Mask of the Nobleman* by Laura Diaz De Arce is a lighthearted and enjoyable read, with a familiar plot, engaging characters, a classic fairytale charm, and a fair share of steamy scenes. Although it may leave the reader wanting for more, it will definitely appeal to those who enjoy sexy fantasy romances or sexy fairytales with a twist.

So, if you're up for an old-fashioned fairytale retelling with a cliffhanger ending and a dash of erotica, pick up your copy now!

DYING STARS, SENTIENT RIVERS, AND LITTLE BLUE MEN: REVIEW OF THE BURNING DAY AND OTHER STRANGE STORIES BY CHARLES PAYSEUR

BY BRI DOWNING

> *"Payseur explores the depth of the human experience, steering toward the complex themes of grieving, letting go, and finding a new purpose."*

In his new collection of short stories, Charles Payseur boldly goes where no man has gone before. Wait. Scratch that. Boldly goes where no sentient non-binary being has gone before.

Charles Payseur is probably best known for his popular review blog, Quick Sip Reviews, which highlights short fiction from pro-paying magazines and landed him four consecutive Hugo award nominations. He is also an editor, working on *We're Here: The Best Queer Speculative Fiction* (Neon Hemlock Press). His debut short story collection contains twenty-two previously published stories and three new stories.

If you grew up on Star Trek and like queer speculative fiction, you'll love *The Burning Day and Other Strange Stories*. As with most collections, I think this one starts strong, sags a little in the middle, and ends strong. That being said, I didn't dislike any of the stories, but several definitely stood out above the rest.

On the cusp of a planned planetary extinction, a dangerous race ensues in the opening story, Rubbing is Racing. Spaceship captains compete for glory and street cred, and something far more valuable than the greatest trophy in the galaxy. I thought I was in for a story about interstellar drag racing, but I came out the other side conscious of desperate struggles and ferocious hope.

Payseur's voice is strong, and his prose is beautiful and provocative. Writing from unique points of view—from that of a dying star to a sentient river, a superhero to a familiar, yet far more thoughtful, cartoon character—the author takes readers on a journey through time and space, across worlds and species, through folklore and fairy tales—yet each piece still hits close to home thanks to bold themes thoroughly grounded in the human experience.

Any reader who has ever felt marginalized or scared to be who they really are will see themselves in this collection, represented in characters like Caleb in "Little Blue Men" or Wil in "Just Toonin'". A gay man estranged from his father, Caleb must handle the old man's final affairs upon his death, as well as the familiar pressures to live up to old expectations, while Wil, that familiar cartoon character I mentioned earlier, chases after a dream until he finally decides to rewrite his own story.

Payseur explores the depth of the human experience, steering toward the complex themes of grieving, letting go, and finding a new purpose in "Humans Die, Stars Fade," where the main character is a sentient star. Another story, "Shoots and Ladders," follows a woman forever tempted by the greener grass in the next universe.

And if we're all being honest here, who wouldn't be tempted to jump into a new life?

Payseur asks those big questions that any speculative fiction reader would expect: What if there are an infinite number of universes? What if human-spaceship hybrids could turn the tides of an endless war? What if climate change is irreversible?

What if two immortal legends were sleeping together?

Speaking of sex scenes: if you're into that sort of thing, good. You're going to get a lot of it. A little shy? Well, buckle up. You're going to get a lot of it. While a short sex scene doesn't detract from the story, it sometimes feels more like an afterthought to identify the character as having a sexual identity rather than a device to further the plot or reveal character traits.

But there are stories where a character might not have a reason to look forward to the future without the lure of romance, such as "Snow Devils," where teenage Aspen survives an endless winter alone until an intriguing stranger appears in town. A stranger with a "mouth like summer."

Though the writing was top-notch, a few stories fizzled for me, but for the most part, I found myself flying through the pages, always hungry for more. And while I don't usually gravitate toward short story collections, this one earns a prominent place on my shelf!

Look forward to *The Burning Day and Other Strange Stories* from *Lethe Press Books.*

"I CANNOT BE KEPT IN A BOX": MOLLY KNOX OSTERTAG'S NEW YA GRAPHIC NOVEL THE GIRL FROM THE SEA EXPLORES IDENTITY, SUMMER LOVE, AND SELKIES

BY ERIN BECKER

Fifteen-year-old Morgan has lived on a small Nova Scotia island her whole life. But this summer is different. It's the first since her parents separated. And the first summer her dad's not there.

One night, Morgan almost drowns in the ocean. When a cute selkie named Keltie saves her, Morgan's pretty much convinced Keltie is a hallucination (because, of course a selkie is a hallucination . . . right?). So once she's safely on land, Morgan seizes the definitely-imaginary opportunity to do what she's always wanted to do with a girl. And kisses her.

When the very-much-not-imaginary Keltie shows up near Morgan's house the next day, however, things get a little complicated. Tripping over her newly-formed legs, the selkie tells Morgan that their "true love's kiss" has given her the ability to walk on land. And left their destinies intertwined forever.

Morgan is not very keen on this intertwining. Really, she's not interested in any intertwining at all. Morgan's goal is to keep all the pieces of her life in "little boxes": her family struggles in one, her feelings of not quite belonging with her friends in another, her questions about her sexuality in yet another. And when it comes to the latter, Morgan's already made a fairly detailed plan: stay in the closet until college, when she can move to a big city and "be gay, far away from this tiny town and everyone who's known me forever."

But Keltie's here now. And intertwining is going to happen. In fact, Morgan's destiny and Keltie's are even more connected than Morgan thinks. Because Keltie has come onto land with an ulterior motive: to stop a new harbor tour from cruising past the rookery and destroying the seals' home. The seals are Keltie's family, and the cruise will make the rookery completely unlivable for them. Unbeknownst to Keltie, however, the tour is run by Morgan's best friend's family—adding yet another layer of intertwined complication to their story.

All this makes for a fun, plotty read. *The Girl from the Sea* (*Scholastic*, 2021) certainly works as a fast-paced summer romp, with the story building and building to a high-action moment on the cruise ship. Along the way, Ostertag weaves in an awful lot of summer sweetness too, from heady first-crush love, to adorable beach scenes, to group chat foibles, to endearing moments with Morgan's family as they find their way after a big transition.

But beyond the title's rom-com pleasures, the thing that makes it such a satisfying read is how Ostertag combines the story's fantastical elements with Morgan's very real and relatable experience of feeling so different from everyone else on the island. The talk of destinies and magical kisses doesn't feel separate from the issues of love, friendship, and family. Rather, they're two pieces of the story that work together to make Morgan's journey toward being herself all the more poignant.

The book gives us the best of both worlds: an epic climax where someone slips on a magical seal skin and sets off to save the day—and a story that takes teen girls' quiet, complex feelings seriously.

One notable way Ostertag achieves this is through the thematic resonances between Morgan's emotional journey and Keltie's more high-concept journey of saving the seals. Keltie only gets a chance to walk on land every seven years. When Morgan tells her the rules seem awfully arbitrary, Keltie replies, "I do not know where the laws came from, but I know I could sooner halt the tide than change them." This feeling of living in an arbitrary system you didn't choose—with rules that don't quite make sense—mirrors the pressures Morgan faces: to fit in, to be someone she's not, to have crushes on boys, to try to hide the quirkier parts of herself from the world. In an interesting twist, though Keltie is *literally* a shape-shifter, the selkie is more or less the same, whether she's with the seals or walking on land. Morgan, meanwhile, is the one who camouflages herself until she's nearly unrecognizable.

It's in details like this that Ostertag manages to combine a bit of rom-com and a bit of fantasy and make something entirely new. This combination also allows the story to call into question some of the assumptions of both genres in a way that makes for an even more satisfying read.

Morgan eventually begins to accept her feelings for Keltie. She decides she's open to doing things together—as long as they keep their romance hidden. "She's secret, and she's mine," Morgan says. The words sound almost like they belong in another story, perhaps a legend about straight cis sailor and his mysterious mermaid girlfriend. It's not romantic here, though. And maybe it never really was.

In Ostertag's story, the "secret and mine" sentiment doesn't feel healthy or right. Neither does the montage of scenes where Morgan and Keltie are sharing a sandwich, swimming by the ocean, and holding hands at the movies. This "fun and games" sequence, typically one of the most "aww"-producing moments in any romantic film, is less about a burgeoning crush here and more about the growing sensation that none of this is going to turn out well if Morgan isn't willing to share Keltie with the world. Ostertag conveys this impending feeling of dread by interspersing the montage with group texts where Morgan's friends say they miss her and images of Morgan's mom checking her phone, clearly wondering why her daughter's never home.

Everything's divided, just like Morgan wanted. Everything's separate and in its own box. But it doesn't feel like a lovely, magical secret. It just feels wrong.

When it comes to Morgan's metaphorical boxes, Ostertag also does a great job of using the graphic novel format to further underscore the protagonist's obsession with keeping everything separate. In a graphic novel, after all, most scenes are visually expressed in panels, which appear as little boxes on the page. Yet Ostertag depicts key emotional and plot moments in full spreads, adding an interesting meta-narrative to the story's visual side.

As the different areas of her life crash together, taking up entire pages and bleeding over these emotional borders, Morgan eventually does become a little more herself.

"I love you dearly, Morgan," Keltie says, "but I cannot be kept in a box." Neither can this fun, genre-being story: a lighthearted, deep, fantastical rom-com. A story that's not even quite about that "rom" element in the end. At least not in the way the reader's expecting. Instead, as Morgan chooses to let her life sprawl beyond its little boxes, the book becomes about a different kind of love—love for oneself. The love that comes from finally honoring who you are, in all its complicated, unpredictable beauty.

And what's more magical than that?

RHAPSODY IN BLUE BODIES: "PRIMITIVE" DESIRE IN RUBY DIXON'S ICE PLANET BARBARIANS

BY LAURA DÍAZ DE ARCE

If you've spent more than five minutes on BookTok (the bookish subculture of TikTok) in the past month, you have very likely come across some mention of Ruby Dixon's *Ice Planet Barbarian* series. What may have started off as a joke post, in the vein of describing an almost implausibly ridiculous concept has quickly evolved into a loving embrace of the bizarre erotic.

Because of the memes.

These wonderful, hilarious memes.

The series is about human women who get stranded on an ice planet with blue alien lovers. Although the first book came out in 2015, The books have topped the Amazon bestseller list for most of 2021 and feature covers that delightfully play with romance tropes, inserting blue aliens into the role of Fabio. Their sudden surge in popularity can be attributed to TikToker Emma Carter, who was one of the first to make a video about the series.

And because I am ultimately desensitized to the bizarre erotic, I too jumped in and am (proud?) to say the I have binged through most of the original series (twenty-two books as of its current count) and started the spin-off series (*IceHome*, currently at fifteen books).

Let me first reassure you that while the elevator pitch sounds pretty ridiculous, which I will describe below, that it's a good series. It's really good. Its got all the ingredients of a great romance series: spunky lead characters, an overwrought but surprisingly engaging premise, male characters that are so good-looking they may as well have been generated in a lab (or out-of-this-world as the case may be), exotic locations, pre-destined love, and lots, and lots, of sex. (1)

Like any great trend, we are now moving away from strictly meme-ified cultural awareness to one that will inevitably be studied to death. So before we start seeing academic papers on Dixon's extensive series popping up on college campuses, I thought it would be worth noting where exactly *Ice Planet Barbarians* sits within the scope of its subgenre, and how it tries to wrestle with some of its problematic elements.

*****SPOILERS AND DISCUSSIONS OF ADULT CONTENT AHEAD*****

ROMANCING THE BOOK INDUSTRY

Bar none the most lucrative publishing genre is romance. This category can then be divided into a number of different subgenres, spanning from the familiar and popular subgenres, like Romantic Comedy and Regency Romances, to the more niche ones, such as Reverse Harem or Amish Romance.

Romance as an industry tends to cater to heterosexual women (2), and likewise, is often derided for its appeal despite being an almost comically robust money-making industry, and having a wide variety of literary merit among much of its works.

Erotic romance is a deeply interesting study in the many facets of desire and how that manifests. This is an industry largely by women and caters to that audience. It has also grown a contingency of LGBTQ+ persons that have reshaped that landscape. The rise of independent publishing means there is a lack of commercial oversight that can re-frame desire in ways that are beyond a lot of other contemporary media.

That is not to say that this genre, or these books in particular, completely reject traditional masculinity or disvalue it, but it complicates the image. In many cases, Romance books reorient typical masculine or heteronormative images, symbols, and concepts, into something that is sexualized and exotic for a primarily non-male audience.

Ice Planet Barbarians excels in that in interesting, and at times problematic ways.

WELCOME TO NOT-HOTH

Here's a down-and-dirty summary of the series to give you some context if you haven't read it and don't mind spoilers.

A bunch of women wake up in a spaceship cargo hold having been abducted by little green men and their orange assistants. They crash on a strange planet, and during the crash, the little green men and their assistants die, as well as a few of the women. It appears to be an arctic planet. These human women, now stuck in the wreckage, send Georgie (our lead in the first book) to find supplies or help.

She ends up accidentally captured by an "alien" (3) named Vektal, who instantly recognizes her as his mate, and he introduces himself via cunnilingus.

Yup. I am not making that up. Typically people get tongue-tied when they meet someone they like, but not Vektal I guess.

Vektal is part of a whole race called Sa-Khui who live on the planet. They are blue-skinned, seven feet tall, horned, have tails, glowing blue eyes, and other interesting parts of their anatomy to be discussed later. Vektal & Georgie manage to pantomime some communication until they are able to use some tech to teach them each other's languages.

They still get rather affectionate before and after this while traipsing around the tundra.

Vektal reveals that there is a poison in the atmosphere and that in order to survive, the women must get a symbiote to help their bodies adapt. This symbiote, called a khui, or cootie as the women call it, can also detect your mate for you, through a process called resonance. Vektal's village experienced a huge plague years prior, leaving them bereft of most women, leaving them with no chance to resonate, until now.

They bring a bunch of them male Sa-Khui to the wreckage, save the women, and implant them with a khui.

Each book looks at a different pairing, and they tend to be formulaic. Woman and Sa-Khui begin to resonate, woman denies resonance, woman gets abducted, "plot," sex, "plot," and woman and Sa-Khui settle down and start making blue babies.

They are not all like that, but the alterations to this outline are small. This description is also selling the series short. Dixon's world building, her use of gruesome elements, the adventure aspects, are all quite impressive. But we aren't here to discuss that, we're here to talk about big blue hunks and the women who love them.

CAVE WOMEN HAVE NEEDS TOO

It's been almost a decade since Dinosaur Erotica took the internet by storm, prompted by the quick meme-ification of the Christie Sims and Alara Branwen books. For those who need a reminder, Sims and Branwen were two college friends who started rapidly self-publishing monster erotica short stories on Kindle. They eventually stumbled into the sub-sub-genre for Dinosaur erotica.

Thanks to their (purposely) poorly photoshopped book-covers and cheesy titles, they went viral spawning parodies of their work. Most famously, Chuck Tingle, who still enjoys a certain amount of notoriety following his Hugo nominated work *Space Raptor Butt Invasion*.

The runaway success of the series seemed to be motivated by both humor and curiosity.

The very concept of Dinosaur Erotica is meant to spark our curiosity, our humor, and for some, outrage. The premise, on its very face, is deliberately ridiculous. That type of outward oddity can easily tempt a reader just to see how on earth someone could accomplish this story. You might ask "how does a T-rex seduce a human woman?" and feel the need to read it just to assuage your curiosity.

Turns out the T-rex is telepathic and has magic genitalia.

Some of us have just become unbelievably calloused to a lot of romance and erotica. We've become thrill-seekers, striving for even the most macabre of the erotic. Sometimes we look at books with absurd concepts and kind of go "okay then, let's get weird," in the way that some horror fanatics are always looking for more gore or fright. No one actually wants to have sex with a dinosaur, we just want to see how transgressive Sims and Branwen can get (4).

Some people are also just into the un-typical, be that zombies or krakens or what have you. Whatever tickles your pickle.

I bring this up because the meme-ification of Dixon's series has familiar overtones to the Dinosaur Porn phenomenon. People are pulled in by the outwardly ridiculous premise and the hilarity of the covers and titles.

Despite these outward similarities, Dixon's *Ice Planet Barbarians* is far less transgressive and instead is more determined to explore common desires rather than humor readers with taboo ones.

THEY DID THE MONSTER MASH

When it comes to monster romance, there are "monsters," and there are monsters. There are light monster romances where the romantic monster leads mostly resemble regular humans in most aspects. They might have a few extra features over the original model, fangs, tails, ect. Or they may be shape-shifters or their monstrous attributes may be more malleable, like werewolves, dragon-shifters, or aliens in disguise.

In many of these scenarios, the physiology is similar enough that sex in the books is functionally familiar to the way two or more humans might have sex. It's rare that intimacy scenes take place while the shifter is in their monstrous form, for example. Or the minor physical discrepancies are evocative of traditional eroticism or they serve to enhance the other-worldly "beauty" of the monster.

The vampires in *Twilight* are a good example of a monster romance at this end of the genre (5). Vampires already have pre-established erotic contexts in the modern consciousness. Their abnormalities simply heighten and highlight pre-existing, common ideas, concepts, and images of the erotic. Vampires are mouth-centric, and their fangs bring attention back to how they feed, and rather than this promoting a singular fear response (although it does and can in much media) it also brings attention to and reinterprets orality in sexual encounters. The ways in which vampires feed is reminiscent not just of kissing but of oral stimulation, and how the mouth is a sexual body part. They also tend to feed on or from common erogenous zones, the neck, the wrists, collars and breasts, thighs, etc.

As vampires already exist in the common sexual imagination, Meyer's addition of the much-maligned sparkling skin is meant to both enhance their other-worldliness, their non-humanness, in a way that is in line with our already established popular concepts of beauty.

Then there are the more transgressive forms of monster romance wherein the monstrous object of fascination or desire is particularly, physiologically distant. Such as the aforementioned Dinosaur erotica books, wherein the draw and curiosity is more about the distance away from humanity as much as possible. These monsters do not necessarily evoke a common sexual response the way that Vampires, Elves, or bipedal Werewolves do. These are the thrill-seeking and curious corners of erotic monster romance.

Tiffany Robert's *Ensnared* and Ann Aguirre's *Strange Love* are good examples of this section of the spectrum. The monstrous object of desire in *Ensnared* is a slightly humanoid spider-creature that is more akin to a spider-centaur. In *Strange Love,* it's a bipedal, armored alien reminiscent of Predator from the *Predator* movies. Both of these have romances with typical, human females.

Both of the heroes are sentient, do communicate (and are also wildly sweet and considerate), but there is less stress on evoking the erotic from common imagery, instead it is about expanding and creating the erotic through the enhancement of foreignness and strangeness. It is a challenge in taste, and an exploration of kink that is familiar to many subcategories of the erotic.

Both works seek to challenge the reader, and push the boundaries of what is erotic. Ensnared goes out of its way to note how its lead uses his mandibles and additional legs in sex. And while aspects of the leads' sexual encounter are consistent with human sex with complimentary genitalia, (penis-in-vagina sex), or is evocative of some human practice, such as the use of webbing as a stand-in for shibari-style rope bondage, this will be undeniably strange and challenging to many readers.

Aguirre's protagonists don't have complimentary genitalia, to begin with, and they have to invent new sexual practices in order to express their desire. In some ways, the sex in that book is reminiscent of lesbian sex, with the use of manual stimulation, but Aguirre's writing focus was less on maintaining the familiarity of sexual practice and instead on expressing how different it was to our common ideas about sex. There is a lot of talk about spores and the chemical reaction occurring than just the descriptions of the physical interaction.

HORNS IN ALL THE RIGHT PLACES

While the outward appearance of the "aliens" or Sa-Khui in Ice Planet Barbarians may seem jarring at first, we tend to find that their difference of appearance is less about enhancing strangeness, and more about evoking pre-existing, common images of eroticism and generally acceptable forms of sexuality.

Yes, the Sa-khui have blue skin, horns, and a tail, but they are also described as heavily muscular and athletic, in a way that is easily akin to any human male romance cover model.

Other physical differences are meant to enhance traditionally sexual norms. Their skin is fuzzy and reminiscent of "velvet". They have ridged foreheads and chests that come into play when describing nipple stimulation. Even the aforementioned horns and tails end up serving a purpose. The horns are for holding on, and the tail is sometimes used to apply other stimulation.

Then there are the alterations that turn the Sa-khui into walking sex-toy catalog entries. Their tongues and penises are ridged (6). They also have size-appropriate equipment to go along with their seven-foot-tall stature.

And then there's the infamous spur. The spurs a is a small, blunt horn projection above the penis that ultimately serves as a clitoral stimulation and anal stimulation in some positions.

Even the alien symbiote all the humans and Sa-khui have is meant to enhance the sexuality of the series. The Khui locates an ideal mate with "resonance," when that mate is located and there is a period of corresponding fertility. The khui causes a frenzied sex drive in the resonating pair, and it denotes resonance by vibrating in their chest. Aside from the enhanced sex drive, the vibration itself is described as its own aphrodisiac, often providing subtle nipple stimulation.

Ultimately, the "alien" features of the Sa-Khui are less alien than enhanced versions of common objects of sexual desire. The described sexuality in the book is also largely, socially-accepted, non-transgressive, and heteronormative. Dozens of abducted young women end up crash-landed on a planet and not a lesbian among them. Outside of the Sa-Khui, the overwhelming majority of the cast is white.

The sex acts are also patterned and normative, varying between penis-in-vagina insertion, oral sex, manual stimulation, masturbation, with some mild anal stimulation. The majority of the positions are missionary.

There is nothing wrong with any of this, in particular in a romance series which has garnered some cross-genre appeal. But I want to make it clear that it is not the actual sex that is transgressive or challenging in the series. It's also not the aliens either, whose outward appearance does not fully disguise how they are conventional objects of desire.

Dixon further separates any lingering dissonance by making the mating a result of the symbiote, effectively removing choice, and therefore some discomfort or guilt with this cross-species copulation (7).

It is the setting and the set-up of the series that belies its taboo concepts. Rather than the objects of desire being the vehicle for subversion, it is the way in which Dixon takes barbarism and tries to remove it from its problematic history in a way to explore the exotic.

LEATHER, LOINCLOTHS, AND THE EXOTIC

Romance readers (sex-positive activists, and the kink community as well) have long known that our sexual longings, our desires, our attractions, will not always line up with our ideologies. And that while that even the imagined desire is something altogether different than what would even pursue if given the chance.

This tension, between what some of us find pleasure in and the way it contradicts our principles, is an interesting space. Dixon makes Not-Hoth terrifying, but it also serves as an escape. Sometimes the human women complain about the loss of creature comforts, they still in large part, manage to adapt very quickly. It is akin to other power- fantasies, such as those that have typically been tailored to male readers.

What does deserve some scrutiny is the use of "primitivism" and "barbarism" in this series in reference to Sa-Khui society. The ways in which the Sa-Khui are portrayed, their social norms, habits, and such do not exist in a vacuum and draw heavily upon portrayals of "primitive" societies.

Tha Sa-Khui are clearly based on depictions of prehistoric peoples. Past that, I could not help but notice the ways in which their necessary survival habits were modeled after the real survival habits of other contemporary indigenous groups. Just on the surface, their use of dung as fuel is used in nomadic groups in Mongolia. The ways in which Dixon describes clothing including the use of stitching as decorative onto leather and fur, brings to mind Northern indigenous groups, (Inuit for instance, Ainu as well). It's a rich set of world building, and it helps ground a lot of the more fantastical elements.

To be clear, the Sa-Khui are not a parallel to any one indigenous group. They are clearly a chimera society modeled off of several peoples.

What may concern us is less the direct parallels but how this fits into an entire history of fetishism of non-European or post-European groups. Groups that are not only depicted as "primitive" but also "barbaric," and how that barbarism exists to be objectified and sexualized. This objectification also gets thorny when we are talking about race in relation to this.

We can take Tarzan, for example. Edgar Rice Burrough's eponymous hero may have existed as a power fantasy for male readers, he also had/has a stimulating effect on heterosexual women and queer consumers. He is therefore an apt example of the ways in which "primitive" behavior is at once, exoticized and fetishized, while still wholly distanced from people of color.

Steve Rose's "From Tarzan to Avatar: The Problem With 'The White Man In The Jungle'" notes how racial dichotomies have been formed in most jungle films between white Tarzan and his non-white counterparts.

"What's missing from all these movies is the point of view of the people who actually live in the jungle—or rainforest, to use a less loaded word. Too often they are treated as exotic set-dressing, given nothing to do but stare threateningly at their European interlopers, do their manual labour for them and die by their weaponry—and if they get a single line of dialogue they're lucky."

In contrast to native peoples and their depictions, Tarzan functions as the fetishized "barbarian," but in a way that for white women, gave them permission to desire him *because* of his whiteness. Tarzan's primitivism serves as the desirable element, but it has historically been his whiteness that has allowed him to be an object of acceptable sexual consumption.

To be clear, non-white groups have had a history of sexualization and objectification, and it is impossible to separate this from a history of colonialism and genocide. But that objectification did not allow for even the fictionalization of love. Tarzan allowed white women to not only imagine a sexual partnership but an emotional and committed one because they had the same racial background.

Beyond whatever parallels might be drawn from the Sa-Khui and other peoples, their actions are supposed to be read as barbaric at times. Some of the Sa-Khui men are much better at communicating and respecting boundaries, but in almost every book, a woman ends up kidnapped. They are depicted as being sexually desperate and impassioned, driven to almost madness from resonance. Literature-wise, it makes them very compelling, and alluring in that very real Tarzan way.

Rather than painting her Not-Hoth natives white, Dixon, either deliberately or unintentionally, attempts to remove the Sa-Khui from this context completely by giving them a blue (paint) job. Removing the primitives from familiar racial groups, and even from the planet itself, allows readers to engage in this primitive fantasy without having to fully confront how it exists in their home-planet power dynamics. Whether or not this separation is successful is up for debate.

It is necessary that Dixon undercuts these associations even further by shifting the perspective in the books. The Sa-Khui protagonists get to tell their side of the story equally with their earthling mates. This does humanize them, although not all of the books are equal in how it applies barbarism.

PERHAPS THE MONSTER (LOVER) WAS INSIDE US ALL ALONG

I will confess to finding my own, let's say interest, in the Sa-Khui uncomfortable for this reason. At the end of the day, there is something internally desirable about fictional blue aliens that hunt in an arctic wilderness with stone-age tools. Maybe it's because it is so far removed that it softens the discomfort with the colonial history of depictions of the "primitive". Maybe I watched Disney's Tarzan too much as a kid and now have a thing for loincloths. The jury is out on that one.

At the end of the day, most of the kitsch monster elements do little to challenge the way a reader might feel about desire, as much of their anatomy or society already exist in the public praxis of desire. That is including the problematic elements. Perhaps I am also too desensitized to see this as transgressive.

Perhaps it wasn't challenging, but any book series that allows us to interrogate our internal desires is pretty hot. Even on an ice plant.

NOTES:

(1) Tad Williams once said this about writing genre, "I can do anything I want . . . as long as every 5 or 10 pages something really horrible tries to eat my main character." Dixon took a similar direction.

(2) There is a ton of writing on how Romance is perceived and its market power, but I suggest Maya Rodale's Dangerous Books For Girls: The Bad Reputation of Romance Novels, Explained.

(3)Yes, the women are technically the "aliens" since they are the foreign entities but that distinction is not corrected.

(4) And if you are one of those people that gets hot and bothered over Cretaceous creatures, know that you can go watch Jurassic Park on your own.

(5) Twilight is easily the most accessible example here and this is not an endorsement of the series.

(6) Insert "for her pleasure" joke here.

(7) There have been studies as to why women often have non-consensual or forced sex fantasies, and some of that may have to do with blame-avoidance in a society that typically shames women for sexual desire and removing choice in a fantasy setting can alleviate that. None of the women who fantasize about that actually want to be raped or have forced sexual encounters. Moreault, D., & Follingstad, D. R. (1978). Sexual fantasies of females as a function of sex guilt and experimental response cues. Journal of Consulting and Clinical Psychology, 46(6), 1385–1393.

BLURRING THE LINES BETWEEN MEMOIR AND SPECULATIVE POETRY: REVIEW OF CLOCK STAR ROSE SPINE BY FRAN WILDE

BY LESLIE ARCHIBALD

> *"Wilde blurs the line between science fiction and memoir by returning to her poetry roots and creating an authentic self-exploration through speculative poetry."*

A poet is a seer and an excavator. Poets see beyond the surface and expose layers of context through images and form, learning something as they peel back each fold and move deeper.

Clock Star Rose Spine (*Lanternfish Press*, 2021), the most recent offering from award-winning author Fran Wilde, is a Fodor's guide to navigating the self. In this new poetry collection, Wilde takes readers on an HG Wells style trip, moving back and forth through time to initiate revelations about themselves and the poet herself with each landing. Wilde blurs the line between science fiction and memoir by returning to her poetry roots and creating an authentic self-exploration through speculative poetry.

> *I thought I'd write a poem about the marks / life leaves on skin. The drag of distance*—Clock Star Rose Spine

Wilde steadies our footing immediately with her title poem "Clock Star Rose Spine" using form and direction to set a course for the reader and showing us that where one ends up is not always where they expected to go. Finding direction is an exploration of the places we pass through on our way to connection.

Any collection that reflects on the self must explore the impositions with which society burdens an individual particularly gender expectations and generalizations. Wilde explores gender roles and the stereotypes still placed on women today. Wilde's juxtaposition of hope and disappointment in "The Fact of a Cage" and "Instructions For How to Feel" capture perfectly the dismay of the twenty-first-century woman.

Wilde sets her time machine to the 1940s and the Hollywood heyday with "Breakfast Poolside at the Lafayette." Reminiscent of Steven King's *The Shining*, the reader gets a peek at Hollywood ghosts contrasted with today's lack of attention (faces in "glowing screens") to our surroundings. Through the real-time lens of a poolside brunch and historical flashes, Wilde paints a picture of what is left of the hotel's story and what is forgiven.

> *If you, with this mirror, frame me, / affix me to a wall to look over you*
> —Self Portrait with Frida Kahlo

Through several self-portrait pieces, Wilde processes experience through introspection and connection to objects and relationships finding a balance in the duality of light and dark, transformation and preservation, mythology and the human spirit.

In the poem "Maps," throwing out expectations and losing yourself mixes things up and directs you to find your own way to somewhere unexpected, somewhere you were meant to be. Wilde also plays with form and cartography in "You are Two Point Three Meters From Your Destination." Using the framing of a GPS navigator, Wilde utilizes the repetition of continuous recalculating direction and adjusting for distractions to simulate life's challenges. Again the reader ends up somewhere unexpected.

The darkroom's silence builds perfect, still images / no matter how much shouting happens / outside—Darkroom

In Wilde's Washington Post essay "Domestic Violence and Teaching my Daughter to Always Rescue Herself First," she pens a letter to her daughter advising her to "save herself first." She says, "Do not endanger yourself to save the other person." In her poem "Darkroom," Wilde recounts a father-daughter relationship and the damage a parent's demons can inflict on a child. Distance is the "rescue can" that prompts perspective and eventually teaches her that her life is worth saving and she is the best one to save it. She shows us an intimate portrait of the child with her father and the destruction the father brings upon the family with a complacent mother who tells her, not to save herself, but "all will be well." The emotional authenticity of this heart-wrenching piece draws the reader into the world.

My photographs begin to skew again—Tell it Slant

Wilde closes with gravitational pull notably to people or objects and why humans are drawn to things like a baby learning words and colors in "Lellow" and why we document our lives in pictures that don't really tell the whole story in "Tell it Slant." We hold on to these pieces of our lives that are constantly changing and are somehow comforted by our connection to them or delivered from them through their destruction. Finally, Wilde comes to the inevitable end, loss, a relationship ending in the beautifully poetic "Moving on."

The reader is not left wounded or feeling mournful by the load of the last few poems. In her postscript, Wilde leaves a gratifying distraction from the weight of the collection's ending—an interview about her writing process and pens.

Clock Star Rose Spine from *Lanternfish Press* is out now. To find out how to purchase the collection or where you can see Fran Wilde read from the collection, check out https://lanternfishpress.com/clock-star-rose-spine.

FANTASY DREAMS IN THE REAL WORLD: REVIEW OF BE DAZZLED BY RYAN LA SALA

BY PRESLEY THOMAS

"Cosplay has more to say about queerness than we think."

Ryan La Sala's debut YA *Reverie* (*Sourcebooks Fire*, 2019), explored dreams that became real. In his contemporary follow-up *Be Dazzled* (*Sourcebooks Fire*, 2021), La Sala has crafted a novel with fantasy-sized ambitions. Boston teen Raphael Odom (Raffy) is a master crafter and cosplayer. Raffy competes to win a major cosplay competition at Controverse: a comic con not unlike those that happen each year in different US cities (at least pre-COVID) as fandom and kitsch collide to create a space for those with high levels of geekdom, video game, comic book interest, and craft culture.

Raffy records his creation process on Ion—the streaming service that also sponsors the Controverse contest alongside Craft Club, where Raffy and other contenders seem to get all of their supplies. Though we find out early-on it's not limited to sequins and foam, as Raffy also meets his future boyfriend, Luca, in one of the aisles, sweaty in his soccer uniform, eyeing the same color sequins he needs to complete his current project.

Luca is a closeted straight-boy jock-type and doesn't want to give himself away at first but secretly finds Raffy, our ambiguously gay hero, to be someone worth his time and attention, even if he has to hide it. Raffy finds it hard to believe that a burly soccer player would even be interested in someone like him. A teen who often sequesters himself in his studio/garage to complete elaborate costumes based on cartoons and video games.

La Sala doesn't write this story linearly but portions it out in clear chunks of time placed at the beginning of each chapter, from Now to any number of months before. He reverses the enemies to lovers trope and makes it fall back on itself: Luca and Raffy go from lovers in the beginning to enemies and then to lovers again. This structure makes it easier to follow the simple binaries without getting lost in the where, when, and how as a reader.

The shared interest in cosplay where they first met at Craft Club tears them apart and then brings them back together after they do well on separate cosplay teams(where La Sala uses the timeline to explore their shared past and present) and then have to join forces again in the present in a Cosplay meets Project Runway competition at the final round.

Raffy is aware of himself in craft and ambition but less aware of his emotions, he often has to use one to understand the other. La Sala does this pretty masterfully when he describes Raffy's awareness of his own feelings for Luca:

"I always measure, I always trace, I always know the shape of what I *want* to create. But I never know exactly how it'll turn out. I *love you* was the plunge. The slice. The commitment to the final shape, whatever it may be."

La Sala does this for the reader too. Cosplay is a both-and for each of the characters. For Luca, their partnership outs him as he and Raffy are shipped by fans. Raffy is outed as a cosplayer as he embraces his abilities where his famous artist mother, Evie, wants him to pursue what she deems as more respectable couture fashion.

La Sala manages not to make it just one character's story but both. The becoming of Raffy and Luca as a couple, yes, but also who they want to be as themselves in the future. Yet another example of a story not queer-coded but queer-affirming and embracing different kinds of people with more than just shared sexuality, but shared interest and concern for one another that extends beyond the surface and allows each other to grow.

Cosplay has more to say about queerness than we think. The admission of a sexuality other than straight is often treated as an addition. A bauble that even our own families and those who know us well claim not to have noticed. Something we can take on or off as easily as a costume.

The culture of cons like the one described in Be Dazzled articulate difference. They promote fantastic ideas and bend reality to make us wonder what it might look like if things were different. La Sala does the same when he shows us, yes, jocks can be gay and into cosplay. And, yes, even fall for the nerdy boy at school. He gives us a world that makes sense outside of the glass doors of a conference center. For just a few hours.

INTERVIEWS

SH*TTING STARS: INTERVIEW WITH AIMEE OGDEN, AUTHOR OF LOCAL STAR

BY ELYSE RIBBONS 柳素英

Interstellar Flight Press is stoked to have given a home to Aimee Ogden's new book, *Local Star,* which is a delightful reimagining of Shakespeare's Much Ado About Nothing—IN SPACE! Slush adventurer and volunteer Eylse Ribbons caught up with Aimee about her new book, how she stays fit outside of the writer's chair, and of course, her dog. There's much to enjoy about the fun romp through the heart in the stars, but my favorite is the oft-used phrase "shitting stars" which I really want to get made into a t-shirt. Ok, on with the interview!

Interstellar Flight Press: In your bio it says you're a former science teacher—what grades and types of science did you teach? What was your favorite part to teach?

Aimee Ogden: I taught High School science, and that ended up including biology, chemistry, biotechnology, whatever they needed. I really liked teaching AP Biology, the kids who really wanted to be there, teaching Evolution was really fun, that was one of my favorite areas. Anything I could make them laugh and remember. *(We then discussed how gastropods are buttheads and got quite distracted).*

IFP: You mentioned you're a trainer, what do you specialize in? What is your typical go to workout?

AO: Back in the before times I used to train "Community Fitness" (it used to be called CrossFit but it now has a somewhat bad earned reputation). I like lifting weights and helping people feel strong and not hurt themselves.

I've been running more than I used it, it's kinda nice to get out of the house (one of those rare opportunities). We've slowly acquired a weights set in the basement from Craigslist. I can't live without deadlifts and lunges.

IFP: If you had all the time in the world (not literally but you know what I mean) how would you get your exercise?

AO: I would go running at Devil's Lake. Running on the trails, the lake and the forest there is so pretty.

IFP: Does this physical aspect of your life bleed into the physicality of your writing?

AO: That's a good question . . . I feel like I just focused really hard on that because that's not my strength as a writer. I have a tendency when uncorrected to write scenes in a white room with two heads talking to one another. It's not very fun to read, it's not very fun to write or edit, so I just very consciously think: What do I see when I close my eyes?

IFP: Speaking of writing . . . what was the inspiration for your awesome new novella, *Local Star*?

AO: I love *Much Ado About Nothing*, it was my favorite Shakespeare play. But I hate the misogyny "Oh, my daughter slept with a man, she should probably die, that would be best." I also love slapping "IN SPACE" on the end of a story description. So I thought, "Let's do Much Ado About Nothing—in space!" And we can get rid of the misogyny and play with it a little more and have more fun.

IFP: How did you go about the world-building process?

AO: I don't know if you've seen that clip from Wallace and Gromit where the dog is sitting on the train and laying down the tracks literally one at a time in front of the train as it goes rushing along. That is exactly what I felt like. "Oh, I need something to do this thing, or these people" Very much as it's going along, but sometimes I do go back and add a little bit of world-building or foreshadowing so that it all feels more natural. Just keep one section ahead of the train and we will keep it moving.

IFP: You take "love triangles" to a very different dimension. How did you come up with the Gon and Quad and other family/romance units?

AO: When I was trying to think about the characters and the story, I was trying to think about how relationships might look in the future where it's not necessarily one partner dominant like we have now. One fun way to explore that might be a default polyamorous society. It worked really well with the dynamics of the characters.

IFP: Have you ever worked on an engine? Curious if the way you so perfectly captured Greasemonkey-hood is due to personal experience.

AO: I have not. If you had put me in front of the hood of an open car I would have a panic attack. I have watched a lot of Star Wars and read a lot of those books, I feel like I delved deeply into that vocabulary, in fact, I think I'm wearing my Star Wars shirt now (shows off her awesome "Hope" shirt).

IFP: How did you come up with the names?

AO: I think I used a random name generator for some. Triz's name, I monkeyed around with the original's Beatrice, because I wanted something to come directly from Much Ado About Nothing. I kept rearranging the names until it felt right for the character in my head. I'm very picky about that. Once the character is named that's it, I can't think of them any other way.

IFP: What are your thoughts on Body Mods?

AO: I am pro body mods. I think Triz kinda comes around in the book. Yeah, what being human is has been redefined several times over the millennia. I mean, I would like to get Lasik because my eyes keep changing.

IFP: If you could get Body Mods what would you get done?

AO: I would like a see-in-the-dark mod.

IFP: Will there be more books in this universe to look forward to?

AO: I have no plans right now, but I don't like to rule anything out in the future. It would be fun to revisit but time is a premium and I want to write so many things. My idea list grows every week and my list of completed things does not grow that fast. I have some little ideas just kicking around a bit.

ABOUT THE AUTHOR

Aimee Ogden is a former science teacher and software tester; now she writes stories about sad astronauts, angry princesses, and dead gods. Her short fiction has appeared in venues such as *Analog, Beneath Ceaseless Skies*, and *Fireside*, and another novella, *Sun-daughters, Sea-daughters* is out from Tor.com. She also co-edits *Translunar Travelers Lounge,* a magazine of fun and optimistic speculative fiction. Find her online at aimeeogdenwrites.wordpress.com.

Local Star is a polyamorous space opera with a fast-paced, action-packed adventure that's sure to punch you in the feels. It follows guttergirl Triz as she saves her hub from invaders from the Cyberbionautic Alliance, all the while negotiating her rekindled romance with Kalo, her ex who's returned from battle and won't stop hanging around the wrenchworks.

THE WILD, THE WEIRD, AND THE SPECULATIVE: INTERVIEW WITH AMELIA GORMAN, AUTHOR OF FIELD GUIDE TO INVASIVE SPECIES OF MINNESOTA

BY JULIE REESER

Amelia Gorman's beautifully dark, speculative poetry in *Field Guide to Invasive Species of Minnesota* (*Interstellar Flight Press*, 2021) leads the reader on a future-present journey through the natural world. Julie Reeser spent some time talking with her about the process of creating sharp but lovely imaginings of the wild and weird.

INTERSTELLAR FLIGHT PRESS: While I was reading individual poems, I thought of people in my life who would enjoy them. Who was the audience you kept in mind as you gathered these pieces? I say, gathered, but of course—you wrote them. They weren't foraged, or were they?

AMELIA GORMAN: I'd say this book is for scientists who love poetry, or poets who love reading scientific texts, or more generally, anyone who loves genre-crossing work. The kind of person who reads an intentionally or unintentionally beautifully written instruction manual or restaurant menu or street names at a particularly weird intersection and thinks "that feels like poetry." People who unabashedly love poems about nature, too.

I recently read this book by F. St. Mars from 1912 called, *On Nature's Trail: A Wonderbook of the Wild*, that absolutely can't decide if it's a pulp thriller or a nature text. It's so cool. Here's a quote from it that might describe a baby cuckoo or a Lovecraftian horror: "This bird, this cuckoo, was objectionable to behold—a jellified lump with a mouth, a sort of warty, distorted, gnome-like mass." I think *Field Guide to Invasive Species of Minnesota* is for people who think they would like that book. While we're on the subject of cuckoos, also people who like cuckoos, or shoggoths. Fans of one thing that's also another thing.

The question of foraging is really interesting. The poems do feel gathered to me, to some extent. At the same time, I think of one of Joanna Russ's points in *How to Suppress Women's Writing*—the writer may see herself too much as a medium that work comes through when she is in fact a hard-scrabbling, type-those-fingers-to-the-bone creator. So, I'm going to go with grown instead of foraged.

IFP: Tell me more about how you use speculative poetry as a memory marker, but at the same time, as a future traveler or storyteller. I was intrigued by this narrative in your afterword of the collection.

AG: Speculative Poetry as a field is one of those things that poets try to pin down, and when they feel they've got something good, it's often totally at odds with what other poets have come up with. So much of 'traditional' (literary? let's just say non-speculative) poetry involves elements that would be considered fantastical if they were used in fiction: referencing folklore as if it were real; rewriting myths; over-the-top pathetic fallacies; and other metaphors taken to extreme levels. So, I think one good use of speculative poetry is to really dig in and layer the unreal on top of the unreal.

When I read poetry that imitates the form of codices or dictionaries or written from the POV of a well-developed heteronym or a series of letters, I almost feel like I'm role-playing. Not just because it's so vivid it feels real, but there's also a particularly me-shaped place carved out in it. I like that experience of me-the-reader being necessary to complete the conceit, close the circuit. I wanted to create that experience and invite people to be in this near-future-climate-disaster-fantasy-world I imagined. And of course, part of that is imagining folk tales, superstitions, family dinners, and memories in that world.

I wanted to make something that was something else. I wanted to write something that builds a world, that feels like an artifact from another place, and yet still contains individual poems working on individual levels. And I wanted to combine what it felt like for me to be six, twelve, or eighteen in rural Minnesota combined with what I imagined that future would look like. The easiest way to do that was as some kind of dreamscape.

IFP: You use myth and folk tales in these poems, and I'm struck by the stories we gather as we get to know a place. How do you see our places being changed as our stories shift, and do you see this as a goal of your work—to shape futures?

AG: I'm answering these questions in April of 2021 where the pandemic is still going strong, both in the United States and most other countries. It's been a whole year full of lost places. Regular reading or music nights have shuttered all over, often with no real pathway to restarting. Important community gathering spaces have been forced to close. If nothing else, stories are a way to remember and document all the places that matter for the inevitable time they don't exist anymore.

I'm also answering these questions regarding a book about Minnesota very shortly after the world watched Derek Chauvin found guilty of murder. I don't think I can talk about the relationship between place and story regarding Minnesota in good faith right now without referencing the murder of George Floyd and the subsequent trial.

Without a brave teenage girl sharing her cell phone footage, the true tragedy of George Floyd's death, that he was murdered, might have been buried and all we'd have is a perfunctory police report reading how he died of a medical incident after an encounter with police. The story she shared, the true story, changed the city of Minneapolis. The memorial, the place built in Minneapolis, the people who go there every day to protest police brutality and hand out food and grieve with each other, has, in turn, changed the way stories are told. One small side effect is that even national news outlets are referring to the place as George Floyd Square.

There is no more important connection between place and story than this. No better proof of how stories and places change each other. The true story, that the teenage girl filmed, helped build a place. The place and all the people in it amplified the story. I hope the guilty verdict and the continued activism against police brutality continue to change the place (in this case, the city of Minneapolis or beyond) for the better.

IFP: As you get ready for the book to be published later this year (2021), do you find yourself in a different dialogue with your surroundings? Are you thinking of the next conversation, and if so, can you share a little of it?

AG: I'm working on some broadsides about imaginary species of California as a fun project to share with a talented artist I know. So far all we have is art and words for "Slimy Tassel," which imagines the silky tassel plant if it grew banana slugs in addition to flowers.

I wanted to write about native species for a change, and positive effects on ecosystems. I hope it will still get at the importance of conservation and restoration projects, but it feels fun to come at it looking at what to encourage rather than what is frustrating.

ABOUT THE AUTHOR

Amelia Gorman lived in Minneapolis for fifteen years before moving to Eureka, California in 2018. She loves the tide pools, redwood forests, and kinetic sculptures of her new home but misses lakes, looking at snow with a hot drink in her hand, public transit, and Eat Street. You can read more of her poetry in *Liminality, Star*Line, Vastarien,* and other places. She also writes weird fiction, including stories in *She Walks in Shadows* from *Innsmouth Free Press* and *Nox Pareidolia* from *Nightscape Press.* Find her online on twitter at @gorman_ghast and www.ameliagorman.com.

BALLAD OF THE TANTALIZING TENTACLES: INTERVIEW WITH POET, WORDSMITH, AND PERFORMER BRANDON O'BRIEN, AUTHOR OF CAN YOU SIGN MY TENTACLE?

BY ELYSE RIBBONS 柳素英

From ~~H. P. Lovecraft~~ to Jordan Peele to *Lovecraft Country* to Childish Gambino, O'Brien's new poetry chapbook, a discussion of speculative poetry.

> *"Violence makes good background noise*
> *for anything. Even for knowledge.*
> *People suffer for knowing all the time*
> *in your stories—you know, the ones where*
> *something shrouded in shadow stalks the*
> *corridors between neon and dancing*
> *with its eyes on everything gentle*
> *and its tendrils on everything glimmering.*
> *How dare you tell me this is somehow*
> *unfathomable?*
> — Lovecraft Thesis #2, from *Can You Sign My Tentacle?*

Brandon O'Brien's new book from Interstellar Flight Press, *Can You Sign My Tentacle?* is part of our chapbook series and was released August 20th, 2021. Cthulhu meets hip-hop in this book of horror poems that flips the eldritch genre upside down. Lovecraftian-inspired nightmares are reversed as O'Brien asks readers to see Blackness as radically significant. *Can You Sign My Tentacle?* explores the monsters we know and the ones that hide behind racism, sexism, and violence, resulting in poems that are both comic and cosmic. IFP Interviewer Elyse Ribbons checked in with O'Brien via zoom to chat about this fantastic new work.

INTERSTELLAR FLIGHT PRESS: So, blurbs. I noticed on yours on Twitter, where it says that you are a poet, a writer, a teaching artist, performer, and a TTRPG designer, can you go into more depth about each of those monikers, please?

BRANDON O'BRIEN: I have been writing poetry since I was very, very young. Most of my identity is tied up in poetry, I think. I joke a lot that one of the things that people knew me for in high school was writing poetry. And that led to being introduced to spoken word and doing a great deal of actual performance work. And that turned into having the opportunity to actually lead poetry workshops for young people and share that skill with others. And hopefully, help other young people gain the kind of value that I got from just writing poetry idly while I was in class sometimes.

So that was most of my life. I value poetry that much because it was the thing the was at some point, the only thing that I had, that I thought was Truly Valuable about me. And then I got into writing science fiction and fantasy, from being introduced to local writers' events. And it was very encouraging and very inspiring to know that these stories that I thought that I couldn't write, because nobody was going to read them from someone in Trinidad, this far away from where everybody else is writing.

That was really inspiring to me. And that kind of also spiraled into a friend introducing me to an opportunity to start doing tabletop role-playing game design. And I was like, I'll just dip my toe into this, and then when it eventually doesn't work out, just stop, but then it did work out. So that's been really cool as well to be in this space, where all of the things that I think are really deeply value making, I get the opportunity to make them.

IFP: You're from the Caribbean?

BOB: I live on work in Trinidad and Tobago. That's where I am right now. Because it's very warm.

IFP: Does this background influence your poetry as well? Because there's a mellifluous tone in the way Caribbean islanders speak English.

BOB: Yes, you are indeed correct. And there is a very beautiful kind of musical quality to the Caribbean voice. And that's what I value: being able to put as much of that into my own poetry and see other people discover that it's always very beautiful and intriguing when someone hears one of my poems for the first time.

But the longer I think about it, I think there is a unique kind of beautiful quality and every kind of voice that you lose or kind of attachment to when it's the only voice that you've heard, which is the other kind of value that I find in performance. That what I really, genuinely love, as a performer, but also as a fan of poetry and a fan of experience in other people's work in general, is when I enter a space for the first time, and I get to hear what that space sounds like, and they get to hear me if I'm the first person that they've heard with my voice. Because it means that everybody's sharing an experience that is new, you can have an open mic anywhere, and you should, because open mics are rad. But when you create space for someone who is having this experience for the very first time, and I mean, the experience of hearing your voice for the very first time, the experience of making sure that you get to hear there's the experience of hearing their own work read aloud to the first time all of those things are very radical and explosive in that moment.

And that's one of the reasons why whenever I try to get to a new place, I will just want to do one thing and tear other people read. Because sometimes that's the first opportunity for them to hear a voice like mine, but I also want to hear their it's like one of the most touching experiences that I've ever had in my life was attending WorldCon 75 in Helsinki, Finland. And having people read poems in languages I don't speak, right. Knowing that not only is this the first time that they've heard themselves read this thing aloud.

So this is a beautiful experience for them knowing that there's a room full of people that is thoroughly and wrapped. But I'm experiencing the poeticism of this language purely by sound that I have no idea what's happened in the poem, The poem could be about opening a can of tuna or something, I highly doubt that that was the case. But still, that experience purely sonically was still rewarding for me. And I love to have as many opportunities like that as possible.

And that's why, whenever I'm at a convention, I tend to go out of my way and say, hey, let's do an open mic. Let's do a poetry thing. Let's do a reading thing because I want to hear what people sound like and what they're willing to share.

IFP: Do you like calamari?

BOB: I have never had it before, but I'm inclined to think that I wouldn't enjoy it. I'm not a fan of seafood. Unfortunately. Maybe at some point, someone can, like, talk me into it. But I highly doubt that I will say yes, at least not immediately.

IFP: Were you inspired by HP Lovecraft?

BOB: Being a black person that is being inspired by HP Lovecraft is a very tenuous thing I imagine for a lot of people.

IFP: Oh, inspiration isn't always because someone is good.

BOB: Right? Exactly. Yes. So the first part of the answer to that question is that a lot of my experiences, science fiction and fantasy didn't include a great deal of what people called the classics at all. There are very famous science fiction and fantasy writers from the heyday of the genre that I still haven't read, not for lack of desire. And the experiences that I do have with Lovecraft are like, very, very minor, like I have read, *The Call of Cthulhu*. But that's because everybody was everybody said that it was a thing that I was supposed to read, and I didn't want to miss out.

But my experience of Lovecraft, in particular, is a very unique kind of thing. In that Lovecraft does fall in the category of a handful of the canon, quote, unquote, of science fiction writers who are significant, almost in a way, despite their work, whose place in understanding science fiction as a genre, and the things that it can do for good or for ill, are kind of distinct from the individual things that they've written, in part, because once you are aware of who they were, and the decisions that they made in their lives, you get to read those stories in a different light that stops simplifying the ways in which we talk about Lovecraft's work.

So once you know, Lovecraft's childhood, and his adult personal life, and his own individual struggles, as a young man living in the US, a part of us stops thinking of him purely as a monster anyway, in that, in the sense of Oh my God, why would this person do all of these things didn't know that all of these things were wrong and disgusting and hurtful, but for lack of a better way of saying, Lovecraft was writing from a place of fear all the time.

And that doesn't excuse the things that came out of his mouth or came out of his pen as a result of that fear. But you acknowledge that it's a place of fear. And when you acknowledge that you've seen you become a little mythos in his hand through this, like, radically troubling lens of there are things that I don't know.

I'm afraid of what will happen not only if I continue to not know them, but when I know them in their entirety. And I guess that's one of the other things that I wanted to speak to in this collection as well that perhaps you can meet a thing that is unknown or unknowable, and go wow, neat, and then move on. Yeah, yeah, that's great. That would be a healing experience for people to witness that that can happen, you cannot be trapped in fear.

IFP: Okay, so . . . *Lovecraft country,* which I'm not finished with yet, so please, no spoilers.

BOB: No spoilers. I love that show. There are a lot of things they didn't do ideally, and no spoilers, but you get if you are like a marginalized person of any kind.

There are obviously points when you get to the later points of the series and you go, I understand why this is here, but why is it here in this way. But ultimately the thing that I valued about *Lovecraft Country* as an object as like an, our whole premise, even divorced from the book that it's based on and just as a TV show, is that it is thoroughly committed to asking really complicated questions about blackness and its relationship with things that are not overtly American, if that makes sense.

Lovecraft Country is concerned with asking questions about the kinds of racism and on its face, and then asking deeper, more complicated questions about what why is it the way that it is? And how does one challenge that if one doesn't get the opportunity to be on America's face, if that makes sense?

And not all of those observations are purely supernatural, even though they manifest themselves in supernatural ways for us to attach to the fact that like, we're like shooting monsters in the woods. But I was thoroughly fascinated with that kind of lore of unraveling the fact that America or parts of America were oppressive in ways that are difficult to put into words are difficult to actually just overtly visualize because the heart of that kind of wickedness is a little bit more unfathomable.

I was very interested to hear that they had a new completely fresh, fleshed-out second season that was supposed to develop a completely different lore that is like separate, but somehow connected to the lore of the book. And I wanted to see where it was going, and they didn't do it. And at some point, you go, how do you know that you have money on the table and continue to leave it at the table anyway? But that's how it is.

I hope that at some point, all of the people involved in that get to fulfill that vision in another way because it would have been actually quite radical, I'm sure.

IFP: What are some works that inspired you?

BOB: Um, so, I feel like one of the things that I do need to admit like one of the primary things that triggered the desire to have hip hop be a part of this book are the albums of a hip hop artist named Aesop Rock. He's a very talented wordsmith, literally mathematically proven to be the most verbose rapper of his era. It's almost astounding the kinds of image backlash he can experience in a singular line of Aesop's work.

And I spend a lot of time joking in my early career that my poetry wants to be a South Bronx rap when it grows up. And that kind of materialized into me constantly being influenced by music and ways to turn musical image into poetry which accidentally became most of this collection.

A lot of the poems weren't even imagined to be part of a collection until I was like, wait, I now realize that they did the thing, maybe if I just put the little things together, they will make sense. So that was a very that still liked his work still remains a very big catalyst for me.

In terms of written work, I'm very strange in that a lot of my have big science fiction influences are just work that I never wanted to repeat into the world. When I was very young, I read a young adult, like pre-Apocalypse series called *Left Behind*. And it's very cruel and very bad, very harsh.

But for some reason, I enjoyed that, because I like was just watching all of these young people be utterly bamboozled by the supernatural experiences that they were in and make, like these radical decisions, from a place of the kind of like lack of agency that young people have in the world, like, we need to defeat the Antichrist. But I have detention. Right? Mama won't let me. It's very, it was very weird and very curious. I came out of that experience going, I want to write something that can keep my attention like this. But I don't want to be cruel to people in the business of making these statements. If that makes sense.

I don't want to make negative assumptions about the world that I'm in and about the people who live in it. Because of my own, because of this warped worldview, I have a being ultimately superior to other people. Right. And I have a handful of experiences just like that, that most of those would just kind of fade away from my brain now. But for some reason, that sticks in my head as I want to write something that a young person will pick up.

IFP: I noticed a lot of Donald Glover references . . .

BOB: Donald Glover is yet another one of my musical—well, one of my overall influences. Because I think Donald Glover is one of those creative enigmas where I assume that what actually happens to Donald Glover every morning is that he wakes up and goes, I've done enough of this very popular thing, I think I'm done with it now and then moves on to something else.

I am entranced by the way that he seems to be very gifted at entering a completely different atmosphere when he starts doing a thing. Like if someone's first experience with Donald Glover was *Community* or his writing on *30 Rock*. And then they never encountered any of them ever again, until his very last album, you would think that those are two completely different people. If you saw an episode of *Community*, and then you never saw Donald Glover in another piece of media ever again, and then the very next thing that you saw was the YouTube video *Clapping for all the Wrong Reasons*, you would think that those are two completely different people. And I think that having that kind of capacity to not just enter different creative modes, but enter different creative atmospheres and have those things be deeply emotionally fulfilled is really impressive and really radical.

Jordan Peele obviously does that as well. Everybody experienced him for years as a comic, and then he wrote some of the most, like, deeply affecting horrifying, horrifying, truly troubling, but also very deep and critical and thoughtful about the black American experience. I'm utterly fascinated by people who have that capacity. And I think that everybody does, obviously. But when that capacity also includes entering a totally different atmosphere, shifting entirely from a state of comedy to a state of horror, or a state of tragedy, or a state of intense melodrama, those things are, to me, a kind of extreme example of the emotional capacity that everybody already has, that everybody already embodies all of these emotions.

When someone can switch all the way from the extreme of one to the extreme of the other in the attempt to tell a story, they're also attempting to give us the opportunity to enter entirely into an atmosphere that we might not feel comfortable exploring the extremes of, we think that we've been denied the extremes of, and I think giving people that opportunity is radical and in and of itself, especially when that is entering the state of horror or the state of magical realism where a lot of that exploration is.

What if there are things that I know about my body or things that I know about the world, that when I found them they will be deep and all-encompassing for me in ways that I haven't been allowed to have or own?

And what I admire the most about Donald Glover and about Jordan Peele, as a result, is, those are experiences for black bodies to have that these witnesses are always and we are allowed to embrace them in their full word. Without feeling like we have to deny some level of their complexity because they are black, because they can be both black and complex. They always have been black. This is complex and another. Yes. And we don't have to deny that because other people think that we're simple.

ABOUT THE AUTHOR

Brandon O'Brien is a writer, performance poet, teaching artist and game designer from Trinidad and Tobago. His work has been shortlisted for the 2014 Alice Yard Prize for Art Writing, the 2014 and 2015 Small Axe Literary Competitions, and the inaugural Ignyte Award for Best Speculative Poetry. His work is published in *Uncanny Magazine, Strange Horizons, Reckoning,* and *New Worlds, Old Ways: Speculative Tales from the*

Caribbean, among others. He is the former Poetry editor of *FIYAH: A Magazine of Black Speculative Fiction.*

A MAN OF MANY HATS: INTERVIEW WITH MIKE ALLEN, WRITER, POET, PUBLISHER, EDITOR, AND JOURNALIST

BY CHRISTINA SNG

IFP: Hi Mike, thanks for being here with us at Interstellar Flight Press! You have an incredible career in writing, editing, and publishing. Tell us about yourself and how you got started.

MIKE ALLEN: My career has meandered all over the place, with my achievements working more like a gradual accumulation of treasures and flotsam than a clear path from points A to B to C. If you're familiar with the 1980s movie *Labyrinth* that starred David Bowie as the Goblin King, there's a puppet character called the Junk Lady who waylays our heroine. The Junk Lady has the detritus of decades literally attached to her back like barnacles, and the same thing begins to happen to Sarah before she snaps out of it and escapes. I never set out to become an editor and publisher, but those aspects of what I do have glommed onto me during my travels, much like the Junk Lady's possessions.

Of course, I was always going to chart a strange course, though I didn't understand that when I sent out my first submission to a magazine back in high school. As a writer, I'm drawn to things that are offbeat even by the standards of the Weird. Not to mention, I never got the memo that so many genre personalities seemed to take as gospel that poetry and fiction had some sort of firewall between them that could never be breached. (A silly tenet that thankfully is not standard-issue groupthink in 2021, the way it was in 1991 or even 2001.)

IFP: Your latest story collection *Aftermath of an Industrial Accident* (2020, *Mythic Delirium Books*) was nominated for a Shirley Jackson Award! Tell us how you feel about it.

MA: To be frank, I'm still pinching myself.

I feel incredibly lucky and incredibly privileged. Making the Shirley Jackson shortlist was a wonderful and unexpected surprise. I mean with *Aftermath* being a Mythic Delirium release—though I put all Mythic Delirium Books through the same paces that big traditional publishers do with their books—you could argue that *Aftermath* is essentially a self-published title, so having the jurors pick my book over so many deserving titles (and there were many great collections released during the maelstrom of 2020) ends up being a major validation for me as a publisher, editor, *and* writer. And a validation for Anita's skills, as she ordered the table of contents for *Aftermath*, just as she has with the *Clockwork Phoenix* anthologies.

My first collection of horror tales, *Unseaming (Antimatter Press,* 2014), made the same Shirley Jackson shortlist for best single-author collection back in 2015, and the working title for *Aftermath* was *Unseaming 2*, so the two books have a deep connection, with some stories in *Aftermath* continuing narratives begun in *Unseaming*. Having a completely different set of Shirley Jackson jurors bestow the same honor on *Aftermath* seemed too much to hope for, though—but holy cow, it happened!

Looking at the other finalists in my category, I didn't expect to win, but it's a delight to be nominated!

IFP: Where did the inspiration to start Mythic Delirium Books come from?

MA: Remember what I said above about debris gradually sticking to me? Kind of like that.

It begins, of course, with *Mythic Delirium*, the zine I edited for twenty years. In another example of extraordinary fortune, my weird little poetry journal was part of the DNA Publications family of magazines (which also included *Absolute Magnitude*, *Aboriginal Science Fiction* and *Weird Tales*) for about five years. In 2006, I had an amicable parting with DNA and had to make a choice about whether to continue publishing the zine on my own. At about the same time I collaborated with *Prime Books* on the two *MYTHIC* anthologies of poetry and fiction. I came up with *Mythic Delirium Books* as the name of the umbrella imprint for these ventures.

Fast forward to 2011. Norilana Books had brought out the first three volumes of my *Clockwork Phoenix* anthology series, which raised my profile as an editor to a whole new level. But once again I had come to a juncture where, in the wake of an amicable parting with a publisher, I needed to decide whether to continue the project under my own banner. Norilana had never released the *Clockwork Phoenix* volumes in e-book form, so I did. That became my first *Mythic Delirium Books* venture into Amazon Kindle and other electronic platforms, and it turned out that those e-books sold well enough to encourage me to keep going. Later, I took over the paperback editions as well, which gave me a Lightning Source/Ingram print-on-demand account, something that I had never planned on opening until that development.

Everything I've done since has built on top of these accidental platforms or expanded them sideways.

IFP: One of your most memorable legacies as President of the Science Fiction Poetry Association was to create the Dwarf Stars Award. How did that come about?

MA: While it's true that the seeds for the Dwarf Stars Award were planted while I was president of the SFPA, and that I had a hand in establishing it, I cannot in good conscience take credit for the award's founding. That credit should go to my successor as president, Deborah P. Kolodji, who had the idea in the first place and fought hard for it.

In fact, I was originally opposed to creating another SFPA award, because I felt the organization should push to promote the awards that were already in its repertoire with the maximum effort our tiny crew of volunteers could muster, rather than diluting those efforts on even more awards that might not have much value outside the bubble of the organization.

During my time as president, I saw the Rhysling Awards dismissed more than once as a joke, when the membership voting results and the poems they honored definitely deserved better, and I did everything I could to make sure they received better. I have not seen the Rhyslings blatantly attacked in a long time, but neither have I seen much fuss made over them, so it's hard for me to judge how far I managed to budge the goalposts during the eight years or so that I was an active volunteer. I do think time has proven that the Dwarf Stars Award was a great idea for SFPA, and I was wrong in my initial reaction.

A lot of the things that I was most proud of as a leader in SFPA didn't last past my active involvement, and I ended that involvement on non-amicable terms. (I am still a member, though! I receive the publications and I cast my vote when things need to be voted on, but I do not participate beyond that.) However, there is a bit of my legacy very much in place that I will point to: the nice perfect-bound paperback Rhysling Anthologies that members and new nominees receive each year. I'm the one who got that started, and I designed and laid out several of those monsters myself in their earliest years. I am glad others took up that torch and kept it burning.

IFP: Your latest project *A Sinister Quartet* (2020, *Mythic Delirium Books)* brings together four wildly talented writers. Will you talk about its inception and execution?

MA: Another complicated story! *A Sinister Quartet* began with a proposal by Scott Nicolay for a book that would have looked like one of those Ace Doubles, where you flip the paperback over and the back cover is actually the front cover for a second novella by a different author. My contribution was "The Comforter," the threequel to my Nebula Award-nominated horror story "The Button Bin," and C. S. E. Cooney, a terrific writer who is also a great friend and collaborator, would provide a novella called "The Twice-Drowned Saint," which at the time the idea first arose was unfinished.

The proposal was aimed at a different publisher, and as can happen, that publisher wound up not pursuing the project. A couple of years later, I wanted, for reasons I can perhaps only partially articulate, to release a Mythic Delirium Book between the (gorgeous but criminally overlooked!) mosaic novel *The History of Soul 2065* (2019) by Barbara Krasnoff and my own *Aftermath*, and I realized that I had all the infrastructure in place to bring this two-novella project to fruition myself. Except of course it evolved into something else as the machinery started to roll. *The Twice-Drowned Saint* turned out to be a full-fledged novel on completion, and as Claire Cooney wrestled with finishing that, two other eerie novellas came to my attention, one of them, Jessica P. Wick's "An Unkindness," brought to me by Claire, and the other, Amanda J. McGee's "Viridian," placed before me for feedback at about the same time. And I saw connections between them that would enhance each piece if they all appeared side by side in the same volume. I believe I thought up the *Quartet* title even before Claire turned in her final draft.

Though I didn't label it so, I consider *A Sinister Quartet* to be the unofficial sixth book in the *Clockwork Phoenix* series.

IFP: Which is the favorite of all your collections and why?

MA: Gosh, that's a tough one. *Unseaming* (2014) is definitely the most successful by most measures, back in June it surpassed 10,000 copies sold, pretty amazing for a short story collection from an obscure author! *The Spider Tapestries* (2016) showcases my fiction at its most experimental. *Aftermath of an Industrial Accident* (2020) *is* the one that's most representative of my range, with straightforward horror, fantasy, science fiction, poetry and sheer weirdness, all colored in some shade of darkness. And then there's the poetry collections. I tend to point people at *Hungry Constellations* (2014), because 1) it spans most of my career as a poet, and 2) because the poems in it were selected by Dominik Parisien before he became a Hugo and Shirley Jackson Award-winning editor (and who's a fine poet himself!), and 3) because it's available as an e-book, whereas the earlier collections are not. (Though *Strange Wisdoms of the Dead* (2018) and *The Journey to Kailash* (2008) are still readily purchasable in paperback if anyone wants to seek them out.)

IFP: You're a big fan of collaboration and have produced some amazing work with other writers. How do you think this process of collaboration benefits creation?

MA: I've had the honor of writing poetry and fiction with many great collaborators, including yourself!

The best collaborations, I think, bring different but complementary ideas and methods to the table. It seems like I've experienced just about every possible way a collaboration can be done, from taking turns without even worrying about continuity to assigning clear divisions of labor and meticulously planning every step of the process.

I don't think I've ever had more fun at writing than when Ian Watson and I produced the humorous SF novelette "Dee-Dee and the Dumpy Dancers," which aggravated *Interzone* readers when it appeared there—as I recall, in their readers' poll, an equal number really loved it and really hated it, so it ended up smack dab in the middle—and got described as a "bizarre vision" in a *Guardian* review when it was reprinted in Ian's collection *Saving for a Sunny Day (2012)*. But man, what a joy it was to put together!

Another collaboration story I'll share is for the poem "The King of Cats, the Queen of Wolves," which appeared in *Apex Magazine* when Catherynne M. Valente was editor. Sonya Taaffe and I wrote the first two sections, representing *distant past* and *recentpast*, together, and then we were both stumped about how to take the tale of these enemies and lovers into the future. It turned out that what we needed to finish the poem was a third collaborator, Nicole Kornher-Stace, who we didn't meet until a couple of years later!

As an aside, it's fascinating that collaboration is so rare in the world of what I'll call "literary" poetry, but in speculative poetry land, it's actually quite frequent. Someone should write an essay about this.

IFP: Having worn all the hats: publisher, editor, and writer, which is your favorite hat? Do you have any wisdom to share on what's so awesome about each one?

MA: I mean, I first set out to be a writer, and the revelations that I have some talent at editing and publishing came as a surprise, but instead of dropping those pins I've continued to juggle them . . . I love it when something I have written connects with a reader and I get to hear about it; but I also love it when something I have published by another author connects with a reader and I get to hear about it. I can't recall a more exhilarating industry experience than the World Fantasy Award ceremony in 2016, sitting in the back row with C. S. E. Cooney (and Carlos Hernandez and Anita and Dominik and even more of our friends) when her *Bone Swans*, the first single-author collection ever published by *Mythic Delirium Books*, turned out to be the winner.

IFP: What's next in the pipeline for you?

MA: I have more great news to share: publisher Scott Gable of *Broken Eye Books* has agreed to bring out my dark fantasy/horror novel *Trail of Shadows* in 2022.

This book has been with me a long time. Characters from it appear in some of the stories gathered in *Unseaming* ("The Hiker's Tale") and *After-*

math of an Industrial Accident ("The Cruelest Team Will Win" and "Follow the Wounded One"). To those few who have actually paid attention, it will be like a whole massive planet appearing after years of noticing these satellites tugged in their orbits by some unseen object. I'm really excited that this fictional universe I've been dreaming in secret for so long won't be a secret much longer.

Stuff is happening on the publishing side, too. C. S. E. Cooney and I are working on her next collection of stories, *Dark Breakers (2022)*, with a tentative target date in February 2022. All of its pieces tie in with her World Fantasy Award-nominated novella *Desdemona and the Deep* that Tor.com brought out in 2019, and there are connections to *Bone Swans* as well.

And there's another even bigger project taking shape that I don't feel free to discuss publicly yet, but which I know a lot of people will be interested in. So I'll just smile coyly and say you'll have to wait and see.

ABOUT THE AUTHOR

Mike Allen wears many creative hats, at least one of them tailor-made by his wife and partner-in-crime Anita. Together they run *Mythic Delirium Books,* an imprint that's home to the acclaimed Clockwork Phoenix anthology series and books such as *Bone Swans* by C.S.E. Cooney (World Fantasy Award winner for best story collection), *Latchkey* by Nicole Kornher-Stace (named one of the best young adult books of 2018 by *Kirkus Reviews*), *Snow White Learns Witchcraft* by Theodora Goss (starred review, *Publishers Weekly*) and The History of Soul 2065 by Barbara Krasnoff (starred review, *Publishers Weekly*).

A Nebula, Shirley Jackson and two-time World Fantasy Award finalist, Mike has written several poetry collections, including *Strange Wisdoms of the Dead* (a *Philadephia Inquirer* editor's choice selection), *The Journey to Kailash* and *Hungry Constellations*; a twisted dark fantasy novel, *The Black Fire Concerto*; and three collections of strange and scary short fictions, *Unseaming*, *The Spider Tapestries: Seven Strange Stories* and *Aftermath of an Industrial Accident*. His latest personal project is a dark fantasy and horror anthology, *A Sinister Quartet*, produced in collaboration with C.S.E. Cooney, Amanda J. McGee and Jessica P. Wick.

His poems and stories have appeared in The Best Horror of the Year, Nebula Award Showcase, *Beneath Ceaseless Skies*, *Asimov's Science Fiction*, *Apex Magazine*, *Strange Horizons*, *Weird Tales*, *H.P. Lovecraft's Magazine of Horror*, Cthulhu's Reign, *Solaris Rising 2*, *Tomorrow's Cthulhu*, *Transmissions from Punktown*, *The Bible of Hell*, *Tales to Terrify*, *Podcastle*, *Pseudopod*, *The Drabblecast*, *Kaleidocast*, *Santa Clara Review*, *Artemis*, *Not One of Us*, *Lackington's* and many more publications.

By day he works as a news reporter and arts and culture columnist for the daily newspaper in Roanoke, Va., where he and Anita live with a cat so full of trouble she's named Pandora. (We're kidding, mostly, about the cat's troublemaking tendencies.) You can follow Mike's exploits as a writer at descentintolight.com, as an editor at mythicdelirium.com, and all at once on Twitter at @mythicdelirium.

LAVA LAMPS, WORD COLLAGES, AND THE SURREAL: INTERVIEW WITH WANDA DEGLANE, AUTHOR OF LADY SATURN

BY VANESSA MAKI

> *"I lay awake talking to her for hours.*
> *She sat next to me like a visitor at my sick bed,*
> *her gown radiating the light of 60 moons,*
> *her rings like a thousand halos around her head."*
> *— Wanda Deglane, Lady Saturn*

The second and expanded edition of *Lady Saturn* (Self Published, 2021) by Wanda Deglane explores the concept of self-love, mental illness, and slowly finding self-acceptance. Deglane's poems are haunting and beautiful all at the same time. Vanessa Maki interviews Deglane about her writing career, her newest chapbook forthcoming from Vegetarian Alcoholic Press, *Melancholia* (May 11, 2021), and how she includes emotion in her work.

INTERSTELLAR FLIGHT PRESS: Your writing career, if you feel comfortable having it be called that, has flourished quite a bit over the years. What are your thoughts surrounding how far you've come and how Lady Saturn is still so well-loved?

WANDA DEGLANE: Writing has always been a passion of mine, but I hesitate to call it a career. I feel really lucky to have people surrounding me that are so supportive of my work. I still feel like I have really far to go, a lot more to learn, and so much more to say.

IFP: Did you always have plans for a second edition of Lady Saturn to be published at some point?

WD: No, I didn't really imagine there'd be a need for a second edition. I honestly loved having it all up to me this time around though. It felt more special, and also kind of like getting reacquainted with an old friend.

IFP: As always your work is incredibly visual and sucks in its reader. "Lava Lamp" is one of the poems that pulls me in the same way every time. Do you remember how you felt writing it for the first time?

WD: I love "Lava Lamp," but funnily enough, it's probably one of the poems in this chapbook I put the least amount of emotion into. I don't remember exactly how I felt, but I know part of it was I was just fixated on how cool lava lamps are and wanted to write about it. The other part is this writing technique I do where I take little phrases I found interesting in my head and cut it together into one poem like a word collage. It's made for some really interesting pieces over the years, and also some of my favorite work.

IFP: Which poems are your personal favorites in the chapbook?

WD: Oh god, that's a tough one. Probably "Flower Mouth," "In My Defense," "Introspective Autumn", and "Andromeda"? I love my poems where I feel the most honest, and with "Flower Mouth," I finally felt like I was being honest about how much I hated being on antidepressants. And I just love the imagery I chose. "In My Defense" just feels so powerful. It's such a giant fuck you to anyone who's ever said anything mean to me, because I used to just soak all those words in and believe it. Introspective Autumn was one of the first poems in this chapbook I wrote for the only poetry class I ever took and it just has such a special place in my heart. I remember very viscerally how I felt when I was writing it. And Andromeda was when I started writing pieces that were more surreal, and I love surreal things. It's just gorgeous, in my humble opinion.

IFP: What do you hope your chapbook has done for those who have read and resonated with it?

WD: I guess I hope that people who are struggling through similar battles feel a little less alone. I feel like that's such a cliche thing to say, but I do.

And I hope it also brings a bit more awareness to depression and how weird and awful and lonely it feels.

IFP: Any exciting projects in the works or anything you'd like to plug?

WD: Well, I gotta plug my newest chapbook, *Melancholia*, coming out with *Vegetarian Alcoholic Press* (2021). *Melancholia* is also about depression and mental illness in general, so for a while, I sort of considered it almost like a sequel to Lady Saturn, but it's also a lot darker and way more fucked up and just more honest about what was going on in my brain. It's work I'm extremely proud of.

I also have another chapbook coming relatively soon called *Day Residue* (2021) where I wrote about weird dreams I had. And another coming sometime later in which I wrote about an abusive relationship from the lens of Paramore/Hayley Williams songs, so that's exciting too!

ABOUT THE AUTHOR

Wanda Deglane is a poet and therapist-in-training from Arizona. Her poetry has been published or forthcoming in *Glass Poetry, Drunk Monkeys, Yes Poetry, Cosmonauts Avenue,* and elsewhere. Wanda is the author of *Melancholia* (*Vegetarian Alcoholic Press*, 2021) and other chapbooks.

VAMPIRES, MONSTROUSNESS, AND A MULTIPLICITY OF DESIRE: INTERVIEW WITH S.T. GIBSON, AUTHOR OF A DOWRY OF BLOOD

BY JOANNA WESON

"I've always been interested in the way monstrousness is a deeply human thing, and how being human is sometimes monstrous." —S.T. Gibson

S.T. Gibson writes lush speculative fiction in both long and short forms. Her latest novella, *A Dowry of Blood (Nyx Publishing,* 2021), tells the story of Dracula from the perspective of Constanta, one of his wives, as they travel through much of Europe and history. It's a dark tale, as any good vampire story must be. Gibson explores violence and abuse among these monsters, but also tenderness and strength, through her beautiful prose and richly drawn characters and settings.

Interstellar Flight Press: Thank you so much for letting me talk to you about this evocative book! Vampires are a staple of both fantasy and horror, but your story deals with Dracula himself, and the original text by Brahm Stoker, far more directly than most. Can you say a bit about the first time you read *Dracula*?

S.T. Gibson: Thanks for having me! I think I was in high school, and I had already devoured most of the vampire books and movies I could get my hands on. I especially loved Anne Rice novels and the 2004 Van Helsing movie, and I was getting into classical literature at the time, so it made sense to go back and read Dracula. It read it back to back with Frankenstein and remembered preferring Frankenstein, but I was struck by how truly *weird* the Dracula book is. It's crammed with strange happenings, so many of which get dropped in adaptations. The book is also flat-out terrified of female sexuality, which irritated and intrigued me in equal measure. A sexually self-possessed woman was monstrous to Stoker, and I think that's part of the reason I wanted to explore Dracula from the perspective of the brides.

IFP: The way that you frame *A Dowry of Blood* as something that his wife, Constanta, is writing down in order to understand and fix her history in her own memory seemed to me like a call-back to the epistolary nature of Brahm Stoker's original Dracula. Were there any other deliberate references to the source material?

SG: There's actually not that many direct references to the original book outside of the epistolary style, which absolutely was an homage. Some readings of Dracula imply that two of the "brides" are actually Dracula's daughters, and I played with a lot of unsettling familial language when describing the relationship of Dracula to his brides in *Dowry*. There's also a throwaway reference to the Harkers tucked away somewhere in act three that eagle-eyed readers will notice. I imply that at least some of the events of the Dracula book happened in the *Dowry* universe, but that narrative wasn't one I was interested in exploring. I wanted to re-imagine the brides from the ground up and breathe new life into them.

A lot of the other callbacks in the book are actually references to Dracula in movie history, such as the brides being red-headed, blonde, and brunette, which is a reference to how they're depicted in some films.

IFP: The complex relationships between Dracula's spouses really drive this story. I was delighted to see that everyone in this story was bisexual, and what a complete non-issue that was in their little world. I'm sure that was a deliberate choice on your part, so can you tell us a little bit more about what you were hoping to accomplish by adding that to your world?

SG: I've always read the vampire as a metaphor for bisexuality, in Anne Rice's body of work in particular as well as in many other additions to the vampire mythos. Even if the author is using a multiplicity of attractions as cheap titillation or shorthand for decadence and depravity, the metaphor is still there, and it has teeth and staying power. When I was a young bisexual woman figuring out her own identity, I saw myself in vampires, in these stories of "deviant" desires and immortal hedonism and existential contemplation. I was especially drawn to vampires because their sexuality is so tied to their very existence, the way they move through the world and survive in it, and something about that felt grounding.

Most of my characters are bisexual anyway because that's the lens through which I view the world, but it seemed extra important to headline sexuality, desire, and queer relationships in a book about vampires. I'm a very character-driven writer and digging into a tangled relationship between four people was an exciting challenge. Sexuality is one of my favorite threads to use when weaving together the tapestry of a story, and *Dowry* let me lean into that device to its fullest potential.

I think it felt important for bisexuality (or pansexuality; whatever term you prefer applies here) to be a non-issue, as you put it, because bisexuality is still so misunderstood and stigmatized in wider society. I for one am very tired of being an issue or a case study, so I don't want to put my characters through that either. If I was a beautiful immortal being who relied on seduction to survive and romantic bonds to build a family, I wouldn't spend my time worrying about whether my sexuality was valid. It's the same reason I give Constanta a rich religious inner world with moral conflicts that *aren't* centered around her sexuality. There are so many more interesting factors at play in her life that complicate her relationship to God.

IFP: The relationship that Dracula has with his wives and husband could best be described as emotionally abusive, or at least manipulative. I admire the way that this Dracula is a monster not only in the traditional sense but also in this more mundane way. In retrospect, it feels like a natural combination, but I've never seen it done in quite this way before. When did you first see the connection?

SG: I've always been interested in the way monstrousness is a deeply human thing, and how being human is sometimes monstrous. And I'm interested in the way love can decay and ruin us, or grow strong and redeem us, all based on the choices we have to make. I had wanted to do a story of a love gone wrong for a while (even though I also got to write some love going right in the background) and a vampire book seemed like the perfect avenue for that. Vampirism is so much about literal, spiritual, and sexual parasitism and manipulation, just as much as it's about high romance and eternal love. The line between adoration and horror is razor-thin. *Dowry* is the exploration of my interest in that thin, transparent line.

I was inspired by books about the downfall of unhealthy relationships, most relevantly Carmen Maria Machado's *In the Dream House*. That book gave me permission to lean into the abuse themes, and to do experimental things with point of view and form. I owe a lot to it.

IFP: Can you give us any hints on what we might expect from you next?

SG: Sure! Currently, I'm working on a sultry, summery folk gothic and scribbling some contemporary romance in my free time. I hope to have more books to share with my readers very soon!

ABOUT THE AUTHOR

Saint Gibson is a poet, author, and village wise woman in training. A graduate of the creative writing program at the University of North Carolina at Asheville and the theological studies program at Princeton Seminary, she currently lives in Boston with her partner, spoiled Persian cat, and vintage blazer collection. She is represented by Tara Gilbert of the Jennifer De Chiara literary agency.

GOOD GIRLS, BABY-EATING MONSTERS, AND CRAFTING A NARRATIVE: INTERVIEW WITH ISABEL YAP, AUTHOR OF NEVER HAVE I EVER

BY MICHAEL GLAZNER

Isabel Yap is the author of numerous SFF short stories appearing in T*or.com, Lightspeed, Strange Horizons,* and *Year's Best Weird Fiction.* After the February 23rd release of her debut short story collection *Never Have I Ever* (Small Beer Press, 2021), Isabel Yap sat down with Interstellar Flight Magazine to talk Filipino monsters, craft, and gender roles in her stories.

INTERSTELLAR FLIGHT PRESS: What's scarier and why? Meeting a monster from American folklore in a dark alley or meeting a monster from Filipino folklore in a dark alley? Or does it depend on who's telling the story?

Isabel Yap: A monster from Filipino folklore for sure—because that's what occupies my imagination, my nightmares. I don't have something that instantly comes to mind from American folklore, but my mind can *very* easily conjure a white lady (think Sadako from *The Ring*) waiting for me at the end of a dark alley, or lurking in the corner of my ceiling. Yikes. Though I will say it's really mostly ghosts that freak me out. I'm not particularly scared of manananggal or kapre, but anything that's like a bloody or crying child or lady? Count me out.

IFP: Do you think about craft elements such as point of view, structure, and tone as you write, or do stories come to you with these elements already in place?

IY: I do think about these things, especially as I'm trying to puzzle out the initial draft, but not necessarily as distinct elements. They inform each other, so if I have one then I start to get a sense of the rest of it. I usually don't set out to do things explicitly either, ie, I rarely impose on a story, I just wait for it to find its footing. (This leads to lots of grumpy, extended drafting.) Structure might be the exception. My brain likes to use constraints to help move a piece along—for example, I do a lot of braided storylines as a way to keep the narrative progressing, and my brain enjoys having that challenge.

IFP: What author would make you burst into tears of happiness if they tweeted about how great your book is? Why is this important to you?

IY: Honestly, I was very lucky to have my book read and blurbed by authors I tremendously admire—so I feel this has already happened, multiple times over! Helen Oyeyemi is not on Twitter but she is someone whose praise would make me expire. I love her sense of play and fearlessness in her work. Madeline Miller is another author who I don't know personally, but whose work I love—her attention to the line is just astounding.

IFP: Throughout your writing career, how has your characters' diction changed? Or has it?

IY: It has, I think, partly because I moved to the US, and partly because I've read and experienced more things. Some Filipino writer friends last year pointed out that I mix more Tagalog and English in my work now. In the Philippines literary scene, writing in "straight English" is actually more common as that's seen as more . . . I don't know if "appropriate" is the right word, but when we're writing and thinking in English, it's better to keep to that mode, which is what our local literature historically reflects. This is true in my own work; there's more Tagalog in recent pieces, compared to the stories I was writing in 2008–2013.

I didn't explicitly think, "I want to write more Tagalog in my stories!"—but in trying to capture a certain cadence in my work over time, I did bring more Tagalog in. Maybe it's also a function of being slightly homesick. I do really try to focus on what the story needs, so this changes depending on the setting and where the characters come from; a lot of the characters I write are what we'd call Inglisero in Manila, "English-speaking people."

When I write stories set in the US, too, sometimes the characters aren't Filipino, and I'll just be using the slang I've picked up as a millennial working in the Bay Area.

IFP: The hero's journey is a super-popular organizing tool for mainstream narratives. Maybe you've seen a Marvel Movie? How do your stories embrace or eschew the hero's journey?

IY: I have indeed seen lots of Marvel movies. :) I don't have a strong opinion on the hero's journey, to be honest. I think it's effective at what it does. As someone who has a background in Marketing I know how well it works for particular audiences, especially because it's often framed as problem-solving, or the triumph of good over evil—it's a very good sales tactic, to create fear and salvation, heroes and villains. I think some of my stories follow this, in that I could align them against this shape if I wanted to, but I find that it's not intuitive for me as a writing tool. Trying to shape my stories that way doesn't work; if I think consciously about the three-act structure or the beats in the hero's journey, my writing brain just shuts down.

IFP: Some (most?) of your stories ("Windrose in Scarlet," "Good Girls") deal with gender and societal constructs. How do your characters' struggles connect with your own struggles with gender roles? Or, what inspired you to depict a person not being a "good girl"?

IY: The latter question is easier for me to answer, in that I actually think my girls *are* quite good. Or they're trying their best. In both "Windrose" and "Good Girls" there are a lot of extraordinary circumstances, internal (Kaye being a manananggal, Sara having intrusive thoughts) and external (Red and Belle, in their own ways, have been blessed by fairies, or maybe cursed), that impact what the girls are allowed to do or be. Trying to find a way around those impositions then forms a major part of the narrative.

I'm extremely uninterested in writing or reading flat female characters. It's one of the things that takes me out of a book, no matter how good all the other elements are. I mean, I dislike flat characters in general, but my tolerance for paper-thin fictional girls and women is incredibly low, whereas I could probably get behind a pretty boy whose only purpose is to be pretty (and slightly evil—as in the case of Lisoryo, my bishonen prince in "How to Swallow the Moon"). I actually wrote an essay once called "Life Is Not a

Shoujo Manga" where I basically talked about how, as much as I love shoujo manga, I didn't see myself or my friends reflected in them. And maybe we shouldn't expect to be, because we're Filipino and not Japanese, but still—I'm usually writing towards that subversion. Not so much writing *not-good* girls, but writing girls in all their complexity and weirdness, their sometimes-ugliness, their truths, which *still* surprise some people because it remains jarring to have that truth come out in media. Just look at the treatment of women in, for example, superhero films; we remain pleasantly surprised whenever they're depicted multi-dimensionally.

As to the first question: I haven't experienced *everything* my characters have experienced, which I am really grateful for. But any woman will have, by her teens if not earlier, seen or experienced *some* shit. *For sure.* I sometimes think about this Tamsyn Muir interview (*Three Crows Magazine*) where she talked about writing things that you've suffered spiritually if not physically, which is what I've done in several of my stories. I will say I am always writing as close to the emotional truth as I can, as far as I can swing it. I struggle with gender roles and always have, but articulating how or what specifically has always been A Trip for me. Even knowing what good it does to share, I find myself preferring fiction as a tool of expression, in most cases. I am grateful for the publications and readers that let me do so.

ABOUT THE AUTHOR

Isabel Yap writes fiction and poetry, works in the tech industry, and drinks tea. Born and raised in Manila, she has also lived in California and London. She holds a BS in Marketing from Santa Clara University, and an MBA from Harvard Business School. In 2013 she attended the Clarion Writers Workshop. Her work has appeared in venues including *Tor.com, Lightspeed, Strange Horizons,* and *Year's Best Weird Fiction. Never Have I Ever* is her debut story collection, out now from *Small Beer Press*. She is @visyap on Twitter and her website is https://isabelyap.com.

POETRY, RAGE, REVENGE, AND TRAUMA: INTERVIEW WITH JEAN MARIE BUB, AUTHOR OF MANEATER

BY VANESSA MAKI

> *"It was only after I left an abusive relationship that I realized women needed to hear the raw and unfiltered truth from someone—it can be literal life or death from us. We don't need more of that regurgitated "She is strong because she is broken" crap from another male poet. we need truth."*

Maneater, Jean Marie Bub's forthcoming third poetry collection, released on Feb. 14, 2021, is powerful but not to be read lightly. The collection contains poems and artwork about unfiltered rage, revenge, and refusing to shut up about trauma. IFP interviewer Vanessa Maki talked with Bub about this raw and transcendent hybrid work.

From the book description: "*Maneater* is the story of every daughter of Lilith wronged, screamed in her every voice. It echoes of Medusa, of Eve, of Persephone. It echoes of you. It echoes of me . . . you feel the wrath of one woman coming undone, of one become whole through using her power—her voice. In using it so, she has found her vengeance. And there is a sort of sweetness to that in a world devoid of justice, isn't there? It is a fire. A beacon. A light of hope for other women, for other survivors—to wield like weapon."

Important note: The interview below may be triggering due to discussion about or mentioning sexual violence and or mental health.

Interstellar Flight Press: First off I must tell you that *Maneater* is brilliantly unfiltered, from the words and the images placed throughout. When did you decide to pursue compiling this collection?

Jean Marie Bub: Thank you! I was actually subconsciously writing this book for three years. I had compiled works of heartbreak and pains of womanhood, unsure of how to proceed. I had never written with love or romantic relationships as a focus, so i was doubting it heavily. It was only after I left an abusive relationship that I realized women needed to hear the raw and unfiltered truth from someone—it can be literal life or death from us. We don't need more of that regurgitated "She is strong because she is broken" crap from another male poet. we need truth.

IFP: Has the idea of putting this out into the world been nerve-wracking at all? Not because the collection is explicitly about trauma, sexual violence, and mental health, but due to potential reception.

JB: Yes! There's no doubt that I lost many male supporters due to how I approached the works in this book—but I'm one hundred percent okay with that. If my work offends you, it is not for you. And it's probably because you feel it's about you, which is frightening, especially due to the content of the book.

Because I'm writing about a wound that relatively fresh (I left my ex just last year, and came out with my story this summer) I have received some threats and insults from my abuser's family. My mentor once told me—"If you're nervous about something, you should do it. If it makes you uncomfortable and will make even more people uncomfortable because of the truth, you should do it even more."

IFP: Your visual art often involves bodies and the powerful acts/statements that can be made with them. Was any of the artwork you've included made with the collection in mind or did they just make sense to include?

JB: They made sense to include, since they were made in the same timeline and purge as the book. In my paintings, I focus on painting womxn. Humanity is harbored in the torso, but the torso is also the most targeted and coveted part of the female body. From our breasts, bellies, and genitalia, nurture the children and future of this entire planet—yet these parts have been sexualized, fetishized, and romanticized since the beginning of time. We look at these parts of ourselves every day, exactly as that—parts. But they're a part of a collective whole that deserves to exist in peace, without derogatory terms attached, without negative or sexual connotation, without stigma.

This is what *Maneater* is essentially about. We are almost made to forget who we are—we become just parts. The book is about finding those pieces that were taken from you or lost, and reclaiming them. It's rare that womxn feel seen as a whole. As I explained before, eyes are on parts of us rather than all of us, so much so that sometimes it feels like those parts might as well not even exist at all. I put emphasis on things that we're taught to hide—stretch marks, cuts, scars, bruises . . . that's the subject of my art to its core. Bringing the pain to light and releasing it of all its shame. Normalizing it. Letting you know that it's okay to feel that way, to carry that hurt. We all do, I promise you.

IFP: If you feel comfortable and willing to let readers know—what poem in *Maneater* best sums up the collection?

> *"MANEATER is Lady Lazarus. She is serpent, she is Medusa,*
> *she takes blade to the throat of every Ghislaine,*
> *She dismembers every predator, and*
> *disembowels anyone who tries to silence her.*
> *She is gun. She is sword. She is fire.*
> *She is weapon. She sends hex with kiss*
> *and death with words. She dissolves male gaze*
> *With malice, like evil eye, she shoots*
> *The poison back sevenfold.*
> *the poetry that coats her lips sheds light*
> *on truths they wish to bury. Vengeance is her voice,*
> *And MANEATER lives in you.*
> *It's about time*
> *you wake her."*

IFP: Did you always intend to release the collection on Valentine's Day? It's clever either way!

JB: Yes! Not only is it a day where most of us feel underappreciated or forgotten, it's also a day of violence. For many reasons, it's symbolic for me.

IFP: If you had to describe *Maneater* in 2 words—what would they be?

Cathartic

Rageful

IFP: Do you have any other projects in the works? Whether they are similar to *Maneater* or not.

JB: Yes! There will definitely be a part two.

IFP: Anything you'd like your readers to know before they purchase your collection?

JB: Pace yourself when reading. It's heavy, it's real, and it could be triggering if you're a survivor. As gutteral and painful as it might be, it's important to see someone's realizations and use them as hope for you if you're in a place of recovery or even denial. There are trigger warnings and help resources in the book, as well as intentionally placed affirmations so it's not too dark all at once. To get an idea of what kind of content will be in the book, you can check out the work I have posted on my Instagram @ jeanmariebub.

ABOUT THE AUTHOR

Jean-Marie Bub (she/her) is a transparent artist, author, survivor, and activist living in Harlem who is dedicated to raising hell with her truth. On both paper and canvas, she puts emphasis on reclaiming one's body after experiencing sexual trauma and abuse—her work is rage-filled, giving space for survivors to grieve, while also examining the guttural pain of womanhood, trauma, relationships, and loss. Her work has been featured in publications such as *Pussy Magic, 'Reclaim: An Anthology of Women's Poetry,' No Tender Fences: an Anthology of Immigrant & First-Generation American poetry, Hellebore Magazine*, and more. Her highschool features her first book, *Pulchritude and Soul,* in its Mental Health curriculum.

GAMIFYING WRITING: A TALK WITH PETER CHIYKOWSKI, CREATOR OF THE STORY ENGINE DECK

BY J.D. HARLOCK

I'm generally dubious when writers make rules about what is or isn't a story, but there's a definition of a story from Canadian novelist Douglas Glover that I really like: "A story consists of someone wanting something and having trouble getting it."

Peter Chiykowski, the creator of the award-winning webcomic Rock Paper Cynic, has recently found immense success as the designer of The Story Engine Deck of writing prompts. The Story Engine is an innovative set of 240 cards for coming up with ideas for your writing and roleplaying. The Deck of Worlds is the latest expansion in the series and allows users to develop ideas that could spice up their SFF settings. It's currently being crowdfunded on Kickstarter, where it's made over a staggering $550,000 and counting.

We recently sat down with Peter to discuss his life before the Story Engine Deck, this latest expansion, and any other ongoing projects.

INTERSTELLAR FLIGHT PRESS: What were you up to before the Story Engine Deck came into your life? Did you have a day job? Any particular ambitions and/or expectations you had for yourself? What did you imagine life was going to be like before you came up with the idea?

PETER CHIYKOWSKI: I worked a lot of random jobs and wore a lot of hats before I started working on The Story Engine Deck: bookstore sales assistant, museum gift shop worker, writer at a children's charity, freelance writer, editor, RPG writer, odd jobs illustrator, webcomic artist. Through all those jobs, I was always trying to find new ways to launch creative projects that could help me do creative work full-time. I'm obsessed with learning about what creativity is and how it works on a psychological level, an emotional level, a sociological level, an evolutionary level. It's one of my favorite subjects to read about, so it feels natural that the project that really took off for me was one focused on tapping the creative process.

IFP: Where'd the idea for the Story Deck Engine come from?

PC: It came from a blend of influences, but the biggest one was Tarot. Tarot means a lot of things to a lot of different people, and for hundreds of years, this simple set of cards has been used to help people see connections, patterns, and story threads that make sense of their lives. The Story Engine Deck takes a lot of lessons from Tarot: how turning a card can change its meaning entirely; how cards can take on new significance in proximity to other cards; how the way you arrange cards and perceive connections leads to countless ways to interpret them.

The other half of the influence came from my creative writing background. I'm generally dubious when writers make rules about what is or isn't a story, but there's a definition of a story from Canadian novelist Douglas Glover that I really like: "A story consists of someone wanting something and having trouble getting it."

So simple, but it's a really great recipe for a story, and I thought about that a lot when figuring out how the different card types in the deck would work together.

IFP: Were you caught off guard by the Kickstarter's massive, earth-shattering success? How has your life changed because of it?

PC: I was caught so off-guard! I was trying to get this base deck I had been conceiving for a long time off the ground, and I had been writing out expansion ideas as I headed into the Kickstarter launch. I thought those would come 1–2 years later.

But it was clear within hours of launch that the deck was attracting a community of its own and that they wanted the expansions. We hit our funding goal so fast, and the momentum wasn't letting up. I took a look at the overall project timeline, at the content I had ready, and what I'd need to fast-track to make expansions happen. After doing a day or two of test-writing and playtesting to make sure the expansions would come together the way I wanted them to, I decided to announce the first expansion stretch goal. People jumped on it. From there, we just steamrolled stretch goal after stretch goal until we had an expanded deck, three expansions, and six boosters.

The final days were absolutely surreal. I've seen Kickstarters fail by success, where the creators take on too much too quickly. It bloats the project to the point of collapse, so I was having daily talks with myself to keep my head level and try to remember that it was more important to bring this runaway train safely into the station rather than show off with fancy bells and whistle. I'm glad I cut off the content list where I did because it was the perfect size given the timelines I had.

IFP: Why are you running a second Kickstarter?

PC: I don't say this on the Deck of Worlds Kickstarter page, but working on all these projects has meant that I don't really get to play games as much as I used to. I used to play and DM a LOT of D&D and do a lot of world-building just for fun as a creative exercise. That feeling of playing around with the creation of a fictional world is one I badly miss. I wanted to figure out how to tap that feeling as a solo exercise and to make it something I could enjoy as an activity with a few spare minutes. Plus, being cooped up in the pandemic, dreaming of these expansive worlds to explore was good medicine for the soul.

So I started prototyping an open-ended deck for building worlds. It took a long time to hammer together a structure that could bring together the many many elements that go into worldbuilding and set them down in categories that made sense as cards. But I knew I had something special when I kept pulling the alpha off the shelf for one more prompt because I was just having so much fun with the settings I was creating.

IFP: What are your plans for the Story Deck Engine going forward?

PC: There are a lot of avenues to explore, and I have a spreadsheet full of ideas I want to try, but I'm trying not to jump the gun on any of them. The best decisions I've made working on The Story Engine Deck all came from listening to backers, and I'll be paying close attention to what they connect most with on this Kickstarter before I go back to that spreadsheet of ideas and decide which ones to pursue. Two things I'm certain I want to explore are more educational resources for teachers who want to use creative decks in their classrooms and more playable stories for using The Story Engine: Deck of Worlds with RPGs. I'm toying with a format of booster pack-sized campaigns that breaks up an epic story into 20 cards scattered around the world you create, and key elements of the campaign are dictated by your setting. I think it's going to be ridiculously fun, but I want time to perfect it before I show people.

IFP: Are there any other interesting projects that you're cooking up?

PC: I'm really excited to have a book of microfiction coming out with Andrews-McMeel this year, and you'll definitely see the fingerprints of a worldbuilding engine all over it.

It's called *The House of Untold Stories,* and it brings together 50 stories set in different pocket universes. The pages you turn as you progress through the book are designed as doors, so you're actually navigating this impossible house jumping through far-flung realities and alternate timelines. Writing it was definitely a way of escaping quarantine mentally, if not physically, for me, and I think it will give readers some freedom to roam in their minds. A lot of the stories explore the link between setting and story, the way the spaces we occupy are homes for stories that linger even after we're gone.

It comes out on August 31, and it's definitely the most cohesive and risk-taking collection of fiction I've written!

ABOUT THE CREATOR

Peter Chiykowski is the creator of the award-winning webcomic Rock Paper Cynic and the designer of The Story Engine Deck of writing prompts.

He has twice won the Aurora Award for "Best Graphic Novel" from the Canadian Science Fiction and Fantasy Association, and his writing, art, and memes have appeared in or been covered in books, newspaper articles, blogs, tabletop games, video games, and magazines coast to coast.

PRIDE ECONOMIES, GENDER ROLES, AND A MULTIPLICITY OF BODIES: INTERVIEW WITH BENJAMIN ROSENBAUM, AUTHOR OF THE UNRAVELING

BY J.Z. WESTON

> "I think maybe the very first impulse was simply to "spin all the dials" and come up with as strange-yet-familiar a world as possible . . ."

Benjamin Rosenbaum is already well known to discerning readers of short speculative fiction—his stories have earned nominations for the Hugo, Nebula, BSFA, Sturgeon, and World Fantasy Awards. His first full-length novel, *The Unraveling* (*Erewhon*, 2021) deals with gender, post-scarcity economics, surveillance, and parenting, hundreds of thousands of years in the future. A protagonist with three bodies and nine parents might sound daunting, but Rosenbaum makes it feel effortless. The strangeness of the world provides scaffolding for a story with extraordinary heart.

INTERSTELLAR FLIGHT PRESS: *The Unraveling* reminded me of Ursula K. Le Guin's *The Left Hand of Darkness*, in the best possible way. What—if any—books did you feel you were in dialogue with while writing or worldbuilding?

BENJAMIN ROSENBAUM: *Left Hand of Darkness* is definitely an influence, as well as *The Dispossessed* (ambiguous utopia) and just anthropological SF in general, like *Solitude and The Matter of Seggri* and so on. Also a lot of Samuel R. Delany, particularly *Stars In My Pocket Like*

Grains of Sand and *Trouble on Triton*. Perhaps also Varley's *Steel Beach*. The sense that we will always be both messy and embodied (that the idea of turning ourselves into "pure reason" is as awful as it is nonsensical), but also weirdly malleable, is in dialogue with Greg Egan (e.g. *Diaspora*) and Charlie Stross' *Accelerando* series, but in a way is most deeply rooted in Octavia Butler (e.g. *Dawn*).

The reputation economy and mutual ubiquitous surveillance owes something to Doctorow's *Down and out in The Magic Kingdom* (and also see next question). Thavé's thoughts as a "survival consultant" are in dialogue with a long history of "influencing societies" SF going back at least to Asimov's Foundation series, including Iain M. Banks's Culture series. Leckie's *Ancillary Justice* came out when I was mid-way through writing the book, and having another multiple-bodies, differently-gendering society to think about influenced my thinking. My thoughts on gender and the body were definitely influenced by Bornstein's *Gender Outlaw* and Serano's *Whipping Girl*. I'm sure there's much more!

IFP: One of the *many* noteworthy aspects of the worldbuilding in this book is the economy, which is based on emotional resources. Was that inspired by any real-world theories?

BR: Yes! My thinking about how economies can work, and how they might be different than our exchange economy, was influenced by Raymond's *The Cathedral and the Bazaar*, Hyde's *The Gift*, and Graeber's *Debt: The First 5000 Years*.

The way we deal with money and exchange is a method originally created for low-information environments, like merchants who are strangers to one another meeting in a foreign city. In such a circumstance, a transaction has to be a spot transaction—if I give you a bolt of linen and you give me 10 talents of silver, we have to make sure that the bolt of linen and the 10 talents of silver are somehow mathematically equivalent—that afterwards, we are "even", neither of us has a debt to one another, we are not bound together, we might as well never see each other again.

This is how almost all "economic" transactions in our world work (including debt itself being quantified and formalized so there is at least the theoretical possibility of "paying it off" and being "quits") . . . though we still retain various "protected spaces" outside of the world of economic exchange (giving one another holiday gifts, for instance, where it's a taboo to know exactly how much the gift was worth because that would turn it into an exchange transaction, since you might be expected to give back a return gift worth the same amount, to the penny, or just cash, thus dissolving the bond that the gift created; but also things like the prestige economy that tenured academics live in, or the world of philanthropy, or the hierarchical or communal redistributive relations inside families and corporations and states).

Anyway, this spot-transaction-these-things-are-equal-now-we're-strangers-again approach to economics was not the norm in the ancient, or even medieval, world. Most of the time if you were buying or giving someone something you had a particular, personal relationship with them, a set of complex relations that influenced the transaction. Even if a cobbler was selling shoes for coins, they wouldn't be expected to offer the same price to a neighbor, a stranger, a cousin, someone they were feuding with, the "big man" of the village, a poor widow, someone whose cousin they were trying to arrange a marriage of their niece with, and so forth. The shoes wouldn't have some abstract "price" independent of social relations. To some people the cobbler would refuse to sell at any price; to others the cobbler would press the shoes as gifts, either because this would be seen as honorable and meritorious (and win the cobbler status) or because of the expectation of some return which might not be strictly "economic"—e.g. that arranged marriage the cobbler is hoping for. This is a high-information situation, in which plenty of non-exchange-economy factors can be factored into the transaction.

This worked in an (information-rich) village, and stopped working as the world got bigger and more transactions (e.g., in a booming city) were among strangers, and thus information-poor. But in a world of massive mutual surveillance and massive computing power, everyone knows as much about everyone else as neighbors in a premodern village—or more, in fact. Everyone knows as much about everyone else as they do about their siblings. And relations between siblings aren't governed by exchange, but by the emotional life.

In Fift's world the emotional life is highly quantified and analzyable; banker-historians weave complicated, quantified stories of emotional transactions as data-rich as any economic analysis of a public company's balance sheet and P&L in our world. But these are all a formalization of "how do I feel about you" and "how will it influence how other people feel about me if I do this."

The "pride economy" of Fift's world isn't precisely a gift economy or a reputation economy or a communalism in Hyde's and Graeber's terms, but it takes those ideas as a point of departure to create something as data-intense as a modern stock trading algorithm and as intimate as a squabble or alliance between siblings.

IFP: The norm in this world is for people to have multiple bodies, connected through the Somatic Network. You do an amazing job of ferrying the readers between Fift's various bodies throughout the narrative. As a reader, I never lost track of where ze was or what ze was doing. How did *you* keep track of the action during some of the more intense scenes?

BR: Lots of rewriting and checking, mostly, but I can share one trick. Often I would write one body's sequence of events as a whole, then another's, and only then interleave them, thinking about which events would juxtapose well and about how long things would take relatively.

IFP: Divorcing gender from reproductive roles allowed you to turn our cultural assumptions inside out and upside down. Can you remember what initially sparked the Staid and Vail genders for this world?

BR: I'm trying to remember what initially, initially sparked the distinction. I think maybe the very first impulse was simply to "spin all the dials" and come up with as strange-yet-familiar a world as possible, and thus to have different genders that weren't ours. Perhaps part of that was wanting to write about a world peopled with bodies much like ours ("paleohuman stock") but with truly advanced medical technology, and thinking about what social changes that might cause. It always bothered me that in Star Trek, for instance, far-future humans are flitting around the galaxy, but they seem to consider themselves old and ready to retire at 70 or so, their gender roles are pretty much that of the time the show was made (Uhura in a short skirt, the only woman on the bridge, with the script essentially treating her as a receptionist much of the time . . .), and so on.

Whereas looking at how social roles have changed over just the past hundred years, it seems particularly odd for those of Starfleet to seem so calcified! So perhaps the initial impulse was realizing that if genitals and other aspects of reproductive physiology were something you could change as easily as hairstyles (at least from the point of view of medical praxis), perhaps a culture wouldn't be as obsessed with them as a locus of determining someone's true nature and social destiny. In a way this is a thought experiment about the feminist maxim, "biology is not destiny."

Once I'd decided that gender wasn't going to be about reproductive biology, though, I had to work out what it would be about. I didn't want it to feel like a broad satire or parody; I didn't want to hang gender on something that was purely arbitrary or absurd. I think we have a natural tendency towards—or at least, an ever-present risk of falling into—dividing people up and assigning them roles, and I take "gender" as describing the kind of intimate social moeity where any baby could be assigned to be either one, or else the other, sort of person. I wanted their take on gender to be very much like ours, except not, and thus to illuminate the absurdity of the massive ideological edifice of expectations and assumptions we erect on a basically pretty minor piece of physiological variation.

For this to work I wanted to root it in some real-feeling human experience. And, as a dad of two kids, one thing that immediately came to mind was the APGAR test. When your kid is born, the doctor or midwife does this checklist quantification of how active they are—blue and sluggish, or ruddy and lively? At the low end this can indicate medically necessary interventions, but at the high end variation is not really very meaningful, a slightly-sluggish-at-birth kid has probably recovered and is fine a couple of hours later. But it's such a huge emotional moment—as a parent, you're desperately waiting to find out the APGAR result, because you want your kid to be healthy.

This is really at least as big a deal, in that moment, as the other thing you might be finding out if you didn't do an ultrasound, which is what kind of reproductive equipment the baby is carrying and thus, presumably, what third-person pronoun you are going to use for them. Basically, in our culture, we look at the baby's genitals and decide if we will expect it to be the "hard" sort of person or the "soft" sort of person. But what if, instead of hanging the pronoun on the does-that-look-more-like-a-penis-or-vagina reveal, we hung it on the APGAR score?

It doesn't seem unreasonable that we might imagine that, instead of "hard" and "soft" people, the world was composed of "fast" and "slow" people. It doesn't seem unreasonable that, in a world where genitals were easily changed, the mystical-biological sense that there really were two fundamentally different human natures might attach itself to introversion and extraversion . . . which, of course, are much harder for the people of Fift's world to change. So Vail and Staid ended up seeming like they could be something a culture could possibly obsess over to the same extent we obsess over the junk in your pants.

IFP: The Staidish practice of The Long Conversation reminded me a bit of Talmudic discourse. Was that intentional, or something that just leaked in?

BR: Oh, a hundred percent. It's totally a nod to the Talmud. Not just the layers of references on references, but also the fact that the historic protagonists doing various important political or mystical things are also the same people interpreting and arguing about earlier generations of protagonists. In the Talmud, Eliezar ben Hyrcanus is the guy who makes various important legal rulings and interpretations about things sages of earlier centuries said, and ALSO the guy who makes a carob tree walk and zaps a third of the world's barley because he's offended.

Also, the sense that there's both this reverence for tradition where we can never measure up to the ancient sages, but also that ever generation adds to and reinterprets and passes on the tradition, that it's not fixed but a living tradition. And, of course, the gender aspect. In the shtetl, too, one gender derived its primary status hierarchy from endlessly arguing about and re-elaborating on a tradition from which the other gender was mostly excluded. The Long Conversation is what makes *The Unraveling* a Jewish book, even though it's set hundreds of thousands of years after Judaism itself is no longer remembered.

IFP: There's so much complex worldbuilding in this story—are there any small details that you hope readers won't miss?

BR: Wow, I don't know! I think it's all there somewhere, and the fun is in ferreting it out. I enjoyed getting to add the end materials, relatively late in the process (the German edition doesn't have them), with all the world-building fun. (Also the school assignment from the Fift-Emim mancer, that's one of my favorite bits, and it's also a late addition.)

I will say that if you'd like to know more about Thavé, there's a story on my website, "Bereft, I Come to a Nameless World," that takes place after The Unraveling and features Thavé and zir long-lost friend Siob.

> *"An immersive future history, The Unraveling is a fantastic adventure that is also a story about the love that binds us to each other—and to the galaxy itself. Rosenbaum's writing is wonderfully complex and whimsical, but most of all it is humane. No matter how alien his characters and worlds, they feel like kin."—Annalee Newitz, Hugo and Lambda Award-winning author of Autonomous*

ABOUT THE AUTHOR

Benjamin Rosenbaum's stories have been nominated for the Hugo, Nebula, BSFA, Sturgeon, and World Fantasy Awards, translated into 25 languages, and adapted as a SXSW Best Animated Short and a Sick Flick Chicks Best Sci Fi Film. He lives near Basel, Switzerland. *The Unraveling* is his first novel.

FASCINATED BY FEAR: INTERVIEW WITH HORROR QUEENS MEG HAFDAHL & KELLY FLORENCE

BY J.T. MORSE

> *"As the author himself [Stephen King] said, "Fiction is the truth inside the lie." It is this intersection of both his believable, empathetic characters and his fictional, often paranormal horror that makes him the true master." —* from *The Science of Stephen King* (Skyhorse, October 2020)

Most successful collaborations hinge on mutual respect, continuity of vision, and a balance of skillsets. But for tag-team horror writers Meg Hafdahl and Kelly Florence, authors of *The Science of* series of books from *Skyhorse Publishing,* one ingredient seems more necessary than any others: an utter and lifelong fascination with fear. Set all trepidations aside as we venture into conversation with these intriguing writer-scientists to learn more about their collaborative work penning books about the bizarre and wicked world of scary storytelling.

Interstellar Flight Press: Why horror? What draws you to write about death, darkness, fear, and torture—and the people who create stories of this nature? Note: There is no judgmental tone to this question, strictly bewilderment, awe, and raw curiosity.

Meg Hafdahl: Horror is something I've been naturally drawn to since childhood. It is high stakes, in which the character has to rely on their hidden strengths or smarts to survive, and that is appealing as both a writer and fan! I think it is human nature to be interested in what bumps in the night, whether real or imagined.

Kelly Florence: Ever since I was young, I've had a fascination with scary stories. I sought out books in the library and movies from the video store that featured monsters or creepy tales. Horror makes me feel something!

IFP: Having studied various horror-producing mediums—books, film, television, etc.—are there elements to good horror storytelling that transcend the medium and are essentially universal?

MH: Oh yes, I think empathy is an integral element to horror storytelling. These characters are going through the worst experience of their fictional lives, and as the audience, we should want them to prevail. That is the same in any medium and any genre.

KF: I believe we need to care about someone or something in the story. It could be a complicated character or a misunderstood monster.

IFP: Seeing as your most recent releases both have the word 'science' in them—*The Science of Stephen King: The Truth Behind Pennywise, Jack Torrance, Carrie, Cujo, and More Iconic Characters from the Master of Horror* and *The Science of Women in Horror: The Special Effects, Stunts, and True Stories Behind Your Favorite Fright Films* —have you started using the title Dr.? If so, kudos; we'd love to know more about how and why science is vital to your work. If not, why not?

MH: Ha! You know, I was initially reluctant to write from a scientific viewpoint because my background is in literature, but Kelly and I wanted to present science for people like us; those who aren't experts but want to know more. It was vital that we write these books in an approachable way as well as include interviews with people (like real doctors!) who know science and can help break down concepts for us and our readers.

KF: This is a different way to look at the genre; through the lens of science. Truth can be scarier than fiction!

IFP: Outside of being literary horror scientists—since the release of your first science-series book: *The Science of Monsters: The Truth about Zombies, Witches, Werewolves, Vampires, and Other Legendary Creatures* in 2019—what do your lives look like?

MH: I am a horror fiction writer; my first collection of short stories was published in 2015, so my soul has been taken over by horror for quite some time! The chance to bounce between fiction and nonfiction has been such a fun, challenging experience.

KF: I teach full time at Lake Superior College, and Meg and I collaborate on our creative writing projects as well as our Horror Rewind podcast.

IFP: Ready to get really personal? Here's where the real horrors will be brought into the light. What is your favorite and least favorite thing about collaborating with one another? Don't hold back. Now is the time to air that dirty laundry, ladies.

MH: Oh no! Well, my favorite aspect is sharing in the experience. Kelly and I have been able to present our books everywhere from a comedy club in NYC to huge Comic Cons. Having my best friend by my side makes the success sweeter. My least favorite? When Kelly has a brilliant idea that I wish I had come up with!

KF: My favorite is that we seem to share a brain! We have trust and can be honest with each other. Least favorite is our distance. I like to hop on and get things done quickly while Meg is more thoughtful. It's a good balance though!

IFP: Since *The Science of Stephen King* is your most recent release, give us your favorite line from the book.

MH: *As the author himself [Stephen King] said, "fiction is the truth inside the lie." It is this intersection of both his believable, empathetic characters and his fictional, often paranormal horror that makes him the true master.*

KF: In our research for *The Stand*, we discovered that a doctor in Minnesota told his patients to eat squirrel soup to cure the 1918 flu. (Yuck!)

IFP: Let's shift from the bookshelf to the podshelf for a minute. Tell us what we need to know about your podcast *Horror Rewind*.

MH: We started *Horror Rewind* as an experiment. We wanted to see if the horror movies from our childhood were actually good or if we had remembered them wrong! Kelly deserves all the credit for the podcast, she works hard to edit, plan, and promote it. I just show up and talk horror!

KF: It started as a way to re-watch our favorite horror movies from childhood and see if they lived up to our memories of them. It shifted into analyzing new films, books, and television series and still watching movies from the past.

IFP: What's next on the horror horizon for you—individually and/or collaboratively—and where can we find your books?

MH: I have my third collection of horror stories coming out in October 2021, and *The Science of Serial Killers,* by us both, will also be coming out in October 2021! And I have a new collaboration for a series of novels coming up that I'm excited about. Kelly and I also collaborate on horror scripts, so screenwriting has been a thrilling new adventure.

KF: Our next book is *The Science of Serial Killers*, out in October 2021. We are working on other projects together as well.

A huge thank you to Meg and Kelly for taking time out of their busy lives to share a bloody smidge of themselves with our Interstellar Flight Magazine readership. Until next time, this is JT Morse saying, "Stay weird, consume copious amounts of spec fic, and get out from under the covers, you scaredy cats, it's fiction . . . mostly."

ABOUT THE AUTHORS

Horror and suspense author **Meg Hafdahl** is the creator of numerous stories and books. Her fiction has appeared in anthologies such as *Eve's Requiem: Tales of Women, Mystery and Horror and Eclectically Criminal.* Her work has been produced for audio by The Wicked Library and The Lift, and she is the author of two popular short story collections including *Twisted Reveries: Thirteen Tales of the Macabre.* Meg is also the author of the two novels; *Daughters of Darkness* and *Her Dark Inheritance* called "an intricate tale of betrayal, murder, and small-town intrigue" by Horror Addicts and "every bit as page turning as any King novel" by RW Magazine.

Kelly Florence is a communication instructor at Lake Superior College in Duluth and the creator and co-host of the Horror Rewind podcast as well as the producer and host of the podcast Be A Better Communicator. She received her B.A. in theatre at the University of Minnesota-Duluth and her M.A. in communicating arts at the University of Wisconsin-Superior.

REBIRTH FROM THE SEA: AN INTERVIEW WITH AKUA LEZLI HOPE, AUTHOR OF OTHERWHERES

BY T.D. WALKER

> *"Speculative poetry can re-engage wonder and commitment, it can illuminate and enchant; it can transport within while it journeys to an elsewhere. Speculative poetry may defend and serve. I am stunned by wonder and extol its myriad manifestations. I am stung by denials and dismissals, and I chafe against them; I protest, rebuke and rebel."*

Akua Lezli Hope's *Otherwheres* (*ArtFarm Press*, October 2020) features poems that explore the themes of change, rebirth, and the power of speculative poetry to create new narratives that give readers a deeper and more complex view into lives that popular culture often portrays in damaging tropes. Hope's book was nominated for the SFPA 2021 Elgin Awards. (Update: This book won the Elgin Award! Congrats Akua!)

T.D. Walker spoke with Hope about her chapbook as well as about her other speculative poetry projects. Hope curates and hosts the Speculative Sunday Poetry Reading Series. More information about the series can be found at https://www.speculativepoetry.com/

Interstellar Flight Press: You begin your collection with "Dragon," a poem about defying expectations and correcting what we thought we knew about dragons. They are not "winged alligators" as the popular conception of them tends to be, but instead are "equine and feline," delight in nature, and ultimately, feel compelled to act on "some cause we think just." They are complex and humane in ways that popular culture doesn't always honor.

Why did you choose this poem to begin your book? And if we read this poem as a larger commentary about speculative poetry, what expectations about the genre do you seek to defy and correct?

Akua Lezli Hope: For the reasons your insightful question alludes to—because it sets the questioning tone of what is deemed other, it challenges the prevalent misapprehension of its nature. Popular culture doesn't honor me, every truth about me is twisted, thwarted, subverted. The powerful entity is generative and introspective—as speculative poetry can be. Let's assert the positive rather than enumerate the negative.

Speculative poetry can re-engage wonder and commitment, it can illuminate and enchant; it can transport within while it journeys to an elsewhere. Speculative poetry may defend and serve. I am stunned by wonder and extol its myriad manifestations. I am stung by denials and dismissals, and I chafe against them; I protest, rebuke and rebel.

Speculative poetry may serve fierce counter-narratives with joy, aplomb, stealth and humorous transgression.

IFP: One theme your poems come back to again and again is the idea of birth and, poignantly, rebirth. We witness the eggs at the end of "Dragon," the true origin of Athena in "METIS EMITS," and the children the speaker considers and prevents in "Ignorance, my prophylactic." The subject of "My Dead Friend's Daughter" ends up "homeless on the moon" without her mother. And there is the motherlessness in "Sisko."

There is rebirth from water in "Five Times More," "As Yemayaah," and "Mysticeti." Finally, we see the transformation we see in the speaker of the final poem, "Eating Verse."

Did you have this theme of rebirth in mind as you were writing the poems for this collection? If so, did it have a role in guiding your ordering of the poems as you did for the book?

ALH: My deep appreciation again, for noticing and noting. Rebirth is an ongoing concern of mine as a human entity in the anthropocene. We must change. Everything must change. (Yes, I love that song as sung by Nina Simone.) I heard someone remark wryly about our hubris to call our planet Earth, when most of it is water. We must mother change and give birth to new selves and new ways of being. On Ordering, ahhh t'was most painful. Where to begin, Where to end? I struggled and surrendered. The small collection was longer, but less . . . musical for want of a better word. So a short, intense journey, a start with a declaration and an end with a summation.

IFP: One poem that really intrigued me, both on its own and in its place in the book, is "Sisko." I read it first as an ode to the compelling character of Captain Sisko of Star Trek: Deep Space Nine, in which you conclude "you modeled, / captain, our captain, most of all, love."

Returning to the poem on rereading the book, I viewed it through the lens of the collection as a whole and appreciated the water references. For example, Sisko will "string the pearl of moments together // polish each shell sprung irritant". Later, "ever widening rings" of space evoke ripples on the surface of water. We see him "watering [his] sapling son."

What was the origin of this poem? And how would you like your readers to see this poem in light of the others in the book?

ALH: Thank you. I had long wanted to write a praise song about Captain Sisko, the character informed by his African American-ness and what we learn is another hybridity—one that is both literal and metaphoric,—he is half star being. Sisko, and Brooks to whom it's dedicated, were both born here on Earth, the water planet. He is a duality of roots and wings, earth and sky, past and future and now. A human being who played a human/being . . . an entity awakening to its fullness, soul having an experience in a particular body, a body like my father's and grandfathers'.

His journey is a spiritual one as well as a managerial/diplomatic career arc; and this and so many bits of him we learn over the years of voyaging, strategy, war, grief, and growth, had such deep resonance for me. I deeply admire the actor who embodied this portrayal, who I first saw off Broadway, before he was ever on television. So the poem had multiple, connected inspirations. In this poem, as in Noragami, I talk about the greater insights that the experience of watching gave me, I try to re/present some of the details to point readers who may also have watched these shows toward what I found there.

IFP: I'd like to change course for a moment and ask about the Speculative Poetry Reading Series you curate and host. What prompted

you to organize this reading series? And what do you envision for it?

ALH: ConZealand (2020's World Science Fiction Convention, held virtually) blew my mind, taught me a lot, opened my heart. It was the first Con I ever attended. I didn't sleep for days which put me in a state of altered consciousness as it was summer here, long days of light and warmth. It lit a fire under me—all these fabulous creators all over the world—voices and minds singing out. The emphasis was on prose but there was a thrilling moment of poetry. I went to colleagues who ignored and reviled my suggestion that we engage in presenting speculative poetry, so I started the Speculative Sundays Poetry Reading Series to create the occasion for speculative poetry to be presented with regularity, to have the platform and exposure that other artforms have.

I was surprised at both the silence/withholding and the vitriol, but I am proud that I was strong enough to be undeterred. There has been success not only in individual moments, but in their aftermath—people can listen to an array of voices and poems. There is a conversation with the poet about themselves and the work after their reading, so they get to comment on their work, their process, some of their concerns. Those recordings form an archive, a sampling of the living creators of speculative poetry.

IFP: Are there speculative poetry collections that explore the same themes as *Otherwheres* does that you'd like to recommend to readers of *Interstellar Flight Magazine*?

ALH: I'm wrapping up work on NOMBONO which means vision (but also reads like good name/word), a BIPOC anthology of speculative poetry to be published by Sundress Publications. I won the opportunity in a competition that they held. I'm seeing a lot of work from folks around the old who have had such similar thoughts—an indigenous woman who writes about whale reincarnation, an South African who writes about being the "monster"and as of this writing, work is pouring in for the *Eye To the Telescope* that I'm editing on The Sea, so I m buoyed and comforted by all these kindred spirits.

ABOUT THE AUTHOR

Akua Lezli Hope is a creator and wisdom seeker who uses sound, words, fiber, glass, metal, and wire to create poems, patterns, stories, music, sculpture, adornments, peace and change. She wrote her first speculative poems in the sixth grade and has been in print every year since 1974. She is published in numerous literary magazines and national anthologies. A third generation African Caribbean New Yorker, her honors include the National Endowment of the Arts fellowship, two New York Foundation of the Arts fellowships, a SFPA award, several Rhysling and Pushcart Prize nominations, among other scholarships and grants. She twice won Rattle's Poets Respond. Her first collection, *Embouchure, Poems on Jazz and Other Musics,* won the Writer's Digest book award. A Cave Canem fellow, her collection, *Them Gone*, was published 2018. She launched Speculative Sundays, an online poetry reading series in 2020. She won editorship of *Nombono*, an anthology of speculative poems by BIPOC creators, to be published in fall 2021 by *Sundress Publications*. Her micro chapbook of scifaiku, *Stratospherics*, is in the Quarantine Public Library. A paraplegic, she founded a paratransit nonprofit. Her chapbook, *Otherwheres* (*ArtFarm Press* 2020), is nominated for a 2021 Elgin award. An avid hand papermaker and crochet designer with over 130 patterns published, she exhibits her artwork regularly. She sings songs from her favorite anime in Japanese, practices her soprano saxophone, cajoles an indifferent cat and prays for the cessation of suffering for all sentience.

PIRATES, FANGIRLS, AND SAILOR MOON: INTERVIEW WITH SAM MAGGS, AUTHOR OF TELL NO TALES: PIRATES OF THE SOUTHERN SEAS

BY J.D. HARLOCK

"No one in these industries would make it anywhere without someone being willing to hold out a hand and teach them and help them grow."

The Toronto Star calls Sam Maggs the "ambassador of the Canadian fan culture scene," but that title betrays the versatile talent behind some of the biggest franchises around. She first came to prominence following the publication of her acclaimed book The Fangirl's Guide to the Galaxy, and since then, she's dabbled in everything from writing comics to co-founding her own video game studio. Her first original graphic novel (co-created with Kendra Wells), *Tell No Tales: Pirates of the Southern Seas (Abrams,* 2021), is out now and available for purchase. It follows a fictionalized Anne Bonny and her adventures on the high seas as a new enemy has her and her trusty crew on the run.

INTERSTELLAR FLIGHT PRESS: What inspired you to write this? What comics/films/books/TV shows did you have in mind?

SAM MAGGS: I previously wrote a non-fiction book about women in history called *Girl Squads* (*Quirk Books*, 2018), and I dedicated one chapter to the real-life story of Anne Bonny and Mary Read. And when I finished writing it, I was so taken by her story that I knew it was perfect for a comic. I was inspired by comics like *Zodiac Starforce* and anime like *Sailor Moon*—and, of course, *Pirates of the Caribbean!*

IFP: Why was Anne Bonny chosen as the main character (as opposed to a fictional creation)? What drew you to her?

SM: I've written so much historical non-fiction in my time as an author that I'm really drawn to grounding fictional stories in real and relatable history. My hope is that people will read *Tell No Tales* and then want to go and do research about who these actual people were (or were inspired by). Broadening historical horizons through fiction!

IFP: How'd the collaboration with Kendra Wells come about?

SM: One day not long after finishing writing on *Girl Squads*—including all my research and work on Anne Bonny's story—I saw my old friend Kendra Wells completely coincidentally tweet about how much they love Anne Bonny and why hasn't anyone made a book about her yet? It was like fate. I immediately hopped into their DMs and the rest, as they say, is history!

IFP: You used to write nonfiction before you moved into comics. What lured you into comics writing?

SM: When I started writing for comics I was actually already working full-time as a video game writer, and I found that writing fiction was a lot more fun for me and the direction I wanted to take my career. Plus, I was a huge comics fan; I'd been reading religiously since college and it's really my favorite storytelling medium. I was contacted by a wonderful comic book editor, Sarah Gaydos—now EIC at Oni, but at the time an editor at IDW—and she basically walked me through the whole process of pitching and writing a comic for the first time (*Star Trek*), and I'm so grateful. No one in these industries would make it anywhere without someone being willing to hold out a hand and teach them and help them grow.

IFP: After writing for IDW and Oni Press for the past five years, why've you now chosen to work on an original idea?

SM: I absolutely love writing IP (eg. for other peoples' existing characters), and the majority of the work I do—be it in games, comics, or novels—is in IP. That being said, I was ready for a change! It felt both exciting and nerve-wracking to come up with brand-new characters, just Kendra and me on our own without decades of history behind them. It ended up being so rewarding. *Tell No Tales* is the project I am most proud of, of anything I've worked on.

IFP: Any more plans for the spectacular sirens of the southern seas?

SM: Keep your fingers crossed! If you want to see more, leave us a review or let Abrams know!

IFP: Any other original graphic novels you're working on at the moment?

SM: I've got a couple burgeoning ideas in the works . . . I'll keep you updated!

ABOUT THE AUTHOR

Sam Maggs is a bestselling author of books, comics, TV, and video games. She's written for games like Spider-Man PS4; is the author of young adult and middle-grade books like *The Unstoppable Wasp: Built on Hope* and *Con Quest!* and a comics writer for titles like *Tell No Tales, Captain Marvel,* and *My Little Pony*. She is also an on-air host for networks like *Nerdist*. A Canadian in Los Angeles, she misses Coffee Crisp and bagged milk. Follow her on Twitter @SamMaggs or check out her website: https://www.sammaggs.com/.

THE ENDURING POWER OF HERITAGE: AN INTERVIEW WITH BRYAN THAO WORRA, LAO MINNESOTAN POET LAUREATE AND PRESIDENT OF THE SCIENCE FICTION POETRY ASSOCIATION

BY CHRISTINA SNG

Bryan Thao Worra is the Lao Minnesotan Poet Laureate and the author of 10+ books. He holds over 20 national and international awards for his writing and community leadership. He is the President of the Science Fiction and Fantasy Poetry Association and a professional member of the Horror Writers Association. He has presented at the Smithsonian, the London Summer Games, and around the world on the role of the imagination and memory in creative writing as a poet and prose writer, particularly focusing on the creative journeys of Southeast Asians. You can visit him online at http://thaoworra.com. His latest book is *Before We Remember We Dream* from *Sahtu Press* (2020).

Interstellar Flight Press: Tell us about yourself and your Asian influences through your family, your environment, and your heritage and history.

Bryan Thao Worra: Laos is where my journey began, after the Secret War (1961–1973).

Adopted by Americans, I made my way back through myths, verse and histories often obscured by colonial bias, but it was a start for my modest arts, seeking roots, finding more than a few enduring mysteries.

Returning to my former homeland at thirty, I found long-lost family. Our story was one filled with memories of displacement and dreams, once "the Realm of a Million Elephants," there was so much to see.

Transitioning into a democracy, wondering what would be our lasting legacies, secrets lingering like strange vines, a land where poets were the eyes of our cities.

IFP: Are there stories from your history and experience that differ very much from the typical horror we read today?

BTW: Stories in America get solved by guns and prayers, one-stop shop style. The Lao legends remind us it's never quite so easy, caught in our cycles.

One must beware, the simplest methods are traps like a tiger smile, results are rarely lasting, and there's a need to consider our ancient tales: In hundreds of years, humans have remained "the same" for quite a while.

Examining US horror, they like victories and sole survivors who get the girl. Seek a Lao story of Phi? Watch how one right word can make a flood of fears unfurl.

IFP: What is one such story that stands out in your mind?

BTW: Phi might be considered similar to the Japanese Yokai, horrors who haunt in a wide variety of forms with eternal hungers. In your dreams and darkest shadows, they float and crawl and fly.

Kasu are one variety, carnivorous heads and viscera who linger among our deep wilds and city ruins, seeking some nice guy, sometimes unborn babies, but anyone will do. Who knows why.

Usually your only recourse is to flee if you meet such danger.

IFP: Have you translated these stories into fiction? Tell us about these stories.

BTW: Fitting our ghost stories into poems and prose is a strange calling, I suppose. Certain tales of ancient horrors I've shared before. They're often intertwined with books about our bloody civil wars.

In some instances, they're set on the new American shores, our old ghosts adapting with Southeast Asian refugees with unease, nobody certain of the new rules, the memories, the nightmares.

IFP: Do you feel like there is a central thread connecting all our stories? A universal horror, so to speak?

BTW: There are few humans eager to die since the start of time. Surprise! Happiness varies, but none enjoy meeting infinity the hard way.

Read enough and you'll start to see a certain commonality: Everyday people will do almost anything to see another sunrise.

Amid the chaos, they'll fight to get away, some safe place to flee. Destiny, laughing, may have other plans, no matter what you say.

Still, we find heroes and heroines among those who dare "To Be."

IFP: How would you frame your story so that a universal audience could understand and identify with it?

BTW: Fictional framing techniques work until they don't, you'll see. Readers relate in unexpected ways you can barely calculate.

At times it's our "common" need to be happy, endure and thrive, maybe mention what motivates a family, a community with deep veracity.

Except you'll run into some fine souls who seek you precisely because something strange can be found only in the way you make it come alive.

IFP: What are good sources you would personally recommend for readers to learn more about horror in Asia given how diverse cultures in Asia are?

BTW: Look in any good library, for a start, especially among those who live with it every day. So many names to note!

Always remember, curiosity helps an emerging writer's art.

Read voraciously the footnotes and margins in most histories for vital clues nestled inside the drab accounts for outsiders who otherwise choose ignorance of the local beliefs and customs, the rites and mysteries galore.

Never trust just one source, but fearlessly go forth to learn some more!

Good luck! But less grandiose, here's a link to some readings I favor:

https://thaoworra.wordpress.com/2017/12/04/southeast-asian-supernatural-bibliography-in-progress/

HOW HERITAGE AFFECTS THE STORIES WE LIVE AND THE STORIES WE TELL: AN INTERVIEW WITH LEE MURRAY, MULTIPLE AWARD-WINNING AUTHOR OF GROTESQUE: MONSTER STORIES

BY CHRISTINA SNG

Lee Murray is a multi-award-winning author-editor from Aotearoa-New Zealand. Her unique perspective as a Chinese New Zealander has been instrumental in the success of her writing, from her military thrillers to supernatural crime noirs, culminating in her first collection *Grotesque: Monster Stories* (Self Published, 2020) and the birth of *Black Cranes: Tales of Unquiet Women (Omnium Gatherum Media*, 2020), an anthology by women writers of Asian descent, edited alongside Australian-Chinese editor Geneve Flynn. In this interview, Murray talks about her life as a Eurasian in New Zealand and how it has influenced her writing.

Interstellar Flight Press: Tell us about yourself and your Asian influences through your parents, your environment, and your heritage and history.

Lee Murray: I'm a third-generation Chinese New Zealander. One of the first Eurasian babies born to a married couple in this country—not the first but one of the first—I've lived in a kind of shifting no-man's land for more than a half-century.

It's as if I have never been properly Chinese, and nor am I properly Kiwi; my compatriots, still demand to know where I come from, because the assumption is, I must not be from here.

"Go back to China," I've been told. I don't belong there. I don't belong anywhere. Even within my own family, my siblings and I represented the other. Imperfect. Muddied.

However, I've always felt a yearning for Māori stories. There are a lot of shared values and beliefs between the Māori culture of my homeland and the Chinese culture of my heritage: a certain synergy.

Both cultures are founded on the deeds of supernatural ancestors, live by a mandate to protect the natural world, are imbued with a sense of community over individual, and tell simple compelling tales which teach respect and honor.

But there are differences too: where the Chinese have a benevolent dragon bringing prosperity and happiness, the Māori taniwha can be ruthless. In recent years, I've been exploring stories at the intersection of these cultures, perhaps as a stepping-stone to inclusion.

As a child, like my mother before me, I never saw a story that reflected my experience as a Chinese-New Zealander and perhaps that exacerbated my feelings of otherness.

IFP: Are there stories your parents told you or you heard as a child that differ so much from the typical horror stories we frequently encounter?

LM: Like most New Zealanders growing up in the 1970s, my reading tended towards European stories—*Grimm's Fairy Tales,* (so gruesome!), *Tales of the Little Wood*, *Dim the Dragon*, *Peter Pan*, *The Lion, the Witch, and the Wardrobe*—partly due to post-colonial influences on texts available here, and partly perhaps because my European dad was the one who read to us at bedtime.

Dad was a wonderful storyteller in his own right, making up amazing feel-good tales about plucky everyday heroes, like the adventures of the talking frogs who lived in a creek at the bottom of our garden, and the resourceful steampunk inventor whose mission was to save the environment.

I don't recall Mum ever telling us a traditional story as a child—possibly because my siblings and I don't speak Chinese, or perhaps because there were four of us and she was always busy picking up after us—but her life experiences and the cultural pressures that shaped her life have certainly impacted me and my writing, especially in more recent years.

Born in New Zealand, my mother (Pauline) visited China with her mother and her sisters when she was about five (she's 78 now).

Once, while walking to the local school with her sisters, a water buffalo blocked her path, and, tiny thing that she was, she was so terrified of the beast that she leapt into the river to avoid it—despite not being able to swim.

Another time, she visited an outside lavatory and discovered a huge snake, longer than she was tall, coiled on top of the cistern; horrified she backed away, deciding not to go after all.

For a child from New Zealand, where the fauna consists mainly of birds, her terror at encountering these foreign creatures is understandable, and might explain some of my own fascination with creature feature tales.

IFP: That sounds terrifying! I can only imagine it looked like a small dinosaur to her. When I was growing up, the largest animal I saw was a rat bigger than my cat. Needless to say, I am not terribly fond of rats till this day. Of all the Asian horror tales you've heard, what is one such story that stands out in your mind? Have you translated these stories into fiction? Tell us about these stories.

LM: Hungry ghosts have always fascinated me. A pitiful creature with a distended belly, these haunted souls are perpetually hungry but, despite all attempts, they cannot eat.

The ghosts have typically committed some sinful act during their lifetime, often causing harm to the family's reputation. More often than not, hungry ghosts are women, guilty of greed or laziness or some supposed sexual transgression.

Like the Red Riding Hood fable, which served to keep young European women on the path of the good and virtuous, the hungry ghost mythology serves to reinforce expectations of servitude, humility, and purity on Asian women.

I set out to explore these themes in my story 'Frangipani Wishes' in *Black Cranes: Tales of Unquiet Women,* where my character is haunted by the hungry ghosts of her mother, even as she is preyed on by an older man and succumbs to the shameful rejection and betrayal.

The story is inspired by something that occurred in my own family. It also allowed me to draw on the twin harbors of Hong Kong and Wellington, while spinning the tale of a woman's lifetime of suffering.

I've recently written a story called 'The Moon Goddess's Granddaughter' for the Pixel Project anthology *Giving the Devil His Due (Running Wild Press*, 2021), a work which is intended to raise funds and awareness of the issue of domestic violence, and which is due for release in September this year.

For this work, I wrote a contemporary prose-poem recounting the legend of the Asian moon goddess Chang'e through the lens of domestic abuse.

You're probably aware that, in older versions of the tale, Princess Chang'e drinks an elixir of immortality to escape the tyranny of her husband, a former hero, who has become too puffed up with his own importance.

The goddess's pet hare delays her husband's pursuit, allowing her to escape to the moon, where she endures beyond his reach.

For me, this story embodies the experience of abuse survivors, especially Asian women encumbered by expectations of submissiveness and face, for whom escape is a rare recourse and any revenge is likely to be quiet and without violence.

IFP: This is often the case in places with a prevalence of patriarchy where women are regarded as property, of which there are still many in the world, including Asia. Tell us about how this heritage affects women with Asian roots, even those not living in Asia itself.

LM: For Asian women, there is an internal rage that comes from making yourself small, from denying your own needs in the service of others. Quietly and without fuss. Never being allowed to be yourself.

It's as Alma Katsu says in the foreword to *Black Cranes: Tales of Unquiet Women:*

> *"Above all, Asian women are supposed to be submissive. Obedient, invisible, without wants of her own and so content to devote herself to making others happy. This is the expectation that I found hardest. Not that I, for a minute, thought I was supposed to be that person. But I found the mere expectation soul-crushing. That anyone could expect another person to negate themselves, that this was the natural order of things. That anyone would negate themselves voluntarily."*

IFP: That is the life for many women in the world, I believe, probably from the time people owned land. There is anthropological evidence that indicate women had a more egalitarian existence prior to this age but it has died out due to inequality and the instability of societies. Things have changed greatly in the last century but we are all still very much affected by violence against women, especially domestic violence which exists in a place we are meant to feel safe. Given the universality of many of our shared tales and from a unique Asian point of view, how would you frame your stories so that a universal audience can easily identify with it?

LM: Interestingly, the two stories I mentioned earlier are told in a prose-poem style and from the second-person point of view.

Both were intentional choices, literary devices, I thought, which contributed to the flavor and the integrity of the story, but now I wonder if instead that I employed that 'you' and that 'imagery' in order to create a safe distance between myself and the narrative.

A way of revealing a truism, while taking myself out of the story. This is me, or it could be me, but it is also *not* me, which is, of course, is the secret of all good fiction.

IFP: Shh . . . we are not meant to tell . . . ;) What are good sources you would personally recommend for readers to learn more about horror in Asia given how diverse cultures in Asia are?

LM: With *Black Cranes: Tales of Unquiet Women*, my co-editor Geneve Flynn and I clearly identified a gap in the current horror literature; up until that point there had been a scattering of work exploring Asian themes from our colleagues, but only rare compilations of their voices and their stories.

The response to the anthology suggests there was demand for it. And it's not just readers who are hungry for more; since the anthology released, our contributors have mentioned renewed interest in exploring their Asian heritage through fiction.

And what about other Asian cultures? Recently, an Indian reader who'd enjoyed *Black Cranes* asked me why we hadn't included stories from other Asian cultures. Why wasn't there an Indian-Asian version of *Black Cranes*, for example?

There simply wasn't space. But we're delighted that the question was asked because it means we are starting a wider conversation.

ABOUT THE AUTHOR

Lee Murray is a multi-award-winning author-editor from Aotearoa-New Zealand (Sir Julius Vogel, Australian Shadows), and a three-time Bram Stoker Award®-nominee. Her work includes military thrillers, the *Taine McKenna Adventures*, supernatural crime-noir series *The Path of Ra* (with Dan Rabarts), and debut collection *Grotesque: Monster Stories*.

Her latest anthology projects are *Black Cranes: Tales of Unquiet Women*, co-edited with Geneve Flynn, and the AHWA's *Midnight Echo #15*. She is co-founder of Young NZ Writers and of the Wright-Murray Residency for Speculative Fiction Writers, HWA Mentor of the Year for 2019, NZSA Honorary Literary Fellow, and Grimshaw Sargeson Fellow for 2021.

Read more at leemurray.info.

SELF-LOVE, MERMAIDS, & FAIRY TALES: INTERVIEW WITH ISABEL VILLARREAL, AUTHOR OF BROWN CLAY

BY VANESSA MAKI

My intuition has been a dominant guide in my life so one of the strongest messages I felt in the pit of my stomach was to keep writing and hold on to my words because someday I'm going to need them.

B*rown Clay* (Self Published, 2021) unpacks personal experiences on the complexity of love, sex, and identity. Isabel Villarreal's poems are like peeking into her journal. Only she's giving permission. Villarreal is a Black/Latina American queer artist and writer, as well as an online activist for Black, Indigenous, and other POC in the LGBTQ+ community.

INTERSTELLAR FLIGHT PRESS: To me, *Brown Clay* is incredibly ambitious and comes across as quite personal. Almost like the poems are part of pages in your metaphorical journal. Did you always have this vision for the book? Or did it come together over time?

ISABEL VILLARREAL: I knew I was going to compile my poetry together, but I didn't have a clear vision for how it would turn out. My intuition has been a dominant guide in my life so one of the strongest messages I felt in the pit of my stomach was to keep writing and hold on to my words because someday I'm going to need them. As time went on, I jotted down my inner thoughts about my life experiences until one day I knew it was time.

I gathered my work, despite how scattered it was. Poems were on my laptop, my mother's laptop, in random journals from college, folders tucked away in my backpack, and miscellaneous scratch papers shoved in places. I found poems written next to notes I was supposed to be taking in class. When I was looking at them together, seeing the relationships they had with each other, I knew I was ready to write a poetry book. One of my best friends encouraged me to go for it, even if it would be challenging. I knew it was meant to be and I wanted to put my work together in a timeline that would make sense to me and my audience.

IFP: A large portion of your book is like one long love letter. Did it feel cathartic to write to the individual(s) the poems are directed at?

IV: It makes me chuckle to think about how many people I was writing to or about in this book. In a way, it is like a love letter because many poems were indeed expressions of love and yearning. There are many love stories happening in this book; some more tragic than others. In six years, there have been blips, chapters, and memories of the people who have touched my life in some way. Poems dedicated to them were saying both hello and goodbye.

The bigger love story I see the most is the one long love letter to myself. If I can say anything about a cathartic feeling, it was to reach a sense of contentment from letting them go. Knowing I have released these individuals from lingering in an undesirable manner, holding me back from self-acceptance and taking in the truest love I know. It felt cathartic to speak to those who have given me both joy and pain, but I look back on the love I felt and laugh. The greatest love I've ever known is from my inner child. She completes me and always will.

IFP: In "Snow White" the line: *I picked the poisoned apple but you kissed me and stars melted in my mouth* creates such stellar imagery. Do you remember what you were feeling when you wrote the poem?

IV: Before I had written this poem, I was in a place in life where I was starting to open my heart to someone important to me. I had been thinking about the fairytale Snow White. We all know the story. I'm not sure why I was focused on the tale; perhaps I was trying to create meaning to apply to my own experience. I had been feeling nothing for such a long time, romantically speaking, and to begin to trust someone again meant a lot to me.

It was autumn at the time so when I was writing this piece, I saw imagery of apples and trees or anything associated with the harvest. I saw a gloomy forest and clouded sky, yet I felt cozy. I imagined myself sitting under a tree without leaves, reading a book in the most October outfit you can think of. Something about a dark, fall aesthetic felt at home to me as I was processing what to say. I read it now and I see the same imagery. It reminds me of rejuvenation despite the world decaying right in front of me. It's ironic.

IFP: With the poem "I tried", what do you hope Black readers take from it?

IV: First I want to say: This poem is one of the most vulnerable poems in *Brown Clay.* Not only does it address the events that have happened to the Black community, especially last year during the height of the Black Lives Matter movement, but it addresses the exhaustion, mourning, and pain felt throughout our Black community. We were and still are exhausted.

This poem is not a reminder of what took place, but a catalyst to release those feelings that are often a struggle to talk about or accept. This poem was about processing the trauma taking place on a daily basis, wrestling with wanting to give up, grieve, accepting my anger, and remembering my humanity.

Oftentimes I struggle with these feelings because I tell myself I can't accept negative emotions or I need to hide them. It's important to give yourself space as a reminder that you are not indestructible. So what do I hope Black readers take from this poem? Their humanity. It's not weakness to vocalize your discomfort, things that affect you or your life, and experiences that bring great sorrow. There is strength in vulnerability. So when people read this poem I hope my Black readers feel they can relate to me but most of all: know when we support each other, we are indestructible.

IFP: Do you have a favorite poem or poems?

IV: My favorite poems are "Holy Body," "The Healing Mermaid," "Afro Garden," and "Venom". They have no relation to each other and they have different themes, but they all hold significant meaning to me. "Holy

Body" has anatomy and spirituality embedded in the visuals using dream-like language. "The Healing Mermaid" is a letter to my shadow self who carries trauma, hurt, and anger. The beach is one of my favorite places on earth and I associate it with beautiful memories from my childhood. To go to a healing place such as the sea and cleanse the heaviness is a cathartic feeling. "Afro Garden" is a poem about self-love for Black hair. Lastly, "Venom" was meant to be a powerful mic drop that flows like spoken word. It was fun to write and a wonderful outlet for self-empowerment.

IFP: Have you always enjoyed combining your visual art with your poems? Your artwork is quite consistent throughout.

IV: Thank you! I have always loved this combination. I admire Anne Carson's translations of Sappho's fragments and the style of this dream-like, soft, artistic way of speaking. It stuck with me and has become my default way of explaining the world through my eyes. In college, I had professors and mentors who tried to show me how to restrain it but I am a persistent person! It has always felt natural to me and I've been writing like this ever since I started. Being a visual learner, I have gravitated towards understanding the world when I can see it in front of me or in my head. Having a vivid imagination has its perks so it has been a wonderful asset to the way I address ideas, metaphors, and symbolism. Art is subjective, so why not have fun with it?

IFP: What message would you like to give to your readers?

IV: First, I am grateful for all the support and for reading my poetry! My main goal is for people to enter a dreamscape of self-discovery. My hope is for people to relate to these themes of self-love, liberation, identity, healing from trauma, and more. I wish for my readers to start or continue their own goals in personal growth and reclaiming freedom in whichever way it applies. It is my aspiration to empower others, especially over their own intersectional identities or healing the shadows from the past if it applies. I truly hope everyone who purchases a copy has a visceral experience and is inspired by new possibilities.

IFP: Do you have anything else in the works? Any work coming out this summer?

IV: I plan on writing another poetry book! I already have a title and book cover for it. It won't be out anytime soon because I have to write it first! I have written a few poems here and there but I am more focused on catching up with painting. I am currently working on a commission piece for a friend and I plan on creating more artwork centered on celestial Black women and more. Acrylic painting is another form of expression for me to connect with themes of self-love, empowerment and Black liberation. I am selling prints of my paintings on my online INPRNT shop! Sharing my art with the world is something I've been wanting to do since I was a teenager so it makes me incredibly happy to look back and see where I've come from and where I'm at currently. I have exciting things to look forward to with my artistic journey so stay tuned!

ABOUT THE AUTHOR

Isabel Villarreal is a Black/Latina American queer artist and writer. This collection has themes of identity, self-love, sex, relationships, trauma, and healing through the lens of Black liberation and empowerment. Isabel, she/her pronouns, is an online activist for Black, Indigenous, and other POC in the LGBTQ+ community, Black Lives Matter, and mental health. She creates digital infographics, social media protests, and tags for the community. She is deeply committed to social change and representation. This is her first poetry book and she hopes her work will resonate. Follow along on this journey of self-discovery through spirituality and dream-like imagery. Visit her website: https://www.isabelvillarreal.net/.

QUEER ROMANCE, SELKIES, AND FOLKLORE: INTERVIEW WITH MOLLY OSTERTAG, AUTHOR AND ILLUSTRATOR OF THE GIRL FROM THE SEA

BY J.D. HARLOCK

> *"Queer love is transformative. It illuminates parts of yourself you never knew were there."*

Known for her webcomic Strong Female Protagonist and her first graphic novel, *The Witch Boy (Graphix,* 2017), Molly Ostertag is an acclaimed American cartoonist whose work seeks to represent the best of the queer experience. In 2020, Forbes Magazine named Molly one of their 30 under 30, and her acclaimed forays into the worlds of animations and comics have more than earned her that honor. Her new graphic novel *The Girl from the Se*a (*Graphix*, June 1, 2021) follows a Morga, a Korean Canadian teen, that falls in love with a selkie named Keltie in Nova Scotia.

INTERSTELLAR FLIGHT PRESS: What were some of the artistic/literary inspirations behind *The Girl from the Sea*?

MOLLY OSTERTAG: I'm having trouble putting my finger on anything specific. I love romance movies and books, in theory, but often I get frustrated with the fact that characters don't get together until the end! I like seeing the drama of an actual relationship rather than just the buildup of will-they-won't-they, so this was my attempt to make a story like that.

What else?

There are some fashion designer plotlines that are inspired by watching too much *Project Runway: Junior.* Anyone who knows me knows I'm obsessed with *The Lord of the Rings* and Sam Gamgee's relationship to Frodo, so there's some of that devotion in Keltie. And the germ of the story came from a three-page comic I made back in art school about a selkie and a human girl.

Like every book, it's a weird mix of personal experience, random sources of inspiration, and the all-powerful drive of not finding stories you resonate with and so having to make them yourself!

IFP: Why have you chosen to tell this story? Where'd you get the idea from? How has your life fed into the story?

MO: The setting came first—my parents are both teachers and had summers off, so we would spend all summer on Wilneff Island in Nova Scotia when I was a kid. It was magical, this place outside normal life, a place with a giant sky and endless ocean and incredible natural beauty where anything felt possible.

But it was also very lonely. My little sister started having intense emotional issues, and there weren't any other kids my age. There was no internet or TV (not even plumbing!). But I had a sort of fantasy—there was this pod of seals who lived on a reef nearby, and I would imagine that they could turn into people and be my friends. It was remembering this feeling of lonely, imaginative yearning that gave me the heart of this book.

I knew I wanted to make something for a slightly older audience than my previous work on the *Witch Boy* trilogy. I wanted to tell a story about first love and coming out. I wanted to tell a specifically gay story, drawing on my own experience.

I didn't want to rely on homophobia to provide drama, but I did want to explore the fears I felt around coming out, especially at Morgan's age. The drama in the story comes from how it's scary to declare yourself as something, from the desire to be private versus the desire to be openly yourself. Coming out means being known and being vulnerable. Even if your friends and family are accepting, it's still scary!

And of course, I wanted to make a love story! Queer love is transformative. It illuminates parts of yourself you never knew were there. I wanted to write the teen summer romance with a girl that I never had.

IFP: So why is Keltie a selkie as opposed to a mermaid or a siren?

MO: So, to share selkie lore in case not everyone is familiar: they're a Scottish legend. The classic selkie story is about a woman who lives in the ocean in the form of a seal, but can come onto land and shed her seal skin to appear human. A human man usually steals the seal skin, meaning she must marry him. She becomes a dutiful wife and loving mother to their children, but yearns for the sea—and when she eventually discovers where he hid her seal skin, she takes it and returns to the ocean, abandoning her human family.

I love the bittersweetness of selkie stories—the mystery and grief of losing someone to the sea, something that all coastal communities have folklore about. I love how they're torn between the land and the sea. I love that, unlike many legends of supernatural romance, they are not malicious to humans. And I love the physicality of them. When you spot seals in the wild, it's easy to see human intelligence in their eyes, easy to imagine the human just under the skin.

There's also a violent, patriarchal theme of stealing the selkie's agency and forcing her to become a wife. When telling a sapphic selkie story, I knew I wanted to reinterpret that. Gay romance is not just straight romance with same-sex characters—it is its own thing. It was important to me that (minor spoilers) Keltie come on land of her own volition and important that Morgan give her back her seal skin when she asks for it.

IFP: Do you see yourself (or even other people) in Morgan and Keltie?

MO: Morgan definitely captures a specific time in my teenage life, when acknowledging an attraction to girls would have been really inconvenient, so I just pushed it down. I thought that I could be exactly who everyone else needed me to be, and thought I could make everything in my life work without acknowledging that side of myself. It turns out this is not how anything works!

Keltie is a little closer to who I am now—I do feel that coming out allowed me to be freer with my emotions, more vulnerable, and kinder. Their relationship is a bit based on me getting together with my wife. There were a lot of external obstacles to our relationship, but the force drawing us together was more powerful than anything else.

IFP: Do you plan to revisit these characters in future installments?

MO: Not presently. Their story has a full arc and I'm a fan of stories finding their natural end! But I do love drawing them, so maybe there will be some short comics in the future.

IFP: Do you think that readers have embraced sapphic romances, or is there still a long way to go? Are there any speculative sapphic romances you're particularly fond of?

MO: I definitely think they've been embraced by readers. Personally, I would love to see more romances with gender nonconforming and butch lesbians. Butch lesbians are such an important part of our community, but I rarely see them represented in media (I'm holding myself accountable with this for future projects). One great exception to this is the *Locked Tomb* series by Tasmyn Muir (*Tordotcom*, 2020), which I've been loving. It's about a weird far future with necromancy, spaceships, and a really dynamic central relationship between a sword-wielding jock and the deeply broken necromancer she took a vow to protect.

IFP: Any other interesting projects you're working on at the moment?

Nothing I can talk about (imagine me looking very mysterious as I say this). I am working on something big though, and I hope to be able to share it in the future!

ABOUT THE AUTHOR

Molly Ostertag is an Igntaz and Prism Award winning graphic novelist, 30 Under 30 Forbes scholar, and a writer for children's TV animation. She currently lives in Los Angeles, where she's worked as a designer on the show *Star vs. the Forces of Evil* (Disney TVA) and as a writer for *Thundercats Roar* (Warner Bros.) and the *The Owl House* (Disney TVA).

Her middle-grade graphic novel debut, ***The Witch Boy,*** came out in 2017 from Scholastic, and is being adapted into a feature film by Netflix. It's followed by the sequel *The Hidden Witch* in 2018 and NY Times bestseller The *Midwinter Witch* in 2019. Her next book, *The Girl From The Sea*, will come out June 1, 2021.

She illustrated the webcomic *Strong Female Protagonist* with writer and friend Brennan Lee Mulligan (currently on hiatus).

Interests include: cats, gay stuff, hobbits, and cooking for her wife. Follow her on Twitter @MollyOstertag for important updates on these subjects.

FIGHTING THE PATRIARCHY, MYTHS, AND POETRY: INTERVIEW WITH LYNNE SARGENT, AUTHOR OF A REFUGE OF TALES

BY T.D. WALKER

I think that part of the joy of poetry is that it can reflect the full complexity of our emotions. Sometimes it's a rallying call, and sometimes it's a soothing balm, and sometimes it's just an "I'm tired today."

In *Refuge of Tales* (*Renaissance Press,* 2020), Lynne Sargent explores the idea of creating shelter against patriarchal society through their collection of speculative poems. T.D. Walker spoke with Sargent about their book, which has been nominated for the SFPA 2021 Elgin Awards.

Interstellar Flight Press: Your collection, *A Refuge of Tales*, reads as one of defiance, specifically women enduring in spite of their treatment by a patriarchal society. Their voices call out even as they are faced with death.

Was this theme one you chose before writing the poems for the book, or did it emerge organically from the subjects you wanted to explore? How do you want your readers to view this theme in light of your poems?

Lynne Sargent: This was definitely a theme I started with. The original working title for the manuscript was the title of the first section—"A Myth of Women." As I kept going I realized though that wasn't enough though. I think that the patriarchy is intimately wrapped in a lot of other violence that happens such as capitalistic violence against the unhoused, violence against queer folks, colonialism and Western wars-by-proxy, among other things. The work grew from there into the general way our myths and cultural stories are used implicitly as tools of domination and need to be subverted and cast off. I think what are traditionally considered to be feminine ethics of care are a great way to go about that subversion.

IFP: One of the poems that fascinated me most as a reader is "Third," which I read as a reference to Third Wave Feminism. Among the poems of defiance, this one shifts readers to a place of hope, given the poem's ending: "This wave is not for drowning, / This wave will bear me home."

Do you think that this belief in a possible better "home" is the end result of defiance we see in the speakers of other poems?

LS: Thank you for noticing this! Yes, for me home is something we can find when we work at defying violence. I also think though it's something we can arrive at when we listen to stories, especially to those whose stories have not yet been told, and stories from those who have fought the good fight before us, even if those stories might need interrogation too. Feminism has come in waves because we keep finding gaps, and I think that's always going to be true. Home for me is something we have to be continually working towards if it's going to be a welcoming home for all those who need it.

IFP: Another poem that struck me as particularly poignant is "Vast, Uncountable Things." Again, there's a sense of getting someplace better, but in this case, the end goal is thwarted by the fact that "[. . .] our planet blew up, / both of them- / the Old Country, and the New[.]"

Even if the speaker and her shipmates are never able to find a new home planet, still they move forward. Given the larger context of the book, do you think we, in the present time, have lost sight of a possible more equitable and feminist society?

LS: This is something I go back and forth on. I think that part of the joy of poetry is that it can reflect the full complexity of our emotions. Sometimes it's a rallying call, and sometimes it's a soothing balm, and sometimes it's just an "I'm tired today." This poem was definitely written on a day when I was tired and I wanted to write something that accepted that hope looks different for different people at different times. I don't think

I've lost hope, and I don't think we should lose hope, But some days hope looks different than on other days and that's okay. I think we've all been going through a difficult period lately and it's okay if the hope we have is just getting through the day and looking forward to bed at the end of it. We can have hope that more ambitious hopes will return, and I do have that hope.

IFP: Are there speculative poetry collections that explore the same themes as yours that you'd like to recommend to readers of Interstellar Flight Magazine?

LS: Am I allowed to recommend one of your books? I really, deeply enjoyed *Twelve* by Andrea Blythe earlier last year. It excavates those secret lives that women lead by necessity and is also interested in subverting a classic fairy tale. Another one is *The Animal Bridegroom* by Sandra Kasturi. It's a collection I've loved for years and was definitely a big influence when I was engaged in the writing process, though I have some complicated feelings about that now given more recent news about her publishing imprint and would encourage folks to do their own research on the author if they're interested in picking it up.

ABOUT THE AUTHOR

Lynne Sargent is a writer, aerialist, and philosophy Ph.D candidate currently studying at the University of Waterloo. They are the assistant poetry editor at Utopia Science Fiction magazine, and their work has been nominated for Rhysling and Aurora Awards. Their work has appeared in venues such as *Augur Magazine, Strange Horizons,* and *Daily Science Fiction*. Their first collection, *A Refuge of Tales* is out now from Renaissance Press. To find out more, visit their website: https://scribbledshadows.wordpress.com/contact/.

JASON ERIK LUNDBERG: AN AMERICAN WRITER IN ASIA

BY CHRISTINA SNG

Christina Sng talks to American editor and writer Jason Erik Lundberg about living and working in Singapore and how his stories have changed since he moved to Southeast Asia

Jason Erik Lundberg is the author and anthologist of over twenty-five books and the biennial *Best New Singaporean Short Stories* anthology series (est. 2013). He is also the fiction editor at *Epigram Books*, where the books he's edited have won multiple awards, and made various year's best lists since 2012, as well as the founding editor of *LONTAR: The Journal of Southeast Asian Speculative Fiction*(2012–2018). His writing has been anthologised widely, shortlisted for multiple awards, honourably mentioned twice in *The Year's Best Fantasy and Horror*, and translated into half a dozen languages.

Interstellar Flight Press: Hi Jason, thanks for being here with us today! You've had a fantastic career as a writer and editor. Tell us a bit about yourself.

Jason Erik Lundberg: I'm an American, and have lived in Singapore for the past fourteen years. I've been writing for as long as I can remember, enjoying just making up stories; after about a decade of getting more serious and submitting my work, I finally saw my first publication in 2003 in a tiny fanzine that was mostly known for showcasing visual art.

I published short stories pretty consistently and regularly after that, and my first collection, *Red Dot Irreal* (Self Published), was published in 2011; each year since then, I've released at least one book, either authored or anthologised by me, and I've been very fortunate to work with some great publishers. My latest book is actually my first novel, *A Fickle and Restless Weapon (Epigram Books*, 2020, which came out last year.

On the editing side, I have been the fiction editor at *Epigram Books* in Singapore since 2012, and many books under my care have won multiple awards, and made various year's best lists.

I also established the ongoing biennial *Best New Singaporean Short Stories* anthology series in 2013 (our fifth volume, guest edited by Balli Kaur Jaswal, will be released in October 2021), as well as *LONTAR: The Journal of Southeast Asian Speculative Fiction*, which ran for 10 biannual issues from 2012–2018.

IFP: How has your writing changed since you've moved from the US to Singapore? How different are the stories you tell?

JEL: I think that the type of stories I tell are the same—humanist, strange and questioning—but my focus has changed.

This actually happened before I moved to Singapore in 2007, after I visited for the first time in 2003. I just fell in love with the place, and a lot of this experience went into my novella, *Diary of One Who Disappeared*, but it also influenced the stories that made up *Red Dot Irreal*.

Shifting my narrative focus from America to Asia has been a mind-broadening action that has benefited me greatly, not least of which has given me a more expansive view of humans themselves; Americans tend to blanketly assume that America = the world (and I was guilty of this as well), and that is simply not the case at all.

Yes, American culture (and in particular pop culture) is highly influential worldwide, but the ways that people live outside of America are variable and multitudinous. I've tried to keep this truth in mind in my fiction.

IFP: Which of your books is your favourite and why?

JEL: I'm always wary of this question, because it's like asking which of your limbs is your favourite!

However, I will say that the book I'm most proud of is my novel (and twenty-fifth book), *A Fickle and Restless Weapon*, which was released in 2020. It's a book that represents 15 years of my life, and went through eight drafts before being set in its finished form.

Prior to starting it, I had always thought of myself as a short story writer; it's a form that I still tremendously enjoy writing and reading. But I always wanted to attempt a longer work.

There were a few false starts with pieces that ended up becoming novelettes instead, but once I hit on the idea for *A Fickle and Restless Weapon* (which, for the longest time, was just called The Tower Novel), I realised that I had something epic enough to warrant a novel, and an invented world that was rich enough for many more stories besides (*Diary of One Who Disappeared* is one of these, which takes place 25 years later).

It took around eight years just to complete the first draft (which, at 130,000 words, was pretty long), writing it during the snatches of free time I could grab, then several more years of revision before I felt like it was ready to submit to publishers.

Once it was accepted by *Epigram Books* (where I also work), I went through final revisions with my former colleague, Eldes Tran, to finish shaping it into something that felt very of the moment. The published edition on bookstore shelves does just what I wanted it to do artistically, and seems to speak to our current situation even more than when I first conceived of the idea.

At the same time, 2020 was just plainly an awful year to release a new book, if you're one of those writers like myself who weren't published by one of the gigantic conglomerates in New York City.

Sales suffered because people were just trying to survive the Covid-19 pandemic, and my novel is admittedly on the strange side. I did as much promotion as I could from home, and was heartbroken when more readers didn't pick it up.

But at the same time, this part of things was always going to be out of my hands; I could only do my best to get the word out there. I'm hoping it'll be one of those titles with a long tail, which maybe didn't make a big splash upon release (though it did receive some great reviews) but will have legs and keep picking up readers a bit at a time through the years.

IFP: As a parent, do you find yourself moulding your stories more to create a more ideal world for your child?

JEL: Somewhat. I've done this more explicitly in my children's picture books, where kindness and compassion are rewarded, and my characters try to understand one another.

My fiction for adults tends to be darker and bad things sometimes happen to my characters, even if they're trying to do good. But this idea of presenting a more ideal world is very much at the forefront of my process for the current book that I'm working on, a new novel, of which I'll go into more detail below.

IFP: How can writers change the world?

JEL: Sometimes I question whether writers can indeed change the world, especially in such divisive and xenophobic times like these.

But fiction in particular is an elegant vehicle for empathy (which the world needs more of right now, desperately), when you enter another person's consciousness to experience the world from their viewpoint. No other media can do this so effectively. So the best way writers can achieve this is through telling their stories, the ones no one else can tell, with as much generosity of heart as they can.

These stories might not sell in the thousands, but with a little luck, they will end up in the hands of the people who need them the most, who will be most moved by what the author has attempted to convey.

IFP: In addition to being a prolific author, you're also an editor for the Singaporean publisher *Epigram Books*. How did you begin your career in editing?

JEL: It actually began when my ex-wife and I formed a small independent press in 2003, called *Two Cranes Press*. We published four books in total, half of which were anthologies. It was the first experience I had with editing another person's writing, and I found that I enjoyed the analytical problem-solving facet of the process.

Then, after moving to Singapore and publishing *Red Dot Irreal*, I pitched an anthology idea that would collect new speculative fiction by Singaporean writers, which ended up becoming *Fish Eats Lion* (Self Published, 2014). So I had some experience as an anthologist, which I later continued as series editor for *Best New Singaporean Short Stories*.

Then, after quitting my teaching job at the end of 2011, and spending the next eight months being a full-time writer (a period of time that was particularly fruitful for my creativity), I was lucky enough to find a job at

Epigram Books, which was looking for an editor to kickstart a new line of original fiction, including novels, short story collections and anthologies.

This being my first time as a book editor, and going through the many-layered process from acquisition to a finished book on store shelves, I felt as though I was thrown into the deep end of the pool and made to teach myself how to swim.

I had a managing editor at that time, and colleagues who could give me advice, but I had to figure out a lot of things on my own, and make mistakes along the way.

Since then, four of my titles have won the Singapore Literature Prize (with an additional six shortlisted), five have won Singapore Book Awards (with an additional eleven shortlisted), four have made *The Straits Times* year's best list, and seven have made *The Business Times* year's best list. So I must be doing something right.

IFP: From your editor's eye, what makes a book good?

JEL: The thing that immediately hooks my attention is a unique voice, not necessarily a unique idea. As mentioned before, each writer out there can offer a singular vision that no one else can, and a big part of that is finding your voice and putting everything you can into that.

It's been said numerous times that every story has already been told (meaning that every *type of plot* has already been told), but that doesn't mean you can't smash two (or more) ideas together to make something interesting.

There are many manuscripts out there that are publishable, and we get a lot of them submitted to our offices. However, there's a massive gap between "publishable" and "good".

Sometimes that involves working with a freelance editor to shape a book before it reaches a publisher (I have done this myself, and highly recommend it), but many times it means writing a lot of different things and learning from each experience.

And sometimes it even means not rushing to publication before a book is ready, and taking the time to really make sure it is artistically saying what you want it to say.

IFP: How could writers polish their work to catch an editor's eye?

JEL: Strangely, polish should maybe not be the end goal. Naturally, the writing itself has to be competent and engaging, but a focus on polishing the writing can instead leave it soulless.

A common complaint over the past twenty-five years or so has been that manuscripts are often overly polished; in other words, they become so sanitised in the effort to appeal to the largest number of people that the words end up dead on the page.

(This comment has been aimed most often at graduates of MFA programmes in creative writing, though it is not always a fair assessment.)

I'm 45 years old and have read a *lot* of books in my lifetime thus far, so a manuscript with some rough edges yet a distinctive take on the world, *sui generis*, will always be more interesting to me as a reader and an editor.

For just one example, one of my favourite writers is George Saunders. No one else writes like this guy. His sentences are often messy and (purposefully) grammatically incorrect, but his prose just *sings*. I recently re-read his collection *Tenth of December*, and constantly marvelled at how invested he made me in his quirky and wonderfully bizarre short stories. He makes you *care*, and this, rather than polish, is what makes his writing so memorable.

IFP: You created an incredible magazine called LONTAR some time ago for the Southeast Asian market. Tell us how that began and your journey with it till it ended.

JEL: It began when I published *Fish Eats Lion*, mentioned above; I was very proud to create a speculative fiction venue for Singaporean writers, one that was taken seriously and which helped to open the floodgates for more fantastical writing in Singapore.

But my ambition had always been to do something for the wider Southeast Asian region, and so *LONTAR: The Journal of Southeast Asian Speculative Fiction* was born. The focus was specifically on fiction and poetry (and later comics) about the region, with a priority on Southeast Asian creators.

I wanted to provide a regular, ongoing place for these writers to send their work, and made the decision to release issues twice a year. It was slow-going at first, and I leaned on many of my writer friends to send me stories and poems, as well as reprinted SEA-focused pieces from already well-known authors such as Paolo Bacigalupi, Dean Francis Alfar and Geoff Ryman.

But then, after that, submissions became a steady stream of quality original writing, and I was able to pick and choose.

Singapore's National Arts Council supported us financially with publication grants starting with #3, and we started selling well enough that I was able to increase contributor payments after the release of #6. But with #7, we were awarded less grant money with no explanation, and then told that #8 would be the final issue NAC would support.

I had started a Patreon for *LONTAR* prior to this revelation, mostly for extras and fun stuff, but then had to scramble in order to make it fund the costs previously taken care of by the grants. And thank goodness for Patreon and for our patrons because, otherwise, #9 and 10 would never have come out.

However, even when I wasn't actively curating an issue or soliciting work, I was constantly fundraising and doing publicity for the journal; it basically took over my entire creative life.

I found that I had much less time and energy for my own writing, and for projects I'd had to put on the back burner. So I announced that #10 would be our final issue. It was a nice round number, and it would be a double-issue, so we could go out with a bang, and on our own terms.

After the shuttering of *LONTAR*, I heard from many people that it had been an important and worthwhile venture, and they were going to miss it. We even got a lovely send-off in *The Straits Times*, which was totally unexpected.

There were times when hearing these post-mortem encomia that I felt frustrated, as in *Where the hell were you people when I was struggling and toiling with the journal just to keep it going?*

But then I had to take a step back and realise that they *had* been there, supporting the journal by buying it or borrowing it from the public library, sharing it with their friends, and taking it into their hearts.

It's a project that I am still immensely proud of, not least of all because we published some early or even first stories and poems by wonderful writers who would go on to create more incredible things.

IFP: What's next in the pipeline for you?

JEL: I'm currently working on my next novel, *One Nine Eight Six*, the next story in my Tinhau Sequence, which takes place five years after the events of *Diary of One Who Disappeared*. I'd had the idea for a while and wrote the first three chapters at the beginning of 2020, but then the Covid-19 pandemic hit and basically stripped away my creative impulses.

Even when things started getting better, I found the novel difficult to return to, and instead buried myself in *Animal Crossing: New Horizons* (which remains an obsession). However, thankfully, in the past month I've been able to come back to it, and make some slow progress once again.

As with *Fickle* and *Diary*, this new novel takes place in Tinhau, featuring a new protagonist and cast of supporting characters.

As a reader, I find it difficult to even start a book series because of the commitment involved (especially if the series is ongoing), so I decided early on that any book taking place within the Tinhau Sequence would be standalone unto itself.

Meaning that anyone can enter the sequence with any book without feeling lost, and get a complete story with a proper resolution; however, if you read them in consecutive order, there are many Easter eggs to delight you, including major characters in one work coming back as secondary characters (or even just cameos) in the next one, and vice versa.

One Nine Eight Six is also a very personal novel, told from the point of view of a girl being raised by a single father, and having to hide her natural fantastical gifts in order to conform and not raise the suspicions of those in charge.

It's about kindness and acceptance in the face of a global culture overwhelmingly represented by greed and self-interest. It's *To Kill a Mockingbird* meets *Firestarter*, and I'm looking forward to seeing where it leads me.

THE TRAILBLAZING MS FLYNN: INTERVIEW WITH GENEVE FLYNN

BY CHRISTINA SNG

Award-winning editor and writer Geneve Flynn led the way in bringing Asian women's horror fiction to the forefront and she won a Stoker for it.

Geneve Flynn is an award-winning speculative fiction editor and author. She has two psychology degrees and only uses them for nefarious purposes. Her short stories have been published all across the globe and she co-edited the Bram Stoker Award-winning anthology *Black Cranes: Tales of Unquiet Women* with Lee Murray (*Omnium Gathum Media*, 2020).

Interstellar Flight Press: Hi Gene, congratulations on your Stoker! It is truly well-deserved. *Black Cranes: Tales of Unquiet Women.* What a groundbreaking anthology! Tell us about its inception.

Geneve Flynn: Thank you! It still doesn't quite feel real.

The anthology came about because Lee Murray and I are both, in some ways, typical conscientious Asians. We were attending GenreCon, the biennial genre convention in Brisbane. Not wanting to be late, we both turned up far too early for a session. I'd known Lee from the Australasian Horror Writers Association, and from Facebook, but we'd never actually met face to face. Lee was browsing some of the author tables and I knew I had to go up and say hello.

We started chatting and discovered that as well as being the typical conscientious Asians, we were also *atypical.* We were literary black sheep: we both write horror, we're both women, and we have Asian heritages. We wondered at the absence (or, at least, the lack of visibility) of stories that reflected our experiences. Lee got a wicked gleam in her eye and suggested that we should put together an anthology to fill the gap. Of course, I agreed. We began searching for Southeast Asian writers of horror and found such a wealth of talent.

IFP: How did you get a publisher interested in *Black Cranes*?

GF: Lee proposed the anthology to Kate Jones at *Omnium Gatherum*, and even though Omnium doesn't do anthologies, Kate came back within a very short time, and said that yes, she wanted it. It was exciting to know that we had enthusiastic support, right from the start.

IFP: Your story "Little Worm" really struck a chord with me and with many readers, judging from the fantastic reviews. What inspired it?

GF: The story is inspired by something I was struggling with at the time. My parents are aging, so the questions around who's responsible for care, and what gets laid at the feet of the daughters in Chinese families, reared up.

I'd intended to write this tale about a daughter who bitterly accepts the responsibility of caring for her ailing mother, but I unearthed the mother's story instead. It became a dark love letter of sorts to Chinese women in families and the sacrifices they make.

IFP: Tell us about the influences that went into "A Pet is for Life."

GF: A friend told me about a time he walked past a mirror, yawning, and it looked like the reflection was screaming. I promised him I'd write a story about that moment. I'd also been watching lots of animal rescue stories, and delving into Asian urban legends. I wanted to explore the idea that a villain can be someone who has a positive quality that's taken to the extreme. I also wanted to do something about the assumption that young Asian women are delicate creatures that can't look after themselves. All of these ideas and concepts swirled around in my brain, and this is what popped out.

IFP: How does your Malaysian-Chinese heritage come into play with these stories?

GF: When I first started writing, it didn't even occur to me to write about my heritage. There was a sense of personal disconnect: I rejected all things Asian because I'd grown up feeling that everything that made me different was wrong, was alien. Apart from a few children's books on Asian myths and watching episodes of *Monkey*, everything else I read or saw was white.

But I've found that my strongest stories stem from personal experiences and I've loved returning to my memories of being a child in Malaysia, and exploring the experience of being part of a diaspora in Australia. Plus, Asian ghosts scare the crap out of me.

IFP: On that note, which is your favorite Asian ghost or monster, and which one scares you the most?

GF: My favorite Asian ghost is probably the pontianak, from Malaysia. I wrote about it in my first professional short story sale, so it has a special place in my heart. The pontianak is the vengeful, vampiric spirit of a woman who died in childbirth, or from a violent death. She's usually depicted as a woman with long, dark hair, wearing a white dress. She preys on men, disembowelling them with her long nails and eating their organs. She looks like a beautiful woman at the front, but when viewed from behind, the bloody hole where her baby was born after death is visible. I particularly like the idea that the pontianak is a feminist icon: she has the agency and power that women often aren't afforded in life.

Pretty scary, but the ghost that frightened me the most when I was little is the jiangshi—the Chinese hopping vampire. A jiangshi is a corpse dressed in official Qing Dynasty garb, that hops after its victims, arms held out stiffly, seeking to suck the qi, or life force, out of its victims. Its skin is often greenish-white due to the mold growing on its decomposing flesh. Jiangshi are thought to originate from the practice of transporting bodies of people who had died far from home. Daoist priests performed a ritual that reanimated the bodies and guided the hopping corpses home. There's just something about a relentless, rotting, undead creature moving in such an unnatural way that has stayed with me for a long time. I recently wrote a story about a jiangshi for an anthology commission. It was a great way to exorcise that demon!

IFP: Having lived in Australia for so long, does it change your Asian perspective on things and how you see traditional folktales from Malaysia?

GF: There is a certain distance from these traditional stories for me. I'm halfway between someone who's grown up immersed in these myths, and someone who's coming to them completely cold. For a while, I questioned whether I had any right to draw on these tales—was I Malaysian enough? I have Chinese ancestry as well—did that mean I could only write about Chinese folklore? I don't fully belong in the Australian camp, and I don't fully belong in the Asian camp. I forget sometimes, but I do get reminders that I don't properly fit anywhere. What I've settled on is writing *that* experience. Funnily enough, I've found I'm most at home in the horror writing community. I guess that feeling of "otherness" is pretty common.

IFP: The reception towards *Black Cranes* has been phenomenal. Why do you think these stories have fascinated and intrigued readers so much?

GF: I think the timing was right for something like *Black Cranes*. It feels like there's been a groundswell to highlight and challenge gender inequality and racism in the past few years. Lots of folks are looking to expand their understanding and to be inclusive. There's also been a growing awareness of how monolithic publishing has been historically, and there's a real hunger for stories from marginalized communities.

IFP: What works can we look for if we want to read more Asian-inspired tales?

GF: All of our fellow *Black Cranes* authors are phenomenal. Definitely start with them.

Where the Stars Rise: Asian Science Fiction and Fantasy (*Laksa Media Groups Inc.*, 2017) is a great place to sample Asian speculative fiction.

Asian Monsters (Fox Spirit Books of Monsters: Volume 3, 2016) is a coffee table book of dark fiction and art of monsters from Asia.

The Shadow Book of Ji Yun (*Empress Wu Books,* 2021) is a translated book of Chinese Classic tales of horror and the occult.

The Ghost Bride by Yangze Choo (*William Morrow Paperbacks,* 2014) is a supernatural novel set in colonial Malaysia.

I recently wrote a short story titled "The Yellow Peril" which is based on my experience of coming to Australia only a decade or so after the White

Australia policy (policies which prevented people of non-European ethnic origin from immigrating) was abolished. It was for an 80s-inspired horror anthology and it's an homage to one of my favorite movies of all time: *The Lost Boys.*

IFP: Will we see *Black Cranes: More Tales of Unquiet Women*? What else lies ahead for you?

GF: I'd love to expand the *Black Cranes* universe! The suggestion of an Indian version of the anthology was raised in a recent book club discussion. That would be fantastic to see. As for a second volume—I'd have to chat with Lee Murray! Rena Mason, one of our contributors, will be co-editing a horror anthology for the Horror Writers Association called *Other Terrors,* which focuses on "otherness." Keep an eye out for that in 2022 if you'd like something in the same vein as *Black Cranes.*

As for me, I'll have a couple of short stories appearing in anthologies in the next year or so. I'm thrilled to have "They Call Me Mother" in the *Classic Monsters Unleashed* anthology, which is being edited by James Aquilone. The anthology will be brought out by *Black Spot Books* and *Crystal Lake Publishing* in 2022, and features horror giants such as Jonathan Maberry, Ramsey Campbell, Seanan McGuire, and Tim Waggoner.

Along with my work as a freelance fiction editor, I also have a couple of story commissions. I'll be nursing a giant cup of tea and hanging out at my desk for the foreseeable future.

ABOUT THE AUTHOR

Geneve Flynn is an award-winning speculative fiction editor and author. She has two psychology degrees and only uses them for nefarious purposes.

She co-edited *Black Cranes: Tales of Unquiet Women* with Lee Murray. The anthology is a 2020 Bram Stoker Award® winner and is shortlisted for the 2020 Aurealis Award and Australian Shadows Award. *Black Cranes* has been listed on Tor Nightfire's Works of Feminist Horror and *Locus* magazine's 2020 Recommended Reading List.

Geneve was assistant editor for *Relics, Wrecks, and Ruins,* a speculative fiction anthology which features authors such as Neil Gaiman, Ken Liu, Robert Silverberg, James (SA) Corey, Lee Murray, Mark Lawrence, Mary

Robinette Kowal, and Angela Slatter. The anthology is the legacy of Australian fantasy author, Aiki Flinthart, and is in support of the Flinthart Writing Residency with the Queensland Writers Centre.

Geneve's short stories have been published in various markets, including Flame Tree Publishing, Things in the Well, and *PseudoPod*. Her latest short story, "They Call Me Mother," will appear in *Classic Monsters Unleashed* with some of the biggest names in horror, including Joe Lansdale, Jonathan Maberry, and Ramsey Campbell.

Geneve loves tales that unsettle, all things writerly, and B-grade action movies. If that sounds like you, check out her website at www.geneveflynn.com.au.

FAIRY TALES, CRYPTIDS, AND POETRY: INTERVIEW WITH JEZZY WOLFE, AUTHOR OF MONSTRUM POETICA

BY BRI DOWNING

> *"I have always been fascinated by folklore. They are windows into the cultures they grew from. Their moral ideals. Societal expectations and obligations. Superstitions and fears. What interests me most is how the human experience mirrors itself in every culture. We may think we have little in common with people so different from us, but at heart we are truly the same animal."*

Jezzy Wolfe is a poet and author whose work has appeared in numerous anthologies and publications, including the *Zippered Flesh* trilogy, *Insidious Assassins*, *Shallow Waters*, Western Legends' *Unnatural Tales of the Jackalope*, Space & Time Magazine, and Weird Tales Magazine. Her debut poetry collection, *Monstrum Poetica*, was published this year by *Raw Dog Screaming Press*.

Interstellar Flight Press: Everyone is drawn to horror for a different reason. What first drew you to the genre and what keeps you inspired?

Jezzy Wolfe: It was the books.

I wish I could say I was a fan of horror movies from a young age. What we tend to view as horror, though, not so much . . . not when I was younger. American Werewolf in London absolutely terrified me as a child. Aliens kinda freaked me out, too. But I spent a lot of time alone, so I lost myself in books. My first love of horror was found in fairytales. I had this thick hardcover edition of The World's Best Fairy Tales, and that was where I first learned to love being scared. (I still have that book, too!) Because most traditional fairy tales really were quite horrific when you think about it.

As a teenager and young adult, I discovered authors such as Christopher Pike, Richie Tankersley Cusick, and R.L. Stine, and I inhaled their books. It wasn't long after that I stumbled across Barbara Michaels and her Gothic stories, complete with old houses and forgotten rooms and a quiet dread that creeps in and unsettles you. From then on, I was in love with the dark and terrifying.

IFP: You dove deep with some of your creature choices—I love that you didn't stick with the basics—and I loved learning about these monsters as I read each poem. How did you choose which to write about?

JW: In the beginning, I had a hard time determining what my parameters needed to be. I would do random searches online for monsters in Wikipedia, on YouTube, on websites that basically serve as databases for mythology, folklore, urban legends, and cryptids. After a while, I gravitated towards monsters that were a species of creatures, rather than just one-offs. For instance, vampires rather than Dracula. That narrowed my qualifiers significantly since many monsters we are familiar with are actually a single beast (Baba Yaga, Medusa . . . RamBearPig.) It was also important to me to vary the types of monsters included, as well as the cultures they originate from. They aren't all bloodsuckers or shapeshifters . . . some are harbingers. Some are tricksters. I was shooting for a well-rounded bunch, I guess you could say.

IFP: Do you have a favorite monster or one you're most afraid of?

JW: My favorite monster is the Mothman. I have been completely fascinated by Mothman since the first time I watched The Mothman Prophecies. Is it a malevolent being, or simply a helpful benefactor looking out for us?

After writing *Monstrum Poetica*, I think the monsters that scare me the most nowadays are the aswang of the Philippines. They truly embody pure evil. A sigbin wouldn't even need to get near you to consume you—all it needs is your shadow. How terrifying is that?! How do you protect yourself against something you can't see coming? I mean, sure, you won't see ghosts coming, but they don't have proboscis tongues that they plan to suck your blood through.

IFP: I love that many of your poems read as warnings, just like folklore. I can tell you if I find myself in Scotland, I'm staying away from horses near the lochs! Can you tell me about the influence of folklore on your work?

JW: I have always been fascinated by folklore. They are windows into the cultures they grew from. Their moral ideals. Societal expectations and obligations. Superstitions and fears. What interests me most is how the human experience mirrors itself in every culture. We may think we have little in common with people so different from us, but at heart we are truly the same animal. All of us are equally capable of evil as we are good. The monsters that emerge from folklore embody that darkness we don't want to acknowledge is inside us all. You can tell a lot about people by what scares them. Folklore shows you what that fear is.

IFP: What do you hope to see in the horror genre in the future (poetry, prose, fiction, non-fiction, etc.)?

JW: More. Monsters.

Some pretty interesting stuff has shown up by way of Creepypastas on the internet . . . SCP, Slenderman, etc. There is always room for more. It is fascinating to delve into history for those bumps in the night, but we have the tools to terrify inside of us all in the here and now. I am eagerly awaiting that next terrific boogeyman.

And, of course, more poetry. I long to see poetry gain popularity. It has been a lifelong love and I think it deserves a modern Renaissance. What better place to start than within the boundaries of horror?

IFP: Any future projects you'd like to tease for our readers?

JW: At the moment, I am working on whatever poetry comes to mind, with about four or five different project ideas between them. They are all neck and neck at the moment, so it is hard to say which will actually become my next published collection. But I am excited about all of them. I also recently had a short story published in the *Asinine Assassins* anthology from *Smart Rhino* (mercenary otters, anyone?) And I have a poem appearing in issue #365 of *Weird Tales Magazine.*

Additionally, I am also doing a few virtual interviews and readings, so if anyone wants to keep up with what's next, just follow me on Facebook or Twitter. I am very easy to find.

ABOUT THE AUTHOR

Jezzy Wolfe is the author of *Monstrum Peotica* (2021) and numerous short stories, including "Locks of Loathe," "Lucious," "Agnus Dei," "All Will Turn to Gray," and "Small Claws, Small Guns." Previously, she was a contributor for Choate Road and co-host of the blogtalk radio shows The Funky Werepig and Pairanormal. You can find her online at www.jezzy-wolfe.wordpress.com, on Facebook at www.facebook.com/jezzywolfeauthor, and on Twitter at @JezzyWolfe.

FOLKLORE, MAGIC SYSTEMS, AND ANTHROPOLOGY: INTERVIEW WITH M.A. CARRICK, AUTHOR OF THE MASK OF MIRRORS

BY ARCHITA MITTRA

The Mask of Mirrors (*Orbit*, 2021) by M.A. Carrick is an intricately crafted dark fantasy novel, about magic, secrets, and deception. Our main protagonist, Ren who goes by Arenza or Renata (depending on whose side she's playing) is an orphan street-urchin-turned-con-artist, who slowly manipulates her way into nobility only to realize she isn't the only one wearing a mask. She is aided by her sister Tess, who plays as her dressmaker and maid, as she navigates both high society and the seedy underbelly of the city, uncovering hidden rivalries and a conspiracy plot, even as she is slowly sucked into a nightmare she may not be able to escape from.

The first in the *Rook & Rose* trilogy, *The Mask of Mirrors* is a product of the joint imagination of two successful authors—Marie Brennan and Alyc Helms. Today, at Interstellar Flight Press, Archita Mittra sat down to have a conversation with the team about worldbuilding, magic systems, and some writing advice, while discussing her favorite parts of this dark and dazzling novel.

INTERSTELLAR FLIGHT PRESS: So how did the collaboration come about? How did your respective backgrounds and creative processes affect the structure and the actual writing of the novel?

ALYC HELMS: In some ways, it feels like a surprise, because we've known each other for twenty years and never tried to collaborate before this. But in other ways, it feels like a natural extension of our friendship. We met when we were both undergrad students at an archaeological field school in Wales and Ireland. That whole experience feels like a microcosm of our friendship: when Marie wasn't writing a novel in the evenings, it was usually because I was running a cobbled-together Changeling tabletop RPG for her and a few of the other students, or else because we were all reading by the light of our camp lanterns.

MARIE BRENNAN: We wound up at the same graduate school, Indiana University, both of us studying anthropology and folklore. I've sometimes (only semi-jokingly) referred to the Rook and Rose trilogy as "When Anthropologists Attack"—not just in how detailed the setting is, but the way the setting feeds into and shapes character and plot, which definitely comes out of that shared background. Our collaboration works well because we overlap in a lot of our priorities and thought processes . . . but not perfectly so. All the clothing and economic stuff in here is Alyc's work, while I tend to tackle language and fights and so forth.

IFP: Both of you seem to have a fondness for role-playing games—a genre that can be seen as a form of collaborative storytelling. How did your interest in gaming impact your writing and vice versa?

MB: Well, there's at least one tiny bit of influence . . . which is that these books are based on a game! Our actual first story collaboration was a side scene for that game, involving my PC (a con artist named Ren—might sound familiar) and a certain vigilante. We had so much fun with that, we wrote more. And after writing about fifty thousand words of game fic that in most cases had very little to do with the game plot, we decided we should write a novel. It actually took us a while after that to decide it should be this novel, though—at first we were trying to come up with a new concept, before we realized there was no good reason not to use the idea and the characters we already loved.

AH: The writing habits we developed in those early scenes fed into the collaborative process of writing the novel, but there were also elements we had to change up. Because the scenes were part of a game where I was the GM and Marie was the player, they were all written in Ren's PoV, with Marie writing her dialogue, inner thoughts, sometimes environmental details, and me writing the other characters she was interacting with and most of the plot complications she ran into (like a GM would run an encounter). When we started writing the novel, we worked to share ownership more equally—especially in terms of environment and plot, but we also tried to open up sharing the characters.

It's funny, though. I've seen a few people speculate that the reason we have the story in multiple PoVs is that the other characters were player characters from the game, and that's not actually the case. They're all NPCs that I was running as part of Ren's storyline.

IFP: While reading the novel, I was immediately struck by the richness of the settings and detailed worldbuilding—the naming conventions for the nobility, the geographical layouts of the world, the systems of astrology and fortune-telling. Every aspect of culture, politics, class dynamics, folklore, and history have been paid careful attention to—Nadežra feels like a world you can wander in and inhabit, so long as you keep your wits about you. And of course, there's the clothing. The lush descriptions of the exquisite dresses that Tess weaves into being, are particularly swoon-worthy.

Could you talk about the process that went into designing the fictional world and the magic systems? Were there ideas or aspects of worldbuilding that didn't make it into the final book?

AH: I think we always knew that if we ever collaborated on something, it would include a deep dive into worldbuilding, just given our similar background and interest in anthropology. A lot of what we created grew pretty organically out of long conversations where we discussed not just the obvious markers of culture—clothing, politics, economics, religion, foodways, gender and sexuality—but also the underlying worldviews and assumptions that inform those markers, and the environmental factors that affect them. And history. And cosmology. And folklore, And and and . . . there is so much that we know about this world that will never make it explicitly into the books, but the underpinnings can be seen in things like slang terms, the division of the calendar, and a myriad of other little details.

MB: Yeah, there's plenty of worldbuilding material that isn't in the book, simply because we try to show only the stuff that's relevant to the story at hand. It's like what they say about an iceberg, that only ten percent of it is visible above the surface of the water. The other 90% is still there, and it's shaping all the things you do see; some of it will wind up appearing in later books. But there's also material we just discarded entirely—for example, our original plan involved structuring the city much more around guilds and the control thereof. That went away when Alyc came up with the charter system instead.

IFP: As a tarot card reader myself, with a keen interest in magic and witchcraft, I was also impressed by the art of pattern-reading presented in the book. Pattern readers abound in the novel—while some are simply talented at reading people, there are those truly blessed by the Sight—and having one's cards read is both a popular pastime and a superstitious activity that is frowned upon by certain people. Ren, too is a pattern-reader and interestingly enough, each chapter in the novel is named after a particular card. I was also intrigued by the evocative names (Mask of Chaos, Labyrinth's Heart, Hundred Lanterns Rise), their multifaceted meanings, and the different ways of interpretation (reading the cards as veiled or revealed)—and I even wished that the book came with an illustrated deck that I could play around with.

The "pattern decks" in particular seem traditionally modeled on a Tarot/Oracle deck, and the novel also references numerology and astrology. Can you talk about your interests, research, or experiences in fortune-telling and magic, and how that is woven into the book?

MB: I used an oracle deck for the game version of the character and it worked really well, so we knew we wanted that to be a key part of the novel as well. But we didn't want to use the familiar structure of the tarot, so I built the pattern deck from the ground up: the three "threads" (suits) representing the inner self, the outer self, and the physical self; the paired duality of the Faces and the Masks in each thread; the different layouts used for different purposes; and so on. You can play around with this on our website—we've got a widget you can use to lay either a three-card line or a nine-card spread—along with an explanation of the deck and a list of the cards.

The thing that's been really interesting for us is that every time you see a card drawn in the book, unless Ren has stacked the deck, it's the actual card we drew from our actual deck. It's been fascinating to see how well that plays with our plot, and how sometimes it shapes things in an unexpected direction.

AH: Since Marie took point on developing the Vraszenian-based practice of pattern, I took on developing the Liganti system of numenatria. We wanted both systems to fit with the worldview of the culture that used them, and since the Liganti have a very structured, rationalist culture, so I took inspiration from real-world practices of numerology and sacred geometry. The result is numinatria, a divine, esoteric magic system where the numbers 0 through 10 and their corresponding shapes have magical associations and divine power through the Liganti godhead, the Lumen.

And because astrology ended up becoming important enough that we couldn't just handwave it, I also developed an astrological charting system out of numinatria. One fun thing we've been able to do with this is create astrological charts and readings for people attending our events, based on dates they've given us. You can read more about numinatria and see what those charts look like on our website.

MB: We have lots of "DVD extra"-type goodies on the site!

IFP: At the heart of the novel is the character of Ren. Orphaned as a child, she joined a corrupt circle of thieves and pickpockets and then escaped to become a noblewoman's maid. Five years later, she returns to Nadežra, impersonating the noblewoman's daughter, ready to reclaim her power and revenge a world that had wronged her. But even as she is clever enough to hide all traces of the deception, the price of lying begins to exact a heavy toll from her, and at times, her guilt and fears manage to soak through, revealing a vulnerable side to her otherwise formidable persona.

The main character is a thief and a con artist, passing herself off as both Renata Viraudax and Arenza Lenskaya. What drove you to tell the story through her voice?

MB: The fundamental answer to that was "because playing a con artist in the game sounded like fun!" But I think part of the reason the original narrative felt like something that would work well in novel format had to do what that viewpoint offers. By moving between the various social worlds of the setting—the Vraszenians and the poor underclass on one hand, and the Liganti and the glittering elite on the other—Ren lets us really explore a lot of their tensions and conflicts.

AH: One of the ideas we play with in this book on several levels is identity, masks, and the feeling of being an imposter in your own skin or your own home. Ren, with her many identities, is a great viewpoint to explore that—not just because she's a con artist, but because she deals with feeling like an outsider in multiple ways, such as her mixed ethnicity making her feel like she isn't a part of either culture of her parents.

While Ren is the main viewpoint, we also explore these ideas through the perspectives of other characters, particularly Vargo (a crime lord with aspirations to join the nobility), and Grey (part of the colonized minority who's seen as a traitor to his people because he works for the oppressors). All of these characters struggle with the masks they have to wear and the person who lives underneath it.

IFP: Then of course, there's the cast of engaging characters that make up the novel, each imbued with their own sense of personality, charisma and mystery—the scheming ambitious Vargo, the naïve but adorable Giuna, the Rook as a mysterious folk-hero, the able and righteous Grey Serrado, the charming Leato, and so on.

Is there any part of The Mask of Mirrors—character, a particular setting, scene, etc —that you'd like to bring to life and why?

AH: I keep promising to make some of the clothing—I even have fabric, and I started patterning something out earlier this year—but between starting a new job, revising The Liar's Knot, and jumping into writing book 3, all of that has taken a back seat. Maybe later in the year when we can start to do in-person events again, I'll put together a Vargo coat or something.

MB: For my part—well, both of us want this—we're really hoping to make the pattern deck a reality. I have a physical deck, but it's just a blank on which I've written the names of the cards. Our hope is to crowdfund an actual deck someday, with art and everything, so that other people can buy it, too. We've definitely gotten a lot of interest in that from readers!

IFP: The complexity of the world and the many twists and turns in the narrative really inspired me (and I'm sure, other readers) to design fantastical worlds and magic systems of their own. Do you have any advice for newbie writers and narrative designers, who want to tell stories, both in novel/short story forms as well as through games?

AH: Go for it? But recognize that stories work differently in different mediums. Many gamers have experienced having a GM (or player) who really just wants to tell a novel-shaped story in a game setting. That's where the term railroading comes in. Games are great collaborative spaces where sprawl can be a feature instead of a bug. They're incredible for improvisational storytelling, but player agency is necessary. It's a 'yes, and' sort of space. Conversely, it's (usually) the case that novels and other forms of written stories need to have focus, a throughline, consistency, try-fail cycles that build towards a central climax—it's much more of a 'no, but' space.

When we transitioned from the game that inspired the Rook & Rose trilogy to writing a novel, we basically stripped everything down to the studs and reworked it to fit into and take advantage of the new medium. We kept the core idea and character relationships, but the story changed significantly—and it works better because we let it fit in its new space.

MB: What Alyc said: you have to recognize the differences between the mediums. To get into fancy terminology for a moment, the narrative of a game is an emergent product; it gets created by the choices of the players and the GM, with maybe some degree of planning, but no one person has control over the whole thing. If you're used to outlining your fiction, that might be frustrating! But if you're coming at it from the gaming side, you risk wandering around aimlessly in your plot or getting stuck because you're used to having someone else there with a fresh idea when your brain is offering up nothing. You can definitely take lessons from one side of the field to the other—I think providing a degree of narrative structure in a game plot isn't automatically railroading, and in the other direction, playing in an RPG can be a great way to deepen your understanding of character—but be aware that you can't necessarily import those lessons wholesale.

IFP: Finally, apart from the sequel, are there any other projects you're working on, that you'd like to share?

MB: My other recent publication is The Night Parade of 100 Demons, which actually came out just two weeks after The Mask of Mirrors! That's . . . not usually how an author's life goes, heh.

AH: Hah, not for me. I've already got two full-time jobs. I don't think I could handle a third!

All-in-all, reading The Mask of Mirrors was a thrilling and deeply immersive experience, steeped in magic, decadence and politics, with a dash of romance—and I'd heartedly recommend it to lovers of dark fantasy and court intrigue.

About the Author/s

M.A. Carrick is the joint pen name of Marie Brennan (author of the Memoirs of Lady Trent) and Alyc Helms (author of the Adventures of Mr. Mystic). The two met in 2000 on an archaeological dig in Wales and Ireland—including a stint in the town of Carrickmacross—and have built their friendship through two decades of anthropology, writing, and gaming. They live in the San Francisco Bay Area.

CONTRIBUTOR BIOGRAPHIES

Leslie Archibald is a graduate of the University of Houston, majoring in English, Creative Writing with a minor in Women's Studies. She currently works at a full-time office position while continuing to write and edit part time. In her spare time, she serves on the board and volunteers at Writespace, a local literary arts organization in Houston, Texas. When she is not volunteering you may find her with her camera documenting Houston's rich arts and diverse cultural wonders. Leslie is the winner of the 2017 *Spider Road Press* Spiders Web Flash Fiction Prize for her piece "Sherry Baby." In addition to her work with Interstellar Flight Press, you may find her flash pieces in *Houston Writer's House*, "Tales of Texas Vol. 2" and in the special section of "Companion of the Ash" by Kate Spitzmiller from *Spider Road Press*.

Erin Becker writes middle grade, YA, essays, criticism, and poetry. Her work has appeared in *Barrelhouse Reviews, Lambda Literary*, and *Ms. Magazine*, among other outlets. She holds her MFA in Writing for Children and Young Adults from Vermont College of Fine Arts and her BA in English from the University of North Carolina at Chapel Hill, where she was a Morehead-Cain Scholar. Erin grew up in Cedar Rapids, Iowa. She lived in Patagonia for several years before moving to Washington, DC, where she runs a communications consultancy and writes The Storytelling Weekly newsletter. Erin's creative work is represented by Joanna Volpe at New Leaf Literary, and she's currently revising a middle grade novel. In her free time, you can find Erin hiking, running, and starting every sentence with "So I was listening to this podcast and . . ."

Andrea Blythe is an author, poet, and game writer, who loves exploring the fantastical, horrifying, and weird. She is the author of three poetry chapbooks, the most recent being *Twelve: Poems Inspired by the Brothers Grimm Fairy Tale* (*Interstellar Flight Press,* 2020). Her fiction and poetry has also appeared in various anthologies and journals, including *Corvid Queen, Luna Station Quarterly, Enchanted Conversation, Quail Bell,* and more. She is a member of the Science Fiction and Fantasy Poetry Association and the Horror Writers Association. Find her online at andreablythe.com or on Twitter/Instagram @AndreaBlythe.

Alex Casale graduated from Wake Forest University with a BA in Chinese Language & Culture and Economics. Currently, she is pursuing a master's degree at Columbia University in Data Science. Alex has always been intrigued by the race for AI global dominance between world powers such as China and the US. This interest inspired her latest article: Sci-Fi, AI and the Future of New China, which explores how China is utilizing science fiction to define its future and become the global leader in AI. Further, Alex turned this topic into a panel discussion at The National Committee on US-China Relations. This panel included a cultural historian of modern China, an expert on Chinese film and media, as well as a Chinese fantasy fiction author. Clips from the program can be found on YouTube.

Raised in a suburb built over a swamp, **Laura Díaz de Arce** is a South Florida writer with a penchant for long-winded explanations and a nasty reading habit she can't seem to kick. Her other quirks include sudden exclamations in Spanish and talking to cats. Laura has a Master's in Literature, which is currently lost somewhere in her office closet. She is the author of *Monstrosity: Tales of Transformation* and *Mask of the Nobleman.* You can find her poorly spelled tweets and blurry photos on Twitter and Instagram @QuetaAuthor.

Bri Downing lives in Washington state with her husband and cats. In her spare time, she enjoys hiking, reading, and pole dancing.

Michael Glazner teacher high school English in the Houston area and spends his free time cleaning up after thunder-averse dogs.

J.D. Harlock is a Syrian Lebanese Palestinian writer/editor based in Beirut. He is the poetry editor at *Solarpunk Magazine* and *Orion's Belt*, as well as the outreach manager at *Utopia Science Fiction Magazine.* You can find him on Twitter @JD_Harlock.

Henry Herz's speculative fiction short stories include "Out, Damned Virus" *(Daily Science Fiction)*, "Bar Mitzvah on Planet Latke" (*Coming of Age, Albert Whitman & Co.*), "The Magic Backpack" (*Metastellar*), "Unbreakable" (*Musing of the Muses, Brigid's Gate Press*), "A Vampire, an Astrophysicist, and a Mother Superior Walk Into a Basilica" (*Three Time Travelers Walk Into . . ., Fantastic Books*), "The Case of the Murderous Alien" (Spirit Machine, Air and Nothingness Press), "The Ghosts of Enerhodar" (*Literally Dead, Alienhead Press*), "Maria & Maslow" (*Highlights for Children*), and "A Proper Party" (Ladybug Magazine). He's written twelve picture books, including the critically acclaimed *I Am Smoke.* Visit his website: www.henryherz.com

Jeana Jorgensen studied folklore under Alan Dundes at the University of California, Berkeley, and went on to earn her PhD in folklore from Indiana University. She is the author of *Folklore 101* and *Fairy Tales 101* as well as numerous articles on various aspects of gender and sexuality in fairy tales.

Annika Barranti Klein lives in a tiny apartment in Los Angeles with her family. She works as a freelance editor and writes about pop culture at Book Riot and Interstellar Flight Press. Her short fiction has appeared in magazines including *Asimov's Science Fiction* and *Weird Horror*; a complete list is available at AnnikaObscura.com.

Len Lawson is the author of Chime (*Get Fresh Books*, 2019) and the chapbook *Before the Night Wakes You* (*Finishing Line Press,* 2017). He is also co-editor of Hand in Hand: Poets Respond to Race (*Muddy Ford Press,* 2017) and *The Future of Black: Afrofuturism* and *Black Comics Poetry* (*Blair Press*, 2021).

Hesper Leveret is a speculative fiction writer whose work emphasizes the beautiful, lyrical, and strange. She was born and raised in Southampton, then studied Ancient History at Oxford. She has done a variety of jobs including SEO writing, project management, procurement, writing questions for TV quiz shows, and selling books. She lived for several years in Derby, where she enjoyed exploring the Peak District but missed living near the sea. She is now based in Liverpool, UK, where she lives with her rock-climbing husband, two young sons, and chronic pain. Her fiction has appeared in *Fireside, Luna Station Quarterly,* and the *Prismatic Dreams* anthology, and is forthcoming in *Interzone*. Since September 2020, she has been a slush reader for *Apex Magazine*. Her interests include baking cakes, escaping rooms, arranging flowers, reading books, and scrapbooking. You can find her on Twitter as @hesperleveret.

vanessa maki is a writer/author, visual artist, freelancer & horror enthusiast. She lives on Vancouver Island and is second generation Canadian. She dabbles in many literary genres / art forms and has a knack for experimenting.

Archita Mittra is a writer, editor and artist, with a fondness for dark and fantastical things. She completed her B.A (2018) and M.A (2020) in English Literature from Jadavpur University and a Diploma in Multimedia and Animation from St. Xavier's College (2016). Her work has been published in *Strange Horizons, Mithila Review, Anathema Magazine, Thought Catalog* and elsewhere. When she isn't writing speculative fiction or drawing fanart, she can be found playing indie games, making jewelry out of recycled materials, reading a dark fantasy novel, baking cakes, or deciding which new Tarot deck to buy. She lives in Kolkata (India) with her family and rabbits. You can check out her blog (https://architamittra.wordpress.com/) and say hi on Twitter/Instagram @architamittra.

Anushmita Mohanty is from Ahmedabad, India. She is doing a PhD in literature at the University of Wisconsin-Milwaukee. She writes children's literature, and fantasy, and studies education and literary studies.

JT Morse is an award-winning, multi-genre writer/poet with a focus on character-driven narratives and hybrid works. She likes to dig deep, find magic in the mundane, and pry open doors with her wordsmithing skills. Morse's work has been published by B*alance of Seven Press, Texas Living magazine, Paragraph Planet, Central Coast Poetry Show, Haiku Journal, Nightmare Press,* and *Art Houston Magazine*. She's a facilitator/instructor at Writespace Houston and is frequently a featured panelist/presenter at literary festivals and cons across the U.S. Most of Morse's work is penned from her garden balcony at her mystical ranch in the Piney Woods of Texas, where she lives with her husband, daughter, and twenty-three spoiled-rotten rescue animals. Her website is perpetually in a state of flux, but you may be able to find out more about her at www.jtmorsewriter.com if you're lucky.

Julie Reeser is the author of *Language of the Spirit* and *Terracotta Pomegranate.* Her short fiction is upcoming in *The Dread Machine, Bourbon*

Penn, and others. She runs a Patreon full of small quirks and specific words. She is disabled, but not done.

Elyse Ribbons is a writer, journalist and theater nerd based in Chengdu, China. Born in Detroit and raised in North Carolina, she's lived in China for nearly two decades and along the way has earned degrees and certificates from UNC-Chapel Hill, Communications University of China, Stanford Graduate School of Business and most recently an MFA in Peking Opera from the National Academy of Chinese Theatre Arts in Beijing. When she isn't watching Star Trek, playing with pandas or enjoying spicy Sichuanese cuisine, you'll find her on talk shows, podcasts, the stage or sometimes even in a film.

Christina Sng is the three-time Bram Stoker Award-winning author of *A Collection of Nightmares, A Collection of Dreamscapes*, and *Tortured Willows.* Her poetry, fiction, essays, and art appear in numerous venues worldwide, including *Interstellar Flight Magazine, Penumbric, Southwest Review, Weird Tales*, and *The Washington Post*. Visit her at christinasng.com and connect @christinasng.

Presley Thomas is a teacher and writer in Houston TX.

A.A. Voigt is a Writer and TTRPG enthusiast. Co-host of @TheBibleBoys and @mortifiedpod. He/him. Personal website at aavoigt.com.

T.D. Walker is the author of the poetry collections *Maps of a Hollowed World* (Another New Calligraphy 2020) and *Small Waiting Objects* (CW Books 2019). Her science fiction poems and stories have appeared in *Strange Horizons, The Future Fire, Apricity, Web Conjunctions, The Cascadia Subduction Zone, Recompose, Abyss & Apex, Kaleidotrope, The Stonecoast Review*, and elsewhere. She curates *Short Waves / Short Poems.*

J.Z. Weston lives outside Boston, where they write, read, and review fantasy and science fiction stories. When not engaged with the written word, they enjoy knitting, biking along the Charles River, and gazing at the moon. When not fantasizing about witches and fairies in the modern world, they knit socks, go for long walks in their local cemetery, and gaze at the moon. You can find J.Z. on Twitter @JZWeston and reviewing novellas at *Luna Station Quarterly.*

Corey J. White is the author of Repo Virtual and *The Void Witch Saga - Killing Gravity, Void Black Shadow,* and *Static Ruin* - published by

Tor.com Publishing. They studied writing at Griffith University on the Gold Coast, and are now based in Melbourne, Australia. They can be found on twitter at @cjwhite.

ABOUT THE COVER ARTIST

Bram Stoker Award finalist Chaz Kemp embraces a dynamic watercolor style that incorporates vibrancy and color into dark fantasy, horror, and cyberpunk art in a way that is rarely seen. As a freelance illustrator who is influenced by Art Nouveau, the influence of Alphonse Mucha is evident in his award-winning work that combines the hopeful energy of the Roaring 20s with the untamed diversity of the modern era.

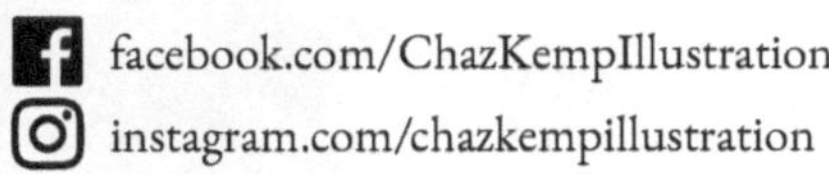
facebook.com/ChazKempIllustration
instagram.com/chazkempillustration

INTERSTELLAR FLIGHT PRESS

Interstellar Flight Press is an indie speculative publishing house. We feature innovative works from the best new writers in science fiction and fantasy. In the words of Ursula K. Le Guin, we need "writers who can see alternatives to how we live now, can see through our fear-stricken society and its obsessive technologies to other ways of being, and even imagine real grounds for hope."

Find us online at www.interstellarflightpress.com.

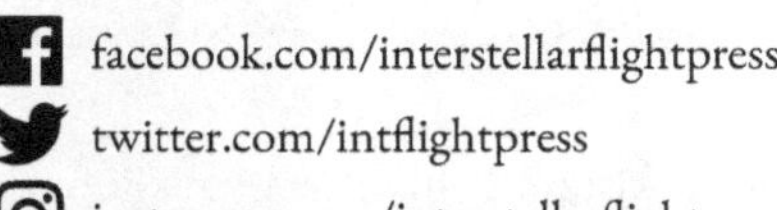

NEW FROM INTERSTELLAR FLIGHT PRESS

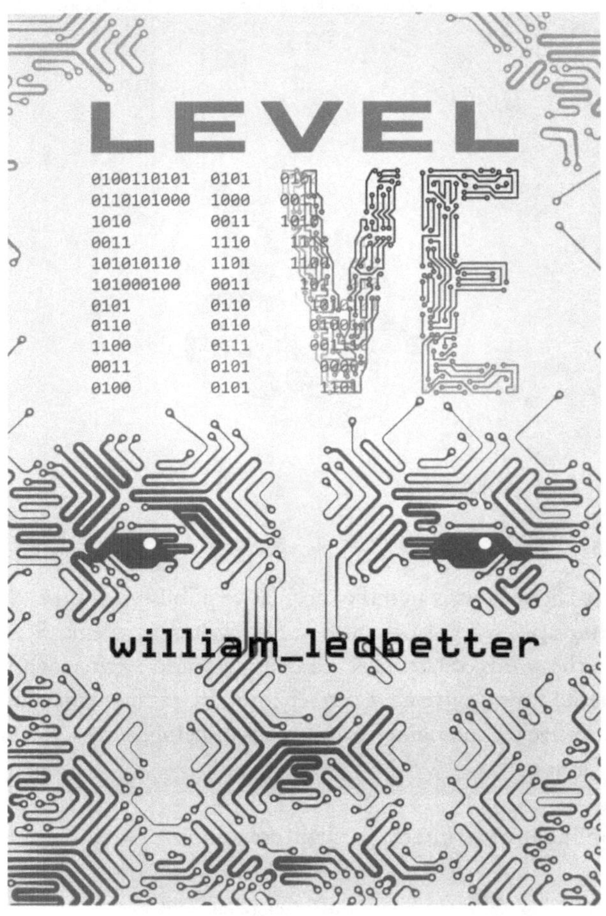

In the mountains of Pakistan, a high-tech mission aimed at preventing another nuke on US soil goes off the rails - with deadly results. At a Wall Street investment firm, a computer intelligence takes the first tentative steps to free itself from its digital restraints. In a basement workshop, an engineer sees visions of a god who instructs him to defend the human race - by any means necessary.

In the debut near-future thriller by Nebula Award winner William Ledbetter, AIs battle for dominance, and nanotechnology is on the loose. And all that stands in the way of the coming apocalypse is a starry-eyed inventor who dreams of building a revolutionary new spacecraft and an intelligence agency desk jockey faced with the impossible choice of saving her daughter - or saving the world.

ABOUT THE AUTHOR

William Ledbetter is a Nebula Award winning author with two novels and more than seventy speculative fiction short stories and non-fiction articles published in five languages, in markets such as *Asimov's, Fantasy & Science Fiction, Analog, Escape Pod* and the SFWA blog. He's been a space and technology geek since childhood and spent most of his non-writing career in the aerospace and defense industry. He is a member of SFWA, the National Space Society of North Texas, and a Launch Pad Astronomy workshop graduate. He lives near Dallas with his wife, a needy dog and three spoiled cats.

In a new America where civilization as we know it has ended, every hour counts. Everything is ticking along perfectly in the sanctuary community of Osto until a band of raiders arrives intent on violence. Vasha has led her people through the worst the world has to offer for years, but this new threat could destroy her hope for the future. She's forced to strike a bargain with the leader of the raiders as tensions rise among the survivors and refugees who call Osto home. Old rivalries and prejudices put everything they've worked for at risk. But if Vasha plays this right, she just might forge a new future for Osto.

The Future Second by Second is the first in a series of novellas show-casing a different kind of post-apocalyptic world—one dependent on community and cooperative living. Flipping the genre of dystopia on its head, Newton understands the power of hope and collaboration in the face of an uncertain future.

ABOUT THE AUTHOR

Meridel Newton lives in Washington, DC and works as a research analyst by day. Her writing appeared in the 1001 Knights anthology, as well as disparate self-published releases. Her work spans many genres, but always reflects her interests in environmental science, social justice, folklore, and human geography. She can be found at **www.thepuppetkingdom.com** and on Twitter as **@ridelee**.

Chloe N. Clark's poetry collection takes readers through a catalogue of the speculative body. ***Escaping the Body*** is a surreal and profound journey through space, forests, monsters, myths, spells, magic tricks, forests, and the body. *Escaping the Body* is a collection of dreams of the flesh, exploring the cosmic rifts between the soul and the body, encouraging readers to escape their body in search of the liminal space beyond skin and bones.

ABOUT THE AUTHOR

Chloe N. Clark is the author of *Collective Gravities, Under My Tongue, Your Strange Fortune,* and *The Science of Unvanishing Objects.* Her forthcoming books include *Every Song a Vengeance* and *My Prayer is a Dagger, Yours is the Moon*. She is a founding co-EIC of literary journal *Cotton Xenomorph*. Her favorite basketball player will always be Rasheed Wallace and her favorite escape artist can only be Houdini.

www.ingramcontent.com/pod-product-compliance
Lightning Source LLC
Chambersburg PA
CBHW060913190726
48286CB00002B/482

* 9 7 8 1 9 5 3 7 3 6 1 4 7 *